PALGRAVE STUDIES IN THEATRE AND PERFORMANCE HISTORY is a series devoted to the best of theatre/performance scholarship currently available, accessible, and free of jargon. It strives to include a wide range of topics, from the more traditional to those performance forms that in recent years have helped broaden the understanding of what theatre as a category might include (from variety forms as diverse as the circus and burlesque to street buskers, stage magic, and musical theatre, among many others). Although historical, critical, or analytical studies are of special interest, more theoretical projects, if not the dominant thrust of a study, but utilized as important underpinning or as a historiographical or analytical method of exploration, are also of interest. Textual studies of drama or other types of less traditional performance texts are also germane to the series if placed in their cultural, historical, social, or political and economic context. There is no geographical focus for this series and works of excellence of a diverse and international nature, including comparative studies, are sought.

The editor of the series is Don B. Wilmeth (EMERITUS, Brown University), Ph.D., University of Illinois, who brings to the series over a dozen years as editor of a book series on American theatre and drama, in addition to his own extensive experience as an editor of books and journals. He is the author of several award-winning books and has received numerous career achievement awards, including one for sustained excellence in editing from the Association for Theatre in Higher Education.

Also in the series:

Undressed for Success by Brenda Foley
Theatre, Performance, and the Historical Avant-garde by Günter Berghaus
Theatre, Politics, and Markets in Fin-de-Siècle Paris by Sally Charnow
Ghosts of Theatre and Cinema in the Brain by Mark Pizzato
Moscow Theatres for Young People by Manon van de Water
Absence and Memory in Colonial American Theatre by Odai Johnson
Vaudeville Wars: How the Keith-Albee and Orpheum Circuits Controlled the Big-Time and Its Performers by Arthur Frank Wertheim
Performance and Femininity in Eighteenth-Century German Women's Writing by Wendy Arons
Operatic China: Staging Chinese Identity across the Pacific by Daphne P. Lei
Transatlantic Stage Stars in Vaudeville and Variety: Celebrity Turns by Leigh Woods
Interrogating America through Theatre and Performance edited by William W. Demastes and Iris Smith Fischer
Plays in American Periodicals, 1890–1918 by Susan Harris Smith
Representation and Identity from Versailles to the Present: The Performing Subject by Alan Sikes

Directors and the New Musical Drama: British and American Musical Theatre in the 1980s and 90s by Miranda Lundskaer-Nielsen

Beyond the Golden Door: Jewish-American Drama and Jewish-American Experience by Julius Novick

American Puppet Modernism: Essays on the Material World in Performance by John Bell

On the Uses of the Fantastic in Modern Theatre: Cocteau, Oedipus, and the Monster by Irene Eynat-Confino

Staging Stigma: A Critical Examination of the American Freak Show by Michael M. Chemers, foreword by Jim Ferris

Performing Magic on the Western Stage: From the Eighteenth-Century to the Present edited by Francesca Coppa, Larry Hass, and James Peck, foreword by Eugene Burger

Memory in Play: From Aeschylus to Sam Shepard by Attilio Favorini

Danjūrō's Girls: Women on the Kabuki Stage by Loren Edelson

Mendel's Theatre: Heredity, Eugenics, and Early Twentieth-Century American Drama by Tamsen Wolff

Theatre and Religion on Krishna's Stage: Performing in Vrindavan by David V. Mason

Theatre and Religion on Krishna's Stage

Performing in Vrindavan

David V. Mason

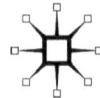

THEATRE AND RELIGION ON KRISHNA'S STAGE
Copyright © David V. Mason, 2009.
Softcover reprint of the hardcover 1st edition 2009 978-0-230-61529-8
All rights reserved.

First published in 2009 by
PALGRAVE MACMILLAN®
in the United States—a division of St. Martin's Press LLC,
175 Fifth Avenue, New York, NY 10010.

Where this book is distributed in the UK, Europe and the rest of the world, this is by Palgrave Macmillan, a division of Macmillan Publishers Limited, registered in England, company number 785998, of Houndmills, Basingstoke, Hampshire RG21 6XS.

Palgrave Macmillan is the global academic imprint of the above companies and has companies and representatives throughout the world.

Palgrave® and Macmillan® are registered trademarks in the United States, the United Kingdom, Europe and other countries.

ISBN 978-1-349-37907-1   ISBN 978-0-230-62158-9 (eBook)
DOI 10.1057/9780230621589

Library of Congress Cataloging-in-Publication Data

Mason, David V. (David Vaughan)
   Theatre and religion on Krishna's stage : performing in Vrindavan / David V. Mason.
     p. cm.—(Palgrave studies in theatre and performance history)
   Includes bibliographical references and index.

   1. Rasalila—Social aspects—India—Vrindavan. 2. Theater—Religious aspects—Hinduism. 3. Krishna (Hindu deity) in the performing arts—India—Vrindavan. 4. Hinduism and culture—India—Vrindavan. I. Title.

PN2886.V75M38 2009
792.0954′2—dc22   2008042620

A catalogue record of the book is available from the British Library.

Design by Newgen Imaging Systems (P) Ltd., Chennai, India.

First edition: June 2009

*For Celia, Sophia, and David,
who played with me in Vrindavan*

Contents

List of Figures ix
Acknowledgments xi
Note on Transliteration xii

1. Introduction: *Râs Lila* Theatre and Its Implications 1
2. Theatre Is God 23
3. Krishna, *Lila*, and Freedom 43
4. Origins of Child Performers in the *Râs Lila* 57
5. Acting in the *Râs Lila* and Real Realism 83
6. Theatre Is Religion: The Acting Audience 115
7. Conclusion 143

Notes 159
Bibliography 183
Index 191

Figures

1.1	The theatre at Jaisingh Ghera	5
1.2	Krishna and Radha in a *jhanki* pose during a performance	7
1.3	The climactic moment of the *phul lila* at Jaisingh Ghera	14
5.1	Young *râs lila* actors preparing for a performance	99
5.2	Vrindavan pilgrims	107
6.1	Krishna adjusts his costume during a worship ceremony	117

Acknowledgments

I am indebted to many for inspiration, guidance, and assistance. Sagaree Sengupta, in particular, helped me find Vrindavan in the first place, and then helped me articulate my interest in it. Velcheru Narayana Rao and James Moy gave patient direction early on. Rick Jarow provided a thoughtful sounding board. John Stratton Hawley gave crucial support to the early stages of this project. Someday, I'm sure, we'll meet in person. Much of the research for this book was possible on account of a Fulbright-Hays Fellowship and by Foreign Language and Area Studies Fellowships administered by the United States Department of Education. I am appreciative of the many, often anonymous, people involved in administering these programs. Assistance came also from the American Institute of Indian Studies. Thanks are also owed to the Emery and Mary Lynn Patten Foundation for additional funding of my work.

People in Vrindavan have been extraordinarily obliging. Everyone at Jaisingh Ghera contributed in some way to this book. Robyn Beeche seems to know everyone and everything, and has moved many mountains on my behalf. Srivatsa Goswami gave much of his much-sought-after time to talk with me about Vrindavan, and he probably does not know that an incidental comment of his so stunned my way of thinking about *râs lila* performers that, years later, I'm still trying to realize all its implications. I owe thanks to Prakash, who has so many things to do, and misses nothing. I also owe Anand, Prabha, Beauty, Amit, and Bitu Malik for making my family part of theirs. *Râs lila* directors Fateh Krishna Sharma, Ramprasad, Amicand Sharma, and Purusottam Lal Gaur generously gave me their expert insight, as did scholars Ram Narayan Agrawal and Vasant Yamadagni.

Recent work on this book was facilitated by a sabbatical leave provided by Rhodes College and the Andrew Mellon Foundation, and by Laura Canon, Cookie Ewing, and David Jilg, who kindly covered for me. I'm also obliged to the Covance Clinical Research Lab in Madison, Wisconsin, without which this book would remain unfinished.

Note on Transliteration

Because this book is not directed toward people with extensive experience with India, its theatre, or its languages, I have tried to simplify my system of transliteration as much as possible. Hence, Krishna, rather than *Kṛṣṇa*. So, also *lila*, rather than *līlā*, since the difference in the way these two forms might sound in English is negligible, and there is no *lila* in Hindi that might cause confusion with *līlā*. However, I have kept the long vowel marking for the word *râs*, so as to avoid confusion with the Sanskrit word *rasa*, which also has to do with theatre, but which is, in the end, a different word. In material I have quoted from other sources, I have kept transliterations and diacritical markings as they appear.

1. Introduction: *Râs Lila* Theatre and Its Implications

Everyone is a little wound up, not only because the play is about to start, but because Holi celebrations have been already going on for a couple of days. A particularly rambunctious Spring holiday in India, Holi gives license to assault perfect strangers with water and dye. Vrindavan, a small dusty town just off the national highway south of New Delhi, is owned by teenagers and other hooligans for the week surrounding Holi, and all in attendance at this morning's *râs lila* performance show the damp and colorful signs of their encounters with the masters of the narrow lanes and streets outside of the ashram. Once sharply white kurta shirts are now splashed purple and red, the patterns of already colorful saris are blotched, and the skin of smiling faces and clasped hands is green and pink—hues that will remain on people for days to come. From his seat located downstage right, the play's director, Swami Fateh Krishna Sharma, has warned the crowd not to indulge in the traditional, messy revelry that proceeds outside, so as to keep the ashram neat. Nevertheless, the crowd is jittery. They anticipate the climax of this morning's play, which employs truckloads of fresh flower petals to transform Holi's typically sloppy revelry into explosions no less colorful, but much less wet.

The *phul lila*—"the flower play"—as it is known, is the brainchild of Purushottam Goswami, the aging patriarch of the Jaisingh Ghera ashram, who is popularly known as Maharaj-ji. Adapting the *râs lila* theatre tradition that has ornamented Vrindavan for a few centuries, he has managed to replicate and reinforce the chaotic joy of Holi while maintaining the sense that the grounds of Jaisingh Ghera are apart from the common bedlam going on outside the ashram's high walls. Maharaj-ji himself seems apart from the common sort. Dressed invariably in traditional saffron, he moves about the pathways of Jaisingh Ghera with the slow shuffle of age, and at every pause some devotee or other steals an opportunity to bend and touch his feet. It is not uncommon to see ashram staff and others fully prostrate themselves as Maharaj-ji shuffles by. He is almost solely responsible for the existence of Jaisingh Ghera, built up in Maharaj-ji's lifetime from the remains of a Rajput prince's eighteenth-century estate. It is one of the most prestigious ashrams in Vrindavan—which means something in a town bursting at the seams with ashrams. He enjoys some renown outside of Vrindavan as well, counting considerable numbers of followers from Rajasthan to Orissa. Maharaj-ji is on the A-list of residents in Vrindavan, where social status has a significance hardly imaginable in the United States. And this is why the play comes to a stop—even at the height of anticipation of what's to come—when Maharaj-ji appears. He steps carefully through an upstage curtain into a far corner of the stage. The music dips, the actors pull back to the edges of the playing space. The audience holds its enthusiasm in check.

But this book is not about Maharaj-ji or the reverence in which the audience of devotees holds him. Rather, it is about what happens next. After a short moment's pause, he lowers himself to the floor, bends toward the actors at the other end of the stage, and touches his forehead to the floor: a sign of contrition and subservience that, given his stature, Maharaj-ji would not be expected to give to anyone in Vrindavan. The actors to which Maharaj-ji defers are mostly just kids. They are Brahman kids, to be sure, but they are from rural Brahman families not approaching even distantly the standing of Maharaj-ji's Goswami lineage.[1] There's more going on in Maharaj-ji's deferral than a simple nod to the actors. The kids on stage, dressed in emerald green saris and shimmering white tunics, are, according to Vrindavan tradition, at least five thousand years old, the children of an idyllic Vrindavan where God spends his time playing games and making mischief as a child. Maharaj-ji prostrates himself before Krishna, the divine boy, and before Radha, the divine girl, and before the *gopi*s, the semidivine, milkmaid girls of the mythical Vrindavan village. He defers to children, to be certain, but to supernal children. At the end of the performance, most everyone present will pay similar respects to this manifestation of God on stage. Devotees regard the presence of God in *râs lila* performances as a matter of fact. His appearance there does not happen by way of trance or mystical projection, but simply *is*, in a way that devotees regard as literal.

Consequently, the *râs lila* of Vrindavan models the way theatre works. We have all caught ourselves, suddenly, *caring* about characters on a stage. Andromache weeps over Astyanax's broken body, and so do we. Stanley hits Stella in the mouth, and a fury rises in us. Oliver asks for some more, and we cringe in anticipation of what comes next. In fact, we all, at one point or another, experience the lovely double-vision of the theatre, in which we see, in a literal way and at the same time, both actors and characters. The ways in which Vrindavan audiences reach, understand, and express this theatrical paradox can tell us much about our own theatrical lives. This book, then, aims at understanding this peculiarity in the *rās līla*, where Gods and actors show up simultaneously, and in articulating how this may not be such a peculiarity, after all, but inherent in theatre experiences of all sorts.

Rās līla theatre also models the close relationship between theatre and religion. One way in which audiences reach the point at which they see Krishna and an actor in the same time and space is through the basic practice of Krishna worship, which trains them in "seeing" from childhood. The image in the temple, or in the household shrine, is both an art object and a manifestation of divinity at the same time. The material fact of the one does not preclude the spiritual fact of the other, and that, perhaps, is not so peculiar in many other religious traditions either. A basic element of religion is that believers "see" both what is there and what is not (empirically) there.

In the *rās līla*, the activity of which is both theatrical and religious at the same time, a distinction between theatre practice and religious practice is pointless, so that theatre is religion and vice-versa, and not because theatre hasn't fully shed the archaic rite from which it arose (the *rās līla* did not arise from an archaic rite) nor because contemporary rites exhibit superficial, theatrical elements such as costume, script, blocking, and so forth. Rather, here, theatre is religion by making the unmanifest manifest—the fundamental thing that both theatre and religion try to do.[2] The explicit convergence of temple rite and theatrical production in the *rās līla* may be implicit in other religious and theatrical practice where the essence of the activity is to make appear what wasn't there before. To the extent that theatre is engaged in making the unmanifest manifest, theatre is religion. And to the extent that religion attempts to make the unmanifest manifest, religion is theatre.

As a consequence of my experience of Vrindavan and of *rās līla* theatre, I am less inclined to distinguish clearly between religion and theatre, though for reasons having to do with human nature and cognition rather than with the coincidental resemblances between the manner of performing theatre and of "doing" religion. The intersection of theatre and religion lies much deeper. Based on neurological research, psychiatrists Eugene d'Aquili and Andrew Newberg have recently asserted what philosophers and theologians have been asserting for centuries: that aesthetic experience and religious experience are not distinct, discrete phenomena, but manifestations of a single mode of human perception.[3] *Râs lila* theatre provides an especially neat model for cognitive theories of religion that seek to correlate religious activity with other human activity as like expressions of a singular human mode of operating, rather than as distinct (and, therefore, normative) ways of interacting with the world.

We find that *râs lila* patrons and performers make little distinction between religion and art; in fact, that lack of distinction extends beyond the walls of the theatre and outside of the timings of performances to the day-to-day lives of actors and patrons and to the general activity of Vrindavan as a whole. The essential notion of religion in Vrindavan is that God *plays*, and being religious means *playing*, so that the *râs lila* stage is only a microcosm of the larger stage that is Vrindavan—a theatre in every strict sense of the word, since it exists and operates only to facilitate the divine play and our (mortal) participation as characters in it.

An hour earlier than Maharaj-ji's advent on the stage, the performance begins in typical fashion, adhering to conventions established in the sixteenth century. The theatre building itself, parts of which date back to the eighteenth century, has been especially constructed for these performances, following an architectural design common to the larger Vrindavan ashrams, combining a theatre and guest rooms for pilgrims and visiting patrons. The theatre's walls, split into two floors, include apartments for Jaisingh Ghera's ever-flowing guests. The doors and windows of the apartments open directly into the orchestra seating on the ground floor and into the shallow balcony on the upper floor. The rectangular orchestra might seat as many as three hundred if it had fixed seating, but, in Indian fashion, there are no seats. Instead, enormous rugs are rolled out over the gray marble floor, and "rump-seating" accommodates many times more than the capacity of fixed chairs. Additional patrons sit on the second-floor balcony, resting their upper bodies on a dangerously low railing (figure 1.1).

Most folks in Vrindavan expect events to begin late, and they are seldom wrong. Those few audience members present at curtain face a plain, proscenium stage, raised about three feet off the floor. Swami Fateh Krishna Sharma, known, like other *râsdharis*, as "Swami-ji," sits on a squat platform downstage right, behind his harmonium, squeezing out moody chords as preparations backstage are being finished. Four additional musicians and an assortment of stagehands squash together behind him with drums, harmoniums, cymbals, and microphones, filling the right wing of the stage to its upstage corner. As Swami-ji's meandering harmonies coalesce into a discernible tune, the curtain goes up to reveal the actors playing Krishna

Introduction 5

Figure 1.1 The theatre at Jaisingh Ghera (Photo by D. V. Mason).

and Radha in brilliant white costumes seated side-by-side on a dais dressed garishly in red, gold, and green material glittering in the stage lighting like tinted tinfoil. These two actors are around fourteen years old, and both are boys. The circumstances in Vrindavan are very few in which women perform.[4] The actors sit by each other with little expression as Swami-ji's opening hymn rolls along, and as six more actors enter.

The additional actors are dressed in gleaming green *saris*, traditional garb for Vrindavan women, though none of these actors, too, are female. The boys in costume saris represent the girls of the mythological Vrindavan village, or *gopi*s, with whom Krishna and Radha spend their leisure time. The oldest of these actors is sixteen, the youngest six, who necessarily follows his compatriots around the stage, since he is only just learning his part, and performances are also rehearsals. The gopis split into lines on opposite sides of the stage, and, facing Krishna and Radha upstage center, perform *arati*: a ceremony borrowed from Vaishnava temple ritual, ceremonially emphasizing Radha and Krishna's appearance in the environment of the play. *Arati* is the first indication that these two teenagers playing Krishna and Radha are something more than actors in a play. John S. Hawley, whose work on the devotional poetry of Braj has included important analyses of *rās līlā* performances and the translation of a few plays, interprets the *arati* thus: "This offering of light is an indispensible part of the worship of *RADHA* and *KRISHNA* as they make themselves present in the temple images: it both honors the objects of worship and makes them visible to the devotees in attendance."[5] The *arati* as performed in the *râs lila* identifies the ritual context the *râs lila* shares with temple worship and the divine identity the actors share with temple images.

When the *arati* concludes, the gopis come together upstage and touch the feet of the divine couple. Reassuming their positions at each end of the stage, the gopis and Swami-ji sing a succession of songs praising Krishna and Radha, praising Vrindavan, praising the river Yamuna, praising the ideal beauty of Braj, and soliciting the divine couple to come and play. This unit of the performance follows a pattern established in scriptural literature and celebrated in devotional poetry in which the gopis seek out Krishna's company, and he, in turn, seeks out Radha's, and the pattern is always played out in roughly the same manner in *râs lila* performances. The gopis get Krishna to come down from the dais, and after some cajoling and pleading, Krishna succeeds in getting Radha to come down as well. The scriptural pattern concludes here with the *râs* dance, in which gopis, Krishna, and Radha collectively participate, and which lends its name to the genre. The dance sequence may last only a few minutes, or might stretch out beyond thirty minutes, or to as much as an hour, depending upon the proclivities of the troupe and the nature of the venue. In this case, the dance sequence runs for about twenty minutes, including a few, short, intervening dialogues between Krishna and Radha, a long series of *jhanki*s, and the climactic *mahârâs* dance.

The *jhanki* is a curious feature of the *râs lila*. In essence, it is a tableau, a picture of the players suddenly coalescing from dance and presenting the characters in iconographic poses explicitly suggesting the poses of temple images and other devotional art (figure 1.2). *Jhanki*s are also arranged behind curtains, drawn by standard stage mechanism on stages so equipped, or held up by stagehands, so that the sudden removal of the curtain reveals a devotionally charged vision of Krishna, Radha, and their associates. These tableaus are extremely important to *râs lila* practice. So central are they to the performance that they may be responsible for the mischaracterization of the *râs lila* by Western scholars of the nineteenth and early twentieth centuries as a kind of mime or dumb-show.[6] In contemporary practice, the *jhanki*s at the opening and closing of the show, and often at moments in the middle of performances, provide an opportunity for worship, as the audience is allowed to enter the playing space and personally approach Krishna and Radha; and audience members do so with all the reverence they exhibit in temple settings. Prabhudhayal Mital,

Figure 1.2 Krishna and Radha in a *jhanki* pose during a performance (Photo by Celia Mason).

author of *Braj ki Râslîlâ*, notes that the chief significance of the *jhanki* is the manner in which it deepens the religio-aesthetic experience (*rasânubhâv*) of the spectators.[7] The *jhanki* certainly appears to be a bridge between *râs lila* theatre and ritual worship in Krishna temples. For Donna Wulff, a scholar of Hinduism whose early scholarship focused on the theological roots of contemporary Krishna worship, "The close parallel with image worship is unmistakable."[8] *Râs lila* theatre, then, is not only theatre, but a worship service. The stage activity quite unselfconsciously crosses boundaries between ritual and theatre, and, in this way, *râs lila* theatre may demonstrate just how artificial those boundaries can be.

On this morning, after dancing apart for several seconds, Krishna and Radha come together center stage and intertwine, turning toward the audience so as to show their two faces atop their one body. They hold this pose for ten or fifteen seconds, while several patrons stand and take photographs. The cycle of dance-pose-photographs repeats several times.

Swami-ji's troop performs the *jhanki* cycle fairly seamlessly, but even here there is an obvious break in the continuity of stage movement as Krishna and Radha search over their juxtaposition to each other to make certain they have their respective limbs in the right places. In other performances with other troupes, the integration of dance and *jhanki* is much less smooth. Many times the actors are obviously untrained in dance, and knock around the stage clumsily until the moment of another *jhanki* arrives, for which they hastily throw themselves together. Among some troupes, dance seems increasingly only to be an excuse to put *jhanki*s together.

Vasant Yamadagni suggested to me that *jhanki*s were introduced to the *râs lila* no more than fifty years ago, and asserted, curiously, that the recent concentration of performances on *jhanki*s has made the *râs lila* less spiritual. I think the confusion of Western scholars such as Sylvain Levi, F. S. Growse, and H. H. Wilson, who described the *râs lila* as mime or dumb-show, suggests that *jhanki*s have been a part of performances for more than a century; but it may be that *jhanki*s have become more the object of performances in the last few decades. In any case, a concern for the degeneration of the art prevails among scholars and older patrons. Ram Narayan Agrawal, author of several books on the *râs lila* and other arts of the Braj region, believes the contemporary tradition lacks the spirituality that characterized it fifty years ago. As opposed to the practice of devotional service to God (*seva*), Agrawal identifies money as the aim of today's performances.[9] To some degree, concerns such as Agrawal's are evidence of a nostalgia for the good old days, which may never have existed. To illustrate this point, Maharaj-ji's eldest son Srivatsa Goswami, who runs Jaisingh Ghera under the auspices of his father, points out with a shrug the five-hundred-year-old allusions to *râs lila* performers in the *Guru Granth Sahib*, which describe performers as beggars with distinctly financial objectives.[10]

Even so, certain aspects of the *râs lila* have certainly changed in the past fifty years, especially those aspects most immediately affected by technology. In recent decades, wire-born electricity has facilitated the introduction of lighting and sound technology to *râs lila* staging, and these technological advances have in turn contributed to the development of the *râs lila* as mass entertainment in addition to devotional practice. The crowd assembled to watch a late-night *râs lila* performance in the public space at Krishna's birthplace in Mathura on Krishna's birthday in the Fall of 2006 was several thousand, and Doordarshan, India's state-run television system, broadcast the event all over India.

But in the recent past, there has been resistance to the technology that has made such *râs lila* spectacles possible and fashionable. In *The Miracle*

Plays of Mathura, the first extended, Western study of *râs lila*, religion scholar Norvin Hein reported that in the Nineteen-Fifties—corresponding with the point fifty years ago at which (so Yamadagni and Agrawal suggest) the sanctity of *râs lila* theatre began to wane—he encountered fierce opposition to his attempts to make audio recordings of *râs lila* performances. Nowadays, both audio recording and video recording of performances is a matter of course, often expressly contracted with media professionals by the patrons who sponsor a given performance. Agrawal may be correct in his assessment of this kind of change as evidence of a diminishing regard on the part of *râs lila* directors themselves for the sanctity of the art they perform in deference to an increasing interest in the money *râs lila* performances can generate. It may even happen that technology and greed will ultimately result in the secular conversion of the *râs lila*, such that it no longer provides a meaningful mechanism of worship and divine reciprocation.

For the time being, however, the *râs lila*'s essence remains spiritual, and its religious character is unlikely to go away except in conjunction with Vrindavan and its peculiar devotion, or *bhakti*, the place and mood to which the *râs lila* is inextricably tied. As long as *bhakti* continues to anticipate the appearance of divinity through material forms such as temple images—of which actors are logical analogs—and as long as Vrindavan's central activity is Krishna worship, the *râs lila* will remain an essentially religious activity, whatever the impositions of technology or distractions of money (and Vrindavan would disappear altogether without Krishna worship). So too, I would argue, as long as devotional activity dominates life in Vrindavan, the town will provide the conditions of day-to-day living that make *râs lila* actors and audience members compelling models for the study of faith, spirituality, and dramatic art.

The next phase of the morning's performance is the *mahârâs* dance, the "Great *Râs*" in which Krishna, Radha, and all the gopis participate. *Râs lila* dancing borrows heavily from North Indian *kathak* dance, involving a high degree of rhythmic stomping (accentuated by a dense collection of small bells on each dancer's ankles) and neat and fluid motions of the arms and hands. But the young *râs lila* actors are not trained in dance with the same degree of discipline as female *kathak* dancers. Many of them hardly know their parts, and they stumble along after the older cast members, while some older cast members—though they clearly "know" their parts—have little concern for the artistry with which they execute their steps. Consequently, *râs lila* dance is often a haphazard affair. But the aesthetic force of the live, devotional music that accompanies it, the opulently gilded scene, and the patrons' own devotional investment combine to easily overshadow the shortcomings of the performers' (mis)steps. Which is to say, the devotional attitude of the audience, rather than the expertise of the performers, determines the quality of the performance. A discussion of *râs lila* theatre is one of audiences and of their active investment in the performance of the event. So active is the involvement of *râs lila* audiences that we can speak of audience members themselves as performers. During performances and in outside circumstances on the Vrindavan stage, *râs lila* patrons develop and play characters of their own. Again, what is explicit in the religious performances and living of Vrindavan may be implicit theatre events, spiritual and secular, generally. Even in the darkened, silent theatres of Western traditions, the experiences that audiences have arise more from their own active acting than from the talent and skill of performers.

The *maharâs* ends the portion of the *râs lila* in which dance predominates with a sequence that seldom fails to impress. As the music reaches a crescendo, Krishna, wearing a broad fan of peacock feathers on his back, spins rapidly around the stage on his knees. Over the combined din of drums and song, stomping, clapping, anklets, and spontaneous shouts of "*Jai ho!*" from company and audience, some musician or other with a microphone inevitably belts out an imitation of the distinctive peacock cry. On this Holi morning, it is a grand moment, and a marked thrill for the audience, which follows Swami-ji with loud shouts of "*Jai, jai Sri Radhe!*" as the curtain falls and there is abrupt silence.

The short intermission that follows divides the course of the show. In this special case, much more than half the performance remains, since the unusual ending of this specially commissioned performance, involving mounds and mounds of flower petals, draws itself out in festive celebration; but, typically, the intermission between a *râs lila*'s "dancing" and "playing" marks a halfway point. As the set is adjusted and costumes changed backstage, Swami-ji lectures on the correlation between God and the utterance of his name. He also considers the significance of Holi, and it is here that he counsels the audience to refrain from typical and messy Holi revelries within the walls of the ashram, so as to keep Jaisingh Ghera clean.

When the curtain again rises, the morning's *lila* commences. As the first half of a *râs lila* is dance, the second half is dialogue-driven drama. The word *lila* means *play*, with as many connotations as the English word, including *theatre*, but with the added South Asian understanding of the physical world altogether as the play of God. The perception of life as God's self-indulgent game contributes to Vrindavan's happily chaotic nature, and also to a sense of blissful futility among residents.[11] Theatrical *lila*s dramatize the mythology of Krishna's childhood play in Vrindavan. There are well more than one hundred of these stories that find play on some occasion or another in a Vrindavan *râs lila*, and more are being developed every year, especially to incorporate the remembrance of sectarian saints and canonical Krishna lore.

The acting style adopted by, or imposed on, the younger actors in these plays is distinguished by a singsong manner of speech, the use of prescribed gestures and hand positions in conjunction with the meaning of particular spoken lines, and very little movement about the stage. This last element may only be a concession to necessity, since mobile microphones are only recently finding their way into the *râs lila*, and actors' movements have been limited to areas close to microphone stands. Even considering the inherent complications, microphones almost always appear in those *râs lila* performances that take place in dedicated venues in town (as opposed to out in the countryside along the pilgrimage trail). At the smallest Vrindavan venues, such as near the shrine at Sudama Kutir, an indoor area that seats around sixty people, none of whom are ever more than eight yards from the actors, at least one microphone on a stand is available to the actors. The musicians who provide continuous music for the *râs* dance similarly provide a nearly continuous stream of music to accompany the dramatic action of the *lila*, and the actors' voices, particularly such small voices, have no chance of competing with the basic musical set up of the *râsdhari*'s piercing voice, a harmonium, a set of tablas, and several sets of finger symbols—each of which may be doubled and tripled in larger troupes—and all of which may very well be electronically amplified themselves.[12]

Older actors—those few men who assume the stories' adult roles, such as Krishna's mother, the divine sage Narada, Gods such as Shiva, and so forth—are patently melodramatic. Their manner of presentation involves strongly asserted physical attributes and gestures, and bellowing, declamatory vocal styles, exhibiting the clear influence of Hindi film acting. The melodramatic nature of *râs lila* acting is emphasized by the fright wigs and Santa beards the adults assume in particular parts.

The hundred-plus stories that play out on *râs lila* stages range from the harrowing drama of Krishna's birth in a prison (and his subsequent nocturnal escape from it) to the heart-wrenching drama of his abandonment of Vrindavan as a teen, and including a full array of comedy in between. As the *râs lila* imagines it, Krishna's association with the gopis is comic more often than not—he steals their food, steals their clothes, undermines their trust, berates them, and castigates them, while they steal from him and conspire to humiliate him. Adult characters are quite often vaudeville-type buffoons, endearing themselves to the audience through boisterous physical slapstick and mental sluggishness. A popular character appearing in a number of stories resembles the stock *vidushaka* clown of Sanskrit drama, the Brahman whose education is limited, but whose appetite is insatiable. In one "Butter Thief" *lila* performed by Swami-ji's troupe, Krishna punches a hole in the bottom of a huge, clay jar of milk, which the gopis have suspended in a net, so as to keep the pot away from him and his cohorts. One of his cowherd friends, a tubby fellow in his twenties, takes up a position directly underneath the jar, and is happily doused by the milk that rushes out, even while he swallows as much as he can.

Even the stories whose content is essentially dramatic have inevitable comic gags. In a *lila* about Mirabai, the Rajasthani poet-saint, performed by Bade Thakur's troupe, the actor playing Mirabai's mother-in-law, driven to distraction by her minions' successively unsuccessful attempts to kill Mirabai, grabs one of the posts that supports the roof of the stage as the nearest thing resembling a stick with which to deliver beatings. Unable to wrench it free, he grabs the nearest substitute, and lashes out at his fellow actors with a microphone stand. The inevitable comic moments do not overwhelm sincere drama in those *lila*s that concern matters of devotional seriousness. In a *lila* performed by Swami Ramprasad's troupe, upon learning that Krishna has gone to Mathura, leaving Vrindavan forever, five or six adult cowherds weep real tears while lamenting the sorry state of Vrindavan in Krishna's absence.

The cowherds of Swami-ji's troupe playing at Jaisingh Ghera this morning are much more festive. Their counterparts are the child actors playing gopis, and the *lila* is a curious theatrical dramatization of annual Holi celebrations in the northern part of Braj, particularly in the town of Barsana. Each year in Barsana, the "battle of the sexes" plays out literally during the days of Holi, as the women of the town take up long, wooden staves and mercilessly beat any man they come across. For their part, the men of Barsana seek out confrontation with the village women, taunting them into fury and retreating when necessary. This *lila* stages this community rite. The cowherds and gopis lob insults at each other from their respective sides of the stage, engage each other in bawdy dancing, slap and kick each other, and generally whoop it up until the staves appear and the gopis go after the cowherds with a very pretended vengeance.

Here, Purushottam takes the stage, and it is time for the flowers. Once Krishna and Radha have been set up on a throne center stage, and with Swami-ji and his musicians in full swing, a stream of wicker baskets filled with flower petals begins to flow from the wings to the gopis, who pour out the petals over the heads of the divine couple. After a minute or two, Krishna and Radha are shrouded by orange marigold petals. After another few minutes, their limbs disappear, and as the baskets continue to pass through the gopis' hands, Krishna's and Radha's faces must be cleared to keep the actors from suffocation (figure 1.3). Still, the petals fall, mounding on the tops of the actors' heads, and piling up around their throne such that all that is visible of the throne and the actors are two pairs of eyes and a couple of noses amid distinct layers of orange, yellow, and red flower petals, painstakingly separated according to their color the previous night and produced onstage in color-coordinated sequence.

Fifteen or twenty minutes go by before the supply begins to wane. Then the gopis scoop up the petals and fling them in damp clumps out over the audience, which dances happily in the floral volleys. Passed as they have over the bodies of Krishna and Radha, the petals are a type of *prasad*— what God graciously discards for the benefit of his devotees. Several devotees take Krishna from the stage on their shoulders and shoulder him back through the gleeful audience, clambering to get close enough to be under the petals Krishna continues to fling in every direction. On stage, the gopis and Radha continue their revelry under a persistent cloud of flower petals, which is spreading inexorably out from the stage as audience members are able to gather handfuls of their own to send aloft again.

Not all *râs lila* performances are quite so raucous, but they all have a kernel of this playfulness, the manifestation of which seems to be facilitated by the genre's dependence on child performers. This study of *râs lila* performance follows my own fascination with the happy chaos that child performers here inspire. To be sure, Krishna devotion (*bhakti*) can transport adult devotees to such heights independent of the immediate presence of children. *Play*, as a concept, is an inherent feature of *bhakti*, and has been essential to it since Krishna *bhakti* emerged as a popular form of worship in the first few centuries of the Common Era (CE). Such contemporary devotional activities as *kirtan*s, in which groups sing and chant together in rather playful celebration of Krishna, can inspire participants to ecstatic levels, quite apart from the direct participation of actual children. But the focus of devotional activity in Vrindavan, with or without the participation of children, is invariably the young Krishna, and it is precisely the peculiar quality of his youth that endears him to devotees. Hence, child actors hold a unique place in theatre connected with *bhakti*, offering as they do a physical manifestation of Krishna's divinely adorable attributes.

Figure 1.3 The climactic moment of the *phul lila* at Jaisingh Ghera (Photo by D. V. Mason).

The topic of chapter two is the religious value of *râs lila* theatre in its own context. The theology handed down to contemporary Vrindavan from the *bhakti* revival of the sixteenth century is a dualistic theology that greatly values emotional experience and the perception of God's presence. The *râs lila* theatre in which emotional experience is intense and the presence of God is taken as a matter-of-fact, then, provides an ideal environment for a devotee—one that, perhaps, even has the same quality as a devotee's desired state of eternal bliss in God's presence. For this reason, I argue that *râs lila* theatre itself acts as a kind of "salvation." *Râs lila* theatre *is* religion. In fact, I am not so concerned with the metaphysical nature of the *râs lila* as I am with showing how theatre resembles religion and very easily lends itself to religious practice. The basic premise of this book follows from this issue. Religion and theatre are so well suited to each other that they are often indistinguishable from each other.

Following this theoretical foundation, I offer a brief summary of the Krishna theme, with a focus on the way his childhood became significant in the first centuries, CE. I also try to connect early Krishna mythology with the South Asian concept of divine play (*lila*), since the two in combination provide the central conceit of *bhakti*. Of course, this exercise in glossing a fairly broad and infinitely complex period of Indian cultural history is vulnerable to accusations of Orientalism, the nineteenth-century version of which too eagerly sought to trace genetic origins, categorize cultural phenomena, and fix boundaries between social movements that might very well have overlapped. The overview of Krishna that I provide here is not intended to suggest an inviolate map of the Krishna figure's conception and evolution, nor do I intend here to assert that we should suppose that any one formulation of Krishna's character excludes other possible and coexistent formulae and practices of worship. Especially with regard to Krishna's earliest appearances in literature, I hope to show in this first chapter how little is certain, in fact, about the Krishna character, while providing for readers approaching my discussion of Krishna theatre, without any background in South Asian studies, a sufficiently clear picture of Krishna and the movements that developed around him. The early popularity of the child Krishna as a popular response to Brahmanic oppression does not exclude the possibility that Krishna as a child might have appealed to sectors of the middle class and upper class for entirely different reasons at the same time (just as is certainly the case today). However, my focus on the child Krishna's popularity among the lower classes leads to a discussion of the childlike abandon inherent in many forms of Krishna worship, which derives from the Krishna character itself.

The fourth chapter in this study is also concerned with the place of children and childishness in Vrindavan theatre, and toward this I reassess Western and South Asian theories concerning the introduction of children to *râs lila* performances in the sixteenth century. Scholars from the East and West have, perhaps unjustifiably, identified the significant developments in *râs lila* practice in the last half of the fifteenth century with the initial introduction of child actors. Although a significant period with respect to *râs lila* form and function—probably the origin of the contemporary form of the art—I would suggest that it was the sixteenth century that saw the transformation of a theatrical practice already utilizing children in its principal roles. The establishment of this assertion is important to the contention that the peculiar nature of child performers has always been a fundamental element of Krishna theatre in the Braj area, which depends upon a "true" representation of Krishna, the divine child, and the village children with whom he plays.

The use of children as principal performers in a theatrical tradition is not unique in India to the *râs lila*. In Western scholarship, the *ram lila*, especially the specific version of this tradition performed annually and on a grand scale at Ramnagar near Varanasi, has long since been recognized for its reliance on local children to hold down leading roles.[13] The similarities between these two kinds of devotional performance extend further, as the children employed in the *ram lila* are similarly regarded as *svarup*s—the incarnations of the divine roles they assume—*arati* fulfills a similar role in the patrons' regard for the actors, and both performance types seek to vivify a sacred past and the sacred geography to which the past is tied. In fact, these two traditions are sufficiently similar in so many respects that most *râs lila* troupes in Braj also perform portions of the *ram lila* cycle. There are, however, some distinctions between the two. Performances of the *ram lila* are tied more tightly to a festival than are *râs lila*s. The *ram lila* appears in northern India each Fall in connection with the celebration of *dussehra*. *Râs lila* performances, while reaching biannual high-points during Holi in the Spring and *janmashtami* during the Fall, nevertheless play in a variety of contexts throughout the year. The *râs lila* has long since developed into a featured activity of Braj pilgrimage, and, hence, enjoys year-round demand. The significance of this difference may be that the *râs lila* provides a better model than the *ram lila* for a study of the way a theatrical tradition is integrated into a culture's method of day-to-day worship (as opposed to the heightened activities of worship that play out in festival and holiday celebrations).

Another significant difference lies in the sacred geography the two performance traditions occupy. As William Sax has noted, for some devotees, the *ram lila* at Ramnagar transforms the space of Ramnagar into the literal manifestation of Ayodhya, Ram's hereditary kingdom, Ravana's Lankan fortress, and the jungle in which Ram lives out his exile. The *râs lila* similarly manifests the Braj of Krishna's mythic childhood, but on the very ground that devotees already accept as Krishna's childhood home. In the case of the *râs lila* the relationship between geography and performance is much more reciprocal, as pilgrims' sacred regard for the land reinforces the *râs lila*'s presumption to manifest it. Here, again, the *râs lila* appears more naturally a part of daily religious activity and more intimately a feature of living than an annual diversion from it. We should also note that *ram lila*s performed by Braj theatre troupes stylistically resemble *râs lila*s, and in this way they are stylistically distinct from *ram lila* performances at Varanasi and elsewhere.[14]

The fifth chapter considers the art of the *râs lila*'s contemporary child actor, who receives little in the way of formal training, but who derives meaningful training in acting from day-to-day living in Vrindavan. Though entirely unstructured, elements of the actor training that devotional life provides *râs lila* actors resemble features of so-called Stanislavskian training. Similarly, other residents of Vrindavan, those who patronize the *râs lila* as a devotional event, partake of the same training by living in the same environment that is permeated by theatricality. Consequently, Vrindavan audiences are well trained in acting and equally participate in *râs lila* performances as actors.

Recognizing the fact that, for devotee patrons of the *râs lila*, the characters who appear on the *râs lila* stage are not representations but incarnations raises some question as to the *râs lila*'s theatrical legitimacy. If *râs lila* actors are not "acting," as such, but "being," can we regard the *râs lila* as "theatre"? Because of the *râs lila*'s confusion of mimesis and ontology, some resist characterizing it as theatre, much as they resist using the term *theatre* to discuss other ritual activities, such as the Catholic mass, in which, for the faithful, imitation and authenticity merge. The argument I develop in chapter six is that theatre is defined more by spectatorship than by stage activity, so that *theatre* need not be defined by acts of mimesis. The audience who appears at Carnegie Hall to watch Andy Kaufman be Andy Kaufman has itself created a theatrical event. So, too, the audience who materializes at a *râs lila* performance to watch God be God creates by their own presence a moment of theatre.

To the degree, however, that we restrict the understanding of theatre in the context of South Asia to canonized South Asian performance theory, the limits of mimesis in *râs lila* performances may not be negligible. The *Natyashastra*, an authoritative treatise on theatrical aesthetics from the fourth century, CE, seems to regard imitation or representation as an essential feature of theatrical performance (*natya*). Certainly, the accepted theory of *rasa*—the heightened aesthetic experience of the spectator as described by the *Natyashastra*—maintains that aesthetic distance between spectators and performers is essential to performing art, since without that distance, an activity is indistinguishable from "real life." This distance depends on the recognition of representation in a performance by its spectators. To the extent that Krishna himself plays in *râs lila* performances, as is understood by *râs lila* patrons, we might suppose that the *râs lila* lacks the necessary distinction between "real life" and performance, and therefore cannot be considered "theatre."

To return to the earlier example, the audience who sits in Carnegie Hall to watch Andy Kaufman be Andy Kaufman nevertheless understands, on account of a variety of elements that frame Kaufman's activity, that they watch both Kaufman and a "Meta-Kaufman" at the same time. I would suggest that the same phenomenon operates in *râs lila*. Krishna himself appears on the *râs lila* stage, but Krishna himself is an actor. Because God's activity itself is theatrical, an audience who sees God on the *râs lila* stage, rather than a ten-year-old actor, sees theatre—a theatrical performance that transcends the material substance of the visible stage, the actor, his costume, and so forth. Consequently, the patrons of a *râs lila* performance see on the stage a "Meta-Krishna" comparable to a "Meta-Kaufman." That is, devotees at a *râs lila* performance see Krishna playing Krishna. Hence, these theatrical performances satisfy the *Natyashastra*'s own demand that patrons acknowledge the representation taking place on stage.

Furthermore, although patrons do, indeed, regard the Krishna actor as Krishna himself, they do not necessarily *not* regard the actor in a *râs lila* performance as an actor. South Asian audiences in general, and devotee audiences in this particular case, do not generally give much regard to ontological exclusivity, such as that a chair, by being a chair, cannot also be an elephant. With this in mind, Radhakamal Mukerjee writes in *The Cosmic Art of India*, "Art in India...knows no antithesis between the immediate and the ultimate, the earthly and the heavenly, even the sensuous and the transcendental, the enjoyment (*Bhukti*) and liberation (*mukti*)."[15] This nonduality in duality is not peculiar to South Asian thought, but it can be a difficult concept to convey in Western terms.[16] In typically cryptic fashion, Herbert Blau has approached this idea. "A real chair used for a real chair in a 'realistic setting' remains, though a real chair, a sign for a chair. It is what it is not though it appears to be what it is."[17] In the *râs lila*, the chair is a chair and a sign for a chair at the same time without paradox. The boy is Krishna and is the boy at the same time, and the duality perplexes no one.

Based upon my observations of *râs lila* audiences, and an understanding of audiences of religious plays in general, and beginning from the premise that religious theatre shares affinities with all other expressions of theatre, I draw some tentative conclusions about the role audiences play in theatrical performances. I am especially keen to show a qualitative similarity between a devotee's exercise of faith at a religious performance and an audience member's contribution of imagination to a piece of so-called secular theatre. In both cases, a theatrical performance depends in the first place on what the *audience* brings to the theatre. *Râs lila* patrons, I argue, following the theories of Rupa Goswami, Donna Wulff, and David Haberman, themselves play roles during a performance, and this active role-playing on the part of the audience creates the effectiveness of the production, almost independently of what the production itself does. *Râs lila* audiences may, thus, tell us something about the Paradox of Fiction, which denotes the problem of understanding how a theatre audience can feel real, authentic feelings about action that is patently fabricated. Secular audiences, too, play roles when attending theatre. As the *râs lila* audience models for us, an audience's creative contribution to a performance accounts for the performance's effect—especially its emotional effect.

Finally, I look ahead to the next ideas. In Vrindavan, theatre and ritual, art and religion, combine so as to be indistinguishable. Western thought has long suspected a relationship between art and religion that runs deeper than the business of shared imagery. The very *experience* in religion and art may be of one substance. Perhaps, as Whitehead suggests, nothing exists but experience. But, even so, experience itself is, in the first instance, ambiguous. Only after interpretation or through subjectivity does experience take on a religious or aesthetic character (or both at once). By reexamining the experiential tradition of Kantian aesthetics, especially as developed in the United States where secularization has been slower than in Europe, and where *experience* has been central to religion, I point, in the conclusion of this book, to some less-trodden paths that would bear walking. Experience in religion and in theatre is often intense, surprising, and bewildering. The ways in which we arrive at such experience may be common mechanisms, distinguished only *post facto* as religious or artistic. Particularly relevant may be the propensity we all have for role-play, which, as the *râs lila* demonstrates quite explicitly, shapes our experience;

that is, the role-play into which we enter (consciously or not) makes our experience, and, hence, our reality. Developing forms of role-play, such as Massively Multiplayer Online Role-Playing Games (MMORPGs), such as *World of Warcraft*, may be the next things to study alongside religion and theatre toward understanding how the reality we know (or acknowledge) derives from the role(s) we choose to play.

The essential choice we exercise in the adoption of a role that shapes our experience may be likened to faith. Twenty years ago, Richard Schechner solicited of Western practitioners a kind of performance that would be the

> ...source of renewal of religion...sacralizing the relations among people: creating special, sacred, nonordinary—you pick your descriptive adjective—space and time. And acting within, or in relation to, such space/time events that resonate significance not only to the audience but also to the performers.[18]

On the face of it, this was a call for a theatre that would fill a spiritual void in the West, apparently (and theoretically) providing for the West new expressions of religious faith, or, at least, new expressions of human brotherhood through venues set apart from day-to-day living. But Schechner's charge is, of course, less an authoritative mandate than an admission that the numerous, foregone attempts of Western experimental theatre (some of them Schechner's own) at fabricating a religious experience through dramatic performance had not, to that point, succeeded—at least, not in any lasting way. The Holy Theatre experiments of the twentieth century—the attempts at artificial religious practice—which have explicitly sought to emulate the transcendent religious effect of ritual and devotional activity, often by imitating elements of specific religious performances that seem to connect their audiences with transcendence, I would argue, have consistently fallen short of their objective, not because their objective is unreachable—there are many more examples than *ras lila* of theatre that touches transcendence—but because the imitation or emulation of activity is not enough. The transcendent experience of a devotee at a *rās lila* depends upon his devotion, a relationship with divinity that derives from a faith, which does not arise spontaneously from the performance itself but which the devotee grows from his life of worship. Just as a Western visitor to Vrindavan is unlikely to see God in a *rās lila* performance, a theatrical experiment that seeks to provide a transcendent experience for audiences who do not come to the theatre in faith, already attuned to the performance's own spiritual content, fights a losing battle. Theatre thus practiced will never be the renewal of religion. As water turns the mill's wheel, and not the other way around, theatre that fills a religious function moves by the force of its patrons' faith.

Even so, although there may be an unbridgeable gulf between religious theatre and attempts at religious theatre, the way in which audience's faith provides for transcendent experience in the *râs lila* may have a counterpart in the audience-performance relationship of wholly secular theatre. Performance theories that try to account for the essential part that audiences themselves play in performative moments suggest that what is obvious in *râs lila* may be common to any theatre, though, perhaps, of a different quality: a performance succeeds only to the degree that its audience allows.

In the hubbub of the *phul lila*'s final minutes, devotees take Krishna on their shoulders and muscle him through the audience, but above their heads, and a train of stagehands stretches out after him, feeding him wicker baskets of flowers, hand-over-hand. As each basket thrusts up at him from the thicket of upraised hands, he flings its contents over the bouncing heads around him, and as devotees snatch them from the air and scoop them from the floor, the same flower petals almost immediately reappear over Krishna in brisk puffs of red and orange, re-flung by the ecstatic crowd. Krishna passes near me and my cameras and bags and notebooks, and for a moment I can't decide if I should protect my lenses or use them. Several years after the event, I still find stray petals among my things.

2. Theatre Is God ℘

POPULAR DEVOTION IN BRAJ

Braj is a geographical region south of New Delhi. Tourists making the day-trip from New Delhi to Agra to see the Taj Mahal pass directly through Braj, the largest city of which is Mathura. Perhaps eighty miles in diameter, Braj encompasses numerous villages and towns in addition to Mathura, including Barsana, Govardhan, and, of course, Vrindavan, the spiritual center of both Braj and Krishna devotion. Still largely rural, Braj straddles the ancient and modern world. Countryside hovels without indoor plumbing are wired to satellite dishes. Laptop computers surfing the net on pirated phone lines illumine the paneless windows of one-room flats darkened by power failure. Large, grimy pigs snout around plastic Coke bottles and organic offal in untended, open gutters running past shops selling mobile phones and DVD players. Old and new around Braj coexist closely without acknowledging any distance between them.

Brajwasis, people of Braj, regard the geographic area not only as the place in which the problems and pleasures of their immediate lives play out, but as a historical record. The landscape itself inscribes a peculiar religious character on the area, outlining Krishna's divine activity in Braj's countryside and in towns. Govardhan Hill, for instance, marks the spot where Krishna preserved the Braj populace from a life-threatening storm, and visitors still swarm the hill daily in ritual remembrance of Krishna's presence. For Charlotte Vaudeville, one of the leading Western scholars on Krishna devotion in recent decades, "Every spot, every rock, pond, tree or creeper in Braj—even its dust—tells of Krishna's presence to his *bhakta* [devotee]."[1] Almost continuous activity in temples all over Braj ever renews Krishna's presence there, invoking his name and his image, and the sense that Krishna, once present in historical fact, remains present in spiritual reality.

The dusty town of Vrindavan at the center of Braj draws Krishna devotees from all over India. In any one of Vrindavan's many temples on a given day one will find piles of sweets amid flowers, coins, and other offerings laid out before Krishna's seats. The theological notion that inspires this largesse is that Krishna personally receives the gifts; that he does, in fact, accept them for his own consumption and pleasure. Food is presented to the image at meal times, and the image is afforded private time to eat; whatever food is left over once Krishna has finished his meal is then regarded as divine grace, and distributed to devotees, sometimes with reverence, sometimes not, but always with a manifest attitude of consideration for the divine significance of the substance. On particular holidays at Radharaman Temple, the Brahman family conducting worship produces baskets of sweets that Krishna has passed over, and tosses them dramatically, piece by piece, from the temple dais, where there are fierce convulsions of the tightly packed crowd as patrons vie to snatch the flying balls of goo from the air, from the floor, and from each other.

For Krishna *bhakti*—the "devotion" that is the religion of Vrindavan—once ritual has established the divine presence in the temple image, it is an accepted fact that the image, be it of clay, wood, stone, or other material, not only *represents* Krishna, but *is* Krishna, and anything offered to the image is therefore offered to Krishna himself—not in a metaphysical or metaphorical sense, but in literal reality. And some Vrindavan temple images, such as the one residing in Radharaman Temple, are supposed to have been originally self-manifest, appearing fully formed and miraculously, obviating the need for formal ceremony to establish their link with divinity. The image, as the manifestation of God, is very much alive for devotees. Particularly during important festival celebrations when crowds create a greater distance within temples between patrons and shrines, temple patrons can be seen holding field glasses that they use to discern the minute movements of temple images, to judge better the degree to which they have gained or lost weight, to determine differences in expression, and so forth.

Great efforts are made in temples to emphasize and accommodate this living, breathing character of Krishna's images. The daily schedule of the temple accords with the waking, eating, resting, and sleeping times of the divine person dwelling there, the images of which are washed and dressed, entertained, and given recreational exercise as suits the season and Krishna's proclivities. For example, images of Krishna are often taken from their permanent shrines for part of the day and set on specially constructed swings elsewhere in the temple as a kind of temple R&R. Patrons take advantage of these moments to exercise their devotion by keeping the swing in the motion imagined to be most comfortable for the deity—it sometimes happens that attending priests scold children and overzealous devotees for pushing God too hard. This attendance to the images' comfort is conducted with the literal understanding that God himself is the object of the attention.

WORSHIP AND *RÂS LILA* THEATRE

In Vrindavan, the *râs lila* actors who portray Krishna and the *gopis*—the village girls with whom he plays—are considered as divine as their inanimate counterparts in temple shrines. There are, actually, many different forms of theatre in India that go under the name *râs lila*, owing to the fact that the term refers not so much to a particular style of presentation but to a particular episode in Krishna mythology in which Krishna and the gopis dance together in the forest at night. The *râs lila* theatre rooted in the Manipur region, for instance, in which women perform in cylindrical skirts, has very little resemblance to its Braj cousin, but concerns the same subject.[2]

To the same degree that a temple image is considered the physical reality of divinity, once he has donned the costume headpiece (*mukut*), a young boy playing Krishna in a *râs lila* is considered by devotees to be Krishna, and devotees afford the *râs lila* actor the same respect they reserve for temple worship. Backstage at one performance, I saw a devotee sit patiently as the *mukut* was tied to an actor's head. When the last knot was tightened and the last Sanskrit *sloka* recited, the devotee crept forward and extended his hands, which held five or six *laddoo* sweets. The twelve-year-old actor touched a finger to his tongue, and "anointed" each one.

What makes the *râs lila* particularly special as a means of worship in the *bhakti* tradition is the manner in which a moving incarnation of God can interact on a human level with his worshipers. Insofar as Marjorie Boulton was correct in identifying what is significant in theatre as opposed to other forms of art by calling theatre "literature which walks and talks before our eyes," the *râs lila*'s significance as religious practice is *God* walking and talking before our eyes—or, at least, before the eyes of devotees who see him.[3] A patron can present a plate of sweets to a temple icon with the devotional understanding that the deity is present, eats its fill, and leaves what it will for the benefit of its devotees. But the devotee at a *râs lila* performance can see God eat the offering, and may even take the opportunity to feed God directly. It is common to see a patron do more than set a plate of carefully arranged sweets on the stage or the set to be sampled leisurely by the actors, but to take a *laddoo* from the plate and place it directly in the

Krishna actor's mouth.[4] The *râs lila* actor at these moments brings God to temporal life in a warm and breathing way beyond the capacity of a temple icon. John S. Hawley, whose work on the poetry of *râs lila* plays has been definitive, has documented a *râs lila* performance in Vrindavan in which food offerings made the incarnation of Krishna in the lead actor evident.

> The bathing is by now completed and the food offerings, the very ones Yasoda and her staff have been toiling to prepare, are ready at hand. We see them spread out across the entire stage and arrayed on raised platforms.... The practiced eye will distinguish milk sweets of all sorts, dough fried and stuffed, mounts of fruit in every color, and complicated preparations from vegetables and legumes. Needless to say, the sight of this gigantic display of food... is one of the high points of the *lila*. Here sustenance itself is the very stuff of worship.
>
> And of life: once presented to Giriraj [Krishna], even in this dramatic form, it becomes the "grace" (*prasad*) of which all in attendance at the *lila* will partake. In fact, the *rasdhari* [director] may caution the audience that no one is to leave before tasting this grace.[5]

The real presence of Krishna in a *râs lila* means that *râs lila* performances exist on many distinct cognitive levels at once. In the first place, there is a distinct difference between the actor/acting reality and the God/playing reality; and this distinction alone can be quite complicated given that *râs lila* harbors no sense that its actors exchange their identities for others' during the performance in any state of shamanic "possession" or other surrender of self.[6] But the ontological levels upon which *râs lila* takes place are many more than this, even given that these two realities can coexist in the same time and space. Once we consider the ways in which contemporary *râs lila* performances are related to the myth they dramatize, and the way that myth is related to the religious life of devotees, we see that the *râs lila* presents a very complicated metatheatrical knot that enables the *râs lila* to provide for devotees not only a religious experience equivalent to temple worship, but temporary access to the ultimate goal of their devotion, and, thus, something equivalent to salvation.[7]

METATHEATRE IN *RÂS LILA*

The *râs lila* dramatizes the stories of Krishna's childhood and adolescence in a mythical Vrindavan just prior to the beginning of *kaliyuga*, the modern age, which began five thousand years ago, according to *bhakti* tradition. In 1972, Norvin Hein catalogued some one hundred and six of these stories, including the very popular stories of Krishna's petty thievery, his miraculous defeat of powerful demons sent to destroy him, and his comic-erotic dalliances with Radha and the other *gopi*s. Considerably more stories actually appear in *râs lila* performances, including narrations of the travails and triumphs of revered devotees such as the medieval poet Mirabai and the *Mahabharata* heroine Draupadi. By offering any one of these stories on a given night, the *râs lila* is able to suit itself to any given occasion. A troupe I accompanied to a command performance at a local dairy presented a *râs lila* that concerned Krishna's involvement with the care of Vrindavan cows; in Udaipur, a city in southern Rajasthan, I saw a *râs lila* whose central character (apart from Krishna himself) was Mirabai, a renowned female saint of Rajasthani origin. This variability creates the illusion that the *râs lila* is a particular dramatic mode through which a variety of stories are brought to life—functionally similar to such styles of presentation as Japan's *nô* or southern India's *kathakali*, which apply specific physical disciplines and aesthetics to the dramatization of a corpus of myths. However, the *râs lila* is much less concerned with a coherent technique than *nô* or *kathakali*, and, in fact, is less concerned with the variety of stories in the repertoire than it is concerned with a *single* story that it dramatizes over and over again in each performance. The *râs lila* sets each unique Krishna tale within a dramatic framework that is consistent from venue to venue, and that contextualizes each story within a uniform narrative. In fact, whatever the occasion or selected story, each *râs lila* performance is a dramatization of the same, single myth, and this mythical framework is, perhaps, the principal element responsible for the *râs lila*'s soteric power.

The singular story through which the *râs lila* presents all the other Krishna stories—indeed, the one story from which the various regional *râs lila*'s take their name—comes from the medieval religious text, the *Bhagavata Purana*, a collection of stories sailing widely over the immense sea of South Asian mythology. The tenth book of the *Bhagavata Purana*'s twelve books concerns the life of God as a child in Vrindavan and offers versions of the most familiar myths of Krishna's childhood among the other Vrindavan villagers. In the tenth book, the baby Krishna demolishes a cart with a single kick, uproots trees as he crawls on the ground, and kills a number of assassin demons, such as Putana who offers the infant a poisoned breast from which to suckle. It is also in the tenth book that the child Krishna lifts Mount Govardhan on a single finger and dances on the head of the snake king Kaliya. The last half of the tenth book describes Krishna's adolescence, dwelling in some detail on his relationship with Braj's village girls and emphasizing the girls' extreme love for Krishna—a love so overwhelming it compels them to transgress mores and abandon domestic responsibilities in favor of scandalous, late-night soirees in the forest. The very fact that these girls are eager to act disreputably is regarded by devotees as an indication of the degree of their devotion, and the girls themselves are regarded as models of piety.[8] For his part, Krishna teases the girls incessantly, and the stories of the older Krishna and the gopis most often concern the steadfast manner with which the girls remain committed to Krishna in spite of the abuses he heaps on them. Chapters twenty-nine through thirty-three offer the most famous of these stories, in which Krishna hides himself from the gopis when he perceives their growing arrogance. The lament the gopis subsequently raise in separation from Krishna is a common theme of devotional poetry, which adopted South Asian literature's already well-established theme of *vipralambha*, the intensity of feeling experienced by the melancholy lover separated from his or her beloved. What the girls do when they find themselves forsaken is ultimately what the *râs lila* is about. The story, summarized here from *Bhagavata Purana* 10.29–33, known collectively to devotees as the *panchadhyaya*, goes something like this:

> On a given night, Krishna decided he was going to call out the gopis to play with him, and so, under the light of the full moon, he went strolling through the forest playing his flute. As the notes reached the gopis' ears, they immediately dropped whatever it was they were each doing and ran *en masse* to the woods. Some left their cows unmilked, some left their cooking on the stove, and some even dropped plates of food while serving them to their husbands. There were even a few who heard Krishna's tune while nursing their children, and left the children hungry to follow it. So determined were they, that husbands and parents could not hold them back, and so singularly were their minds focused on Krishna that they were essentially one with him. At that moment their sins were consumed and they attained salvation.
>
> Krishna looked at them all standing there, panting and sweating, and told them to go home. What were you thinking? he asked. The woods at night are no place for girls. Go home to your husbands and your kids.
>
> The gopis were shattered, but undeterred. You're more important than our families, they said. You drew us here. We'll stay here whether you like it or not.
>
> Well, at this point, what could Krishna do but relent? He began to dance and play with them, entertaining them with his flute and treating them each like lovers; and pretty soon each of the gopis began to feel as though she were the most important

woman in the world. When Krishna sensed this was happening, he figured he'd teach them a lesson and purify them at the same time, and he disappeared.

For a moment, the gopis' world fell apart. They'd been enjoying the best anyone could hope for, and the next thing they knew—poof. Back to earth. But because their minds were so attached to Krishna, it wasn't but a few seconds before he was present again in their thoughts; and so clearly could they see him there that they began to feel like him. Hey, look at me, said one, I'm Krishna—look how I'm walking!

You can imagine where this went. Pretty soon all the gopis were acting Krishna's part in one story or another. One girl played at kicking over a cart, another crawled on the ground like a baby. One of the girls danced on the head of another, like Krishna dancing on the serpent king's head. One of the girls lifted her shirt into the air as though it were Mount Govardhan on Krishna's finger, and another sucked at a companion's breast as Krishna did to kill Putana. The list of plays goes on and on, and the gopis went on and on like this throughout the forest until some time later they gathered on the banks of the Yamuna and sang together about Krishna, certain he would show up any minute.

Krishna, of course, couldn't stay away, and he returned like breath, and the delighted gopis flocked around him, and began to dance. Krishna joined in the dancing, and miraculously danced with each of them at the same time. In this way, Krishna embraced them, kissed them, and smiled at them, as though flirting with his own reflection.[9] Of course, they couldn't keep this up forever, and as the sun began to come up, Krishna persuaded them all to go home again.

Devotees who hear and tell this story reach the highest level of devotion (*bhakti*).[10]

Every *râs lila* performance aspires to reenact this event, regarded by devotees as always ongoing in a supramundane way. As Hawley suggests, "The *râs lîlâ* imitates this eternal dance every day..."[11] The structure of the performance identifies it very clearly as primarily a retelling of this story concerning the *gopi*s, for which the variety of other Krishna stories are subservient elements. A formal *râs lila* performance always begins with a dance sequence, in which the Krishna actor and the *gopi* actors dance together an assortment of dances suggesting the playing of the characters of *Bhagavata Purana* 10.29. This opening sequence can last anywhere from fifteen to forty-five minutes and longer. Its length is partly determined by the activities that accompany it: recitations of Sanskrit verses, devotional singing, and sermons as delivered by the performance's director or an important patron. But whatever the length of the *râs lila* preliminaries of dance, song, and the spoken or chanted word, they always culminate in the *maharâs* dance. In this part of the dance sequence, the actors form a circle, and maintain that circle through a range of dances, often including the Peacock Dance as Krishna and others whirl around the circle's inner perimeter by way of a dizzyingly fast movement executed entirely on the performers' knees. The circle of the *rås* dance explicitly represents the final moments of the *gopi*s' supernal night when Krishna danced with each of the girls equally and individually, and they were all singularly engaged with their lord at the same time.

What occurs in a typical *rås lila* performance is, then, a representation of a representation of a representation, or, in performance terms, a play-within-a-play-within-a-play. The contemporary actors play at being the mythical *gopi*s on that celebrated night when the *gopi*s themselves play at being Krishna; so contemporary performers are playing at being *gopi*s playing at being Krishna. This is the equivalent of a play-within-a-play. A twist is added to the knot when we see that Krishna himself is a representation. The kind of Hinduism called Vaishnavism in which Vishnu is the preeminent divinity generally regards Krishna as an *avatar*, or divine incarnation—one of several physical manifestations of God, including, among others, a turtle, a dwarf, the fierce man-lion Narasimha, and the epic hero *Rama*. In each of these cases, God assumed what Donna Wulff calls an "embodied form" so that he might act directly upon the physical world.[12] No single *avatar* fully *was* God, but each in form and function was particularly suited to a particular divine task. Narasimha, for instance, appeared in order to kill a demon who was wreaking some havoc in the world after receiving the promise from a respectable source that no man nor animal would be able to kill him. In a case of equivocation of mythical proportions, God's partly human and partly lion *avatar* made short work of the demon. As much as Narasimha was God incarnate in the world, he was, nevertheless, rather deficient as a representation of God, and the same can be said of all the *avatar*s, including Krishna—with some significant qualifications, as discussed below.

In the apotheosis of the *Bhagavad Gita*, the hero Arjuna dramatically discovers the limitations of *avatar*s. At the crucial moment, Arjuna hesitates to instigate a tremendous battle in which family members would brutally kill each other, and he appeals to his charioteer, the adult Krishna, to relieve him of his indecision. The *Bhagavad Gita* is the impromptu sermon on human action that Krishna gives in response to Arjuna's appeal, standing in a charioteer's clothes, on a chariot, between two armies on an epic battlefield. The text culminates in a grand vision, in which Krishna shows Arjuna the degree to which his physical form fails to represent what he is.

O King, saying this, Krishna,
the great lord of discipline,
revealed to Arjuna
the true majesty of his form.

It was a multiform, wondrous vision,
with countless mouths and eyes
and celestial ornaments,
brandishing many divine weapons.

Everywhere was boundless divinity
containing all astonishing things,
wearing divine garlands and garments,
annointed with divine perfume.

If the light of a thousand suns
were to rise in the sky at once,
it would be like the light
of that great spirit.

Arjuna saw all the universe
in its many ways and parts,
standing as one in the body
of the god of gods....

[Arjuna:] I am thrilled,
and yet my mind trembles with fear
at seeing
what has not been seen before.
Show me, God, the form I know—
be gracious, Lord of Gods,
Shelter of the World.[13]

It turns out that there is much more to Krishna than meets the mortal eye, even back in the epic days. In the Puranic period, Krishna's "secret identity" is sometimes manifest to those close to him, even when he is a young child. In *Bhagavata Purana* 10.7, Krishna's adoptive mother Yashoda has a vision similar to Arjuna's, in which she sees Krishna's universal form when she looks into her child's mouth to investigate the report that he has been eating dirt.

> 39. Seeing in the body, nay in the gaping mouth of her child, this marvellous universe consisting of a variety of organisms... she was seized with terror....

43. The Omnipotent Supreme Lord cast over the Gopa-lady who had thus realized the truth, his deluding *Vaisnava* (divine) charm which filled her with maternal affection for (her) son.
44. Instantly the Gopa-lady lost her memory (regarding the real nature of the Lord). She placed her son on her lap. Her heart overflowed with intense affection as before.[14]

Arjuna and Yashoda both experience what lies behind the physical Krishna facade, and it is more than their mortal senses can bear. Yashoda seems greatly relieved when Krishna closes the vision and returns to being her infant son.

Insofar as the Krishna *avatar* is a representation of the divine Krishna, there is a further metatheatrical layer to recognize in the *râs lila*. The actors play at being *gopi*s, who play at being Krishna. But Krishna—the physical Krishna whom Yashoda nurses, alongside whom Arjuna fights, whom the *gopi*s imitate—is himself only a physical representation of something more than physical. The child Krishna who lies to his mother, the adolescent Krishna who steals other men's wives, the adult Krishna who goads cousins into war, is only playing at being that divine Krishna whose play is eternal and metaphysical. Like the temple images that only partly manifest eternal quality, Krishna's stories, even as he played them out himself in sacred history, only manifest an eternal activity. Regarding the Bengali or *gaudiya* sect's understanding of these two aspects of Krishna's activity (*lila*), De writes, "This Lila or beatific sport may be Prakata or Manifest and Aprakata or Unmanifest, according as it can or cannot be apprehended by phenomenal beings."[15] Wulff summarizes briefly how both the *Vishnu Purana* and the *Bhagavata Purana* characterize the physical Krishna as "a form of pretense." Specific passages Wulff cites refer to Krishna and the other *avatar*s as *nata*s or actors. Wulff concludes, "The traditions surrounding Kṛṣṇa thus have drama at their very center, for the evolving conception of the Lord in relation to his devotees, as represented in texts from the *Bhagavadgîtâ* to the *Bhâgavata Purâṇa*, is a fundamentally dramatic one."[16]

We might distinguish between the physical Krishna *avatar* and the divine Krishna by adopting for the former the name "Krishna-Gopal," by which name devotees commonly refer to the child Krishna. The *gopi*s who, in the Vrindavan forest, imitate Krishna-Gopal and act out his mythology, represent Krishna-Gopal's equally representational imitation of Krishna's divine activity. In the *râs lila*, then, we see actors playing at being *gopi*s playing at being Krishna-Gopal playing at being Krishna. At the least, this is an example of a play-within-a-play-within-a-play-within-a-play.

How does the *râs lila* provide a spiritual experience for devotees? Given the layering of representations in a performance, the succession of cognitive gaps between devotees and the divine Krishna in a performance, how does the *râs lila* facilitate for devotees the experience of the divine? In the first place, we need not suppose that *representation* excludes *presence*. The South Asian *avatar* idea gives some indication of the way in which the representation and the represented can be one and the same, and devotees' appreciation for the way in which the divine is manifest in the physical world through the phenomena of the physical world lends the *râs lila* much of its spiritual force.

In fact, some schools of thought, principally the Bengali sects, contend that Krishna-Gopal, the child of the *Bhagavata Purana*, is not an incarnation or *avatar* at all.[17] The *avatar*s of God, they agree, are diminished representations of God, come into the world with the express purpose of saving the world from a more or less specific ill. Krishna, on the other hand, appears in the *Bhagavata Purana* as the full and complete manifestation of God, not *incarnate* in a physical form with its obligatory limitations, nor with the purpose of lightening the world's burden, but God in spirit and in truth. "One of the most fundamental doctrines of Caitanyaism," writes S. K. De in his summary of *gaudiya* devotion, "is that Krsna as the supreme personal god of the cult is not an Avatara but the divine being himself in his essential character."[18] Nevertheless, these same schools readily acknowledge the dual nature of Krishna's activity in Vrindavan, and the dual nature of Vrindavan itself, as both temporal and eternal. Even in the doctrine of Bengali *bhakti*, which strongly resists characterizing Krishna in anything but divine terms, the sense is evident that there are two versions of Krishna, his activity, and his homeland—all real and present in the same space and time. "Krishna's exploits," writes Alan Entwistle in a broad survey of culture in the Vrindavan area, "are envisaged as taking place on a different plane, in another dimension of time and space.... Because of the correspondence between contemporary Braj and the transcendent realm of Krishna the pilgrims and residents of the sacred centre are encouraged to experience what may be called a place and moment 'in and out of time.'"[19] That is, the Vrindavan that pilgrims experience with their physical senses coexists with a transcendent Vrindavan, which devotees might also experience—along with Krishna's play there—through devotionally refined senses.

ROLES AS DESCRIPTIONS, NAMES, AND MANIFESTATIONS

A performer's role exists not in the theatre, nor on the pages of a play, nor even in the mind of an author, but in an indefinable "out-there." The ideal against which we judge whether a performance of the Hamlet character is "good" or "bad"—the ur-Hamlet—lives with undefined attributes in a nebulous unreality.

In the formalist language of Bertrand Russell, we could say that a performer of a role acts as a *description* of the role. A *description* enables us to speak about things that do not exist, as opposed to a true proper *name*, the meaning of which is the thing it names, itself. In place of a dramatic character's actual existence, we have a coagulation of descriptive phrases, including what seems to be a proper name. Our individual conceptions of Hamlet's nature are solely the products of the combination of these descriptions. In a summary of Russell's "Theory of Descriptions," Avrum Stroll and Richard H. Popkin put it thus:

> All I know about Hamlet, therefore, I come to know through the media of statements containing descriptive phrases—namely that "Hamlet was the prince of Denmark who spurned Ophelia" or "Hamlet was the prince of Denmark who killed Laertes," and so on. The word "Hamlet" is thus, for Russell, a disguised description—or more accurately, an abbreviation for a descriptive phrase like "the prince of Denmark"—and not a genuine proper name.[20]

Olivier's portrayal of Hamlet can seem like a proper name, as though Olivier while on stage has some ontological affinity with an actual entity we describe as "the prince of Denmark who killed Laertes." Hamlet's presence, however, is an illusion, as the performance is an almost infinitely complicated, descriptive statement ("the prince who nodded his head this way and sighed in such a manner…"). Each of our individual notions of who Hamlet *is* reaches in some measure into this dim world behind the descriptions to provide us with a vague standard next to which we measure each performance of the role we encounter.[21] Authors and performers together are under the same constraints as the audience as they summon up not characters themselves but *descriptions*—or *representations*—of characters, and a variety of means by which those *representations* might more effectively appear to name characters.

Characters which do, or at one point did, have an actual existence—historical characters such as Henry VIII, Mark Twain, and Roy Cohn, for which we do have true proper names that are coequal with the entities they name—do not *live* in performance, either, but appear represented in performance, since the performance environment distinguishes itself as a place of description rather than being. Even a character that is ostensibly a performer's own identity is not the performer herself, but a representation of the performer. Joan Rivers playing herself in a made-for-TV movie, for example, represents herself through actions that *describe* her rather than *are* her. Even a character that is a performer's own contemporary persona offered to an audience in an immediate setting, such as is commonly found in performance art, is, nevertheless, not the performer herself since the performance setting, indeed, *time* itself, prevents such a complete expression, but is a representation of the performer's self, constrained by the dictates of the time and space in which we live.

The ur-Hamlet finds its way into time and space by way of a temporary persona that looks a lot like that guy who was in *Marathon Man*, only younger. For a time, Olivier represents Hamlet, without *being* Hamlet in any ontological sense. Through the course of a performance of *Swimming to Cambodia*, an ur-Spalding Gray cannot appear whole and complete because of the limitations of time and space, but still finds temporary expression through a representation that looks an awful lot like that prefab building salesman in *True Stories*.

But it would not be entirely accurate to suggest that Spalding Gray is not Spalding Gray during a performance of *Swimming to Cambodia*, nor is it entirely right to suggest that Olivier is not Hamlet to some degree. Bert O. States, Joseph Roach, and most recently Marvin Carlson have noted the peculiar way that audiences conflate the identities of actors and characters. In a more complex way even than the affliction of mere typecasting, actors and their roles do blend in public consciousness, so that we not only speak of Arnold Schwarzenegger as The Governator, but interpret his manner of governing California as the method of a mindless robot assassin from the future. Carlson quotes Anthony Sher's frustration with the opening lines of *Richard III*:

"Now is the winter..."
God. It seems terribly unfair of Shakespeare to begin his play with such a famous speech. You don't like to put your mouth to it, so many other mouths have been there. Or to be more honest, one particularly distinctive mouth. His poised, staccato delivery is imprinted on those words like teeth marks.[22]

Some of Olivier has rubbed off on King Richard, and vice-versa.[23] States says much the same thing about a different character: "There is *still* a Hamlet in Olivier."[24] However rational, dualistic, or empirically minded we may consider ourselves, the experience of theatre shows us that we easily slip into a mode of both/and rather than either/or.

THEATRE AS AN IDEAL

Thus we return to South Asian thought, which much more openly regards *identity* as a both/and idea. Krishna's various incarnations, or *avatar*s, including Krishna-Gopal, the butter-filching child, are to some extent a description, as are performances that represent Krishna in his various guises. As has been suggested, Krishna *is* the temple icon, and he also *is* the ten-year-old actor, because, for devotees, the descriptions are coequal with Krishna himself. Krishna's divine playing can occur in the divine Vrindavan and in a play on a stage at the same time, owing in part to Vrindavan Vaishnavism's fundamental notion that everything proceeds from Krishna, and nothing, therefore, can ultimately be distinct from him, and also to an understanding of the nature of Vrindavan and devotional activity that may be unique to *bhakti* among Hindu sects.

Love, which Krishna inspires in his devotees, is itself the ultimate end of devotional practice.[25] Scriptural texts, commentaries, and contemporary sermons, using terms suggestive of the English words *bliss, joy, ecstasy,* and such others, regard what individuals subjectively experience when, through worship and service, God's pleasure is foremost in their minds, as tantamount to God's presence. According to S. K. De, what partly identifies Krishna as the complete manifestation of God is the bliss associated with him.

> In the Krsna-Bhagavat [god] there is the fullest display of all the divine Saktis [attributes of power], but what is prominent is the highest expression of the Hladini Sakti or the attribute of bliss which absorbs and supersedes all other aspects.... As such, Krsna...is superior to such lower expressions [*avatar*s] of the deity as Narayana and Vasudeva in whom only the aspect of divine might or Aisvarya is displayed.[26]

De further suggests that the bliss that is the essence of God's character is naturally available to those who, through devotional service, approach God, since "the divine being...produces delight in others."[27] The contemporary doctrine of Krishna devotion in Vrindavan, and in many other parts of India, emphasizes the identification of divine bliss with the divine personage, such that the presence of one is the presence of the other. Margaret Case, in her history of Purushottam Goswami, the Vrindavan Brahman who presides in part over Radharaman Temple, and whose following of devotees stretches from Rajasthan to Orissa, makes clear the significance of bliss in Vaishnava teaching. Describing the substance of the many sermons she has heard Purushottam Goswami (to whom she always refers as Maharaj-ji) deliver, Case writes:

> The individual atma, he says, is a small part of Paramatma, the eternal Soul of the universe. Just as a cup of water drawn from the ocean is of the same material as the ocean, though it does not have the same power to float a ship, so too the individual soul is of the same substance as the great Soul. And what is that substance? *Ananda*, bliss. Bliss is identical with Krishna.... This is the recurring theme of Maharaj-ji's talks, to a large group or a small one.[28]

In popular devotional thought, God's real presence is not different from the devotee's experience or from the Russellian descriptive mechanisms that evoke that experience—the sound of God's spoken name, service to the temple icon, the stories of God's life as recited from scripture, or an actor in the Krishna role.

Here, aesthetic and religious life blend explicitly, as theatre per se becomes not only a means of salvation, but salvation itself. The presence of God as experienced by devotees means that, in the practice of *bhakti*, acts of devotion are not necessarily a means to an end, but are themselves the desired end of devotion. Theorists of religious experience, at least since William James, have asserted that religious experience, such as the bliss inherent in various acts of Krishna devotion, looks toward an alternative reality, which the individual may just as well regard as a more legitimate reality. "Religious experience," writes Joachim Wach, "is a response to what is experienced as ultimate reality; that is, in religious experiences we react not to any single or finite phenomenon, material or otherwise, but to what we realize as undergirding and conditioning all that constitutes our world of experiences."[29] The central strands of post-Vedic Hinduism, developing in the first few centuries, BCE, conceive of the ultimate reality such as Wach speaks of as thorough non-differentiation, a condition perhaps best characterized as "distinction-less." Aims of religious practice in Hinduism, then, include the acknowledgment of this non-differentiated condition as the ultimate and an ever-after state of not experiencing differentiation. As an eternal objective, *moksha*, in Sanskrit, is understood as a discontinuance of the conceived and the actual distinction between an individual and the rest of existence, such that an individual and the absolute are forever after one and the same.[30]

The intent of Krishna-*bhakti* is similarly to provide a kind of *enlightenment* and *liberation*, but its grand objective is much less interested in a profound ellipsis of distinctions. While *bhakti* philosophically acknowledges Krishna's ultimate existence, it retains a devotional attachment to dualism. For the Krishna devotee, enlightenment comes in the recognition of one's true relationship with Krishna, that the individual consists of the same "material" as God, as explained in Purushottam Goswami's comments on *ananda* above. And because this recognition is facilitated by the experience of bliss, as he or she is engaged in devotional service, a devotee might experience enlightenment on a daily basis. Charged as it is with divine presence, this day-to-day experience may very well be for the devotee the qualitative equivalent of *moksha*, since it releases the devotee from every attachment but to God. Clifford Hospital shows how the concept of eternal devotion as liberation plays out in the *Bhagavata Purana*, stressing the power of *bhakti* to free devotees of the concerns of the world. The *Bhagavata Purana*'s references to liberation, Hospital shows, exhibit traditional Hindu thinking as well as a uniquely devotional character. "The lotus feet of the Lord..." writes Hospital, "are seen as a way of extinguishing the miseries of those who take refuge...a way of eradicating the suffering of transmigration..."[31] The bliss that devotion finds overcomes all the desires of physical life from which sorrows derive, leaving the devotee as liberated from the world of perpetual incarnation as any enlightened soul. "Those who find refuge in the dust of your feet long not for heaven," reads *Bhagavata Purana* 10.16.36–38, "There is supreme bliss for him now / such as he desires—even while he lives/revolving on the wheel of rebirth."[32] Supreme bliss now may very well become supreme bliss later, though this *bhakti* concept diverges from classic Hindu ideas associated with *moksha*. The *bhakti* notion of conclusive *liberation*, which naturally follows from the idea that supreme bliss is available to the living devotee, is less concerned with the end of personal identity (*moksha*) and more concerned with the freedom to continue the experience of divine bliss (*uddhara*).

Adherents of the *pushtimarga sampradaya*, one of the principal sects of Krishna *bhakti*, accept that the consciousness of a one and impersonal reality may indeed lead to *moksha*; but for them this kind of liberation can be nothing more than an extension of the material illusion under which an individual labors in mortality, because reaching it depends on an individual's identification with an impersonal, and, consequently, deficient, manifestation of Krishna. More *real* (in a manner of speaking) than this apparent liberation, a loftier objective, is a consciousness of Krishna's divine, personal, and physical reality. In his outline of *pushtimarga* theology, Richard Barz discusses the highest goal of devotion.

> Finally, the follower of the *Pustimarga*...does not want the absorption into *aksara* Brahman [the impersonal absolute]...he wants, instead, to have continual association with the divine body of Shri Krsna.... For Vallabha's followers,

the culmination of delight in the physical presence of Shri Krishna, the Supreme Being and the source of all existence, is the highest experience (*anubhava*) of *seva* [service to god].... By means of the *alaukika* [un-earthly] capability, the *bhakta* shares in the essence of Bhagavan Shri Krsna and consciously and physically enters with him into the eternal *lila*.[33]

Because devotees hold that Krishna is, ultimately, personal, no impersonal relationship with him will ever satisfy them; and they hope, by aiming conclusively to eternally continue their material lives of service to their lord, to find themselves participants in the lord's eternal play.[34]

The other great sectarian division in Krishna *bhakti*, the *gaudiya sampradaya*, often associated with Bengali devotees, similarly emphasizes the *uddhara* type of liberation over *moksha*, a living-liberation, or *jivanmukti*, that may be found even while a devotee remains alive.[35] Joseph O'Connell connects the Gaudiya devotee's understanding of his origin with his eternal intent. "[E]very human soul is a minute part of the divine source Krishna.... The eternal duty of each soul is to turn in devout service toward the divine source.... The very act of prostration proves to be not only an expression of one's urgent need for deliverance but...a disclosure of one's timeless relationship to the divine."[36] *Liberation* in *bhakti* becomes a state in which the devotee might remain forever attached to Krishna's feet—an impossible relationship if the devotee surrenders his or her individual identity. As Srivatsa Goswami remarked to me, "You must experience something to have pleasure, and you can't experience something without duality."[37]

The child Krishna (Krishna-Gopal) who steals butter, rather than the immutable Krishna, best facilitates this relationship of attachment and separation. Krishna's physical form encourages an immutable distinction between himself and devotees. When Krishna reveals his universal form in the *Bhagavad Gita*, Arjuna shouts out. The terror Yashoda experiences when she sees the universe in Krishna's mouth is assuaged when Krishna closes his mouth and coos again like a child. Krishna's mortal *avatar* is easier for his devotees to love; consequently, Krishna is said to mercifully adopt a physical form in order to make an experience of him bearable for a devotee. And not only bearable, but enjoyable. Arjuna's and Yashoda's love for and personal attachment to Krishna-Gopal returned only after the frightful vision closed and Krishna went back to acting the part of the beloved friend and cherished child. The precocious child, the form Krishna assumes in order to endear himself to his devotees, is an illusion of the same kind as the rest of the physical world, but it is an essential illusion that, unlike the dream of the physical world around us, exists for the benefit of devotees. Krishna-Gopal intends to be lovable in the way that best suits his devotees, and grants the distinction between himself and them in order to foster in devotees an attachment that does, in fact, transcend the illusion of differentiation eschewed by other strands of Hinduism by lasting eternally.

The Krishna-Gopal mythology manifests this saving grace. The stories themselves have become a central feature of *bhakti*, since they act as the means whereby devotees-after-the-fact have access to Krishna's endearing form and endearing activities—that is, to what is eternal and real as opposed to what is merely transitory. Krishna's divine play is regarded as real activity, and eternally ongoing in an ideal, ever-present, but unmanifest, Vrindavan. David R. Kinsley, in *The Sword and the Flute*, writes of the Vaishnava concept of Krishna's mythological homeland as eternal but undetected:

> Krsna's sport in Vrindavana is not held to have happened simply once upon a time. His life as set forth in the *Bhagavata-purana*, in particular his sojourn in Vrindavana, is a description of both an earthly manifestation *and* the eternal movement within the essence of the Godhead.... Krsna's earthly sport in Vrindavana is simply a making manifest of what is normally unmanifest. Or, to put it the other way, Gokula (the name of Vrindavana and its surrounding area) has been translated into Goloka (Krsna's eternal realm...). Krsna's childhood, adolescence, and love for Radha and the *gopis* are forever taking place in the paradise of Goloka. Each aspect of his biography, every incident, is therefore eternal.[38]

The unmanifest Vrindavan is not simply *represented* in the physical Vrindavan, nor do recitations of Krishna's activities merely *describe* his eternal playing there. The unmanifest and the manifest come together in Vrindavan. According to De, "[Krishna's] highest Paradise, which is set above all other Lokas, also exist [*sic*] on the phenomenal earth, so that the terrestrial Gokula or Vrndavana is not essentially different but really identical with the celestial Goloka, and the Bhagavat-Krsna exists in both places..."[39] When recited, Krishna's mythology makes his unmanifest activity manifest. Consequently, since at least the time of the *Bhagavad Gita*, which precedes the *Bhagavata Purana* by a few centuries, the telling and hearing of Krishna stories has been an important part of *bhakti* practice, and an act that itself saves. *Bhagavad Gita* 10.9 suggests a connection between the recitation of Krishna's mythology and enlightenment.[40] The *Bhagavata Purana* is more explicit, and more consistent, stating clearly in several verses how eternally valuable the stories of Krishna's childhood can be. "The repetition of the glories / of that One who is worthy of the highest praise," declares the text in 8.12.46, "exhausts and destroys the entire process of transmigration."[41] Devotees regard the recitation of Krishna's stories as the way by which Krishna's qualities are made available and attractive to the devotee. To the degree that a devotee finds salvation in surrendering his attachment to the world in favor of an attachment to the Krishna of some particular stories, the stories themselves have a soteric function.

This is all the more so when the stories are dramatized, or *re-played* as opposed to *re-cited*. Not merely recitations, but walking and talking objectifications of Krishna's divine playing, *râs lila* performances provide an immanent salvation for devotees in attendance. In some respects, *râs lila* performances are the epitome of metatheatre, since, by dramatizing Krishna's eternal playing, they rather self-consciously represent what is already theatrical and cognitively exist as play-within-play—actors play the gopis who play Krishna-Gopal (who plays himself). Regarded this way, the performances' spiritual value is limited to what inspiration a devotee might derive from dramatic representation. Given, however, Krishna's own real presence in the play of a *râs lila* performance, a devotee at a *râs lila* finds himself or herself seeing the paradisiacal Goloka, or unmanifest Vrindavan, and, thus, playing out the very experience of the gopis in the *Bhagavata Purana*. In this case, the *râs lila* no longer exhibits a metatheatrical character, but provides a direct religious experience unmediated by nested degrees of theatrical reality; and in this case, the performance is even *more real* than the material reality in which it seems to play.[42]

This condition as facilitated by the *râs lila* may fulfill the devotee's highest spiritual aspirations. David L. Haberman, in his study of some specific meditative practices in Vrindavan, builds on the argument that religious experience connects an individual to an alternative reality, which the individual may just as well regard as a more legitimate reality. "The religious person," writes Haberman, "seeks to participate fully in a reality that stands qualitatively above all others."[43] For the Krishna devotee, the qualitatively highest reality is Krishna's eternal play in Vrindavan, and the qualitatively highest aspiration one could have is access to that reality, or, as Haberman writes, "an eternal participation in the emotional world of the Vraja-lila."[44] A devotee's emotional experience of a *râs lila* performance is Krishna's own divine bliss. Through the experience of bliss the devotee has a direct experience of the divine Krishna, and he or she transcends the metatheatrical levels of the *râs lila* drama of which Krishna's identity and play is a part. No longer is the devotee imagining Krishna through actors and the roles they have adopted, but seeing

Krishna himself. Through the same feeling of bliss, the devotee transcends the metadramatic levels of the physical world of which the performance and he himself are a part. The devotee, then, does not imagine the spiritual Vrindavan through the concrete buildings and dusty streets that physically sit on the site, but lives in Krishna's eternal playground.

In this way, *râs lila* performances are not a means to an end—a practice by which a devotee might approach liberation—but the end itself. A devotee seeks release from the confines of existence, which derive from his or her spurious attachments, by attaching his or her desires exclusively to the eternal Krishna. Krishna facilitates this attachment by making himself supremely desirable through the form in which he is manifest and in the bliss that accompanies the form. To the degree that a devotee at a *râs lila* desires Krishna, the devotee enters into Krishna's eternal play in Vrindavan through the performance, and finds there the fulfillment of his or her ultimate desires in the experience of Krishna's divine play.

3. Krishna, *Lila*, and Freedom

INTRODUCTION

The Braj *râs lila* commemorates what devotees regard as the historical advent of Krishna in Braj, with an emphasis on his unpretentious childishness, his disregard for custom and propriety, his seductive beauty, the elements of the Krishna story that most delight devotees—that is, the elements that most effectively fulfill devotees' yearning for the bliss associated with divine presence. Performances often assume a rather festive and rambunctious tone that further inflates the joy associated with Krishna's childhood antics. Consequently, the dramatic depiction of Krishna almost requires a space that ignores mundane regulations and concerns. John S. Hawley indicates the tendency of *râs lila* theatre in his description of some of the action of the "Butter Thief" *lila*, as Krishna and his cowherd friends have gained unchecked access to a large supply of soft butter hanging in pots overhead:

> At every stopping point [Krishna] and his cohorts wrangle over who is to get the milk sweets cached away there in lieu of butter, and some are thrown out into the crowd seated nearby, which receives this prasad with a hundred outstretched arms. As the procession returns to the stage, the antics of the COWHERDS become more and more rowdy. Whole potfuls of milk and yoghurt are slung from one COWHERD to another, and so much the better if some prominent devotee gets caught in the crossfire.[1]

Led by Krishna, the stage action devolves here into chaos, which spills over (literally) into the audience, so as to catch up all present in a meta-dramatic free-for-all.

This example illustrates well an essential quality of *râs lila* theatre in Braj as opposed to the various other *râs lila* traditions found throughout northern India. The defining quality of Braj *râs lila* may be the chaos it actively seeks out. Not only does the narrative content of the plays often concern Krishna's transgression of rules and norms, but the theatricality very often aims at engendering a spirit that is unconcerned with conventional social mores. In this way, the Krishna figure and *râs lila* performance sustain each other. The essential quality of the *lila* concept in South Asia is freedom, and, at least from the medieval period in India, Krishna's fundamental characteristic has been a flagrant disregard of restrictions. *Lila* and Krishna are, to some degree, coequal. *Râs lila* theatre's ostensible interest in social license makes it a natural environment for Krishna, whose own contrary nature provides the perfect dramatic premise.

In popular worship in Braj, Krishna is a chubby, blue-skinned child. Calendars and greeting cards picture him at toddler age with one hand in a butter-jar and with a rather beatific smile on his face, and similar artistic representations show up in the ubiquitous household shrines of Braj. Temple images, such as the modern one installed in the temple at *Krishna-janmbhoomi* (Krishna's birthplace) in Mathura, sometimes represent him as slightly older, but this is unusual. More commonly, especially in Vrindavan, the temple images, which are most commonly black and are said to have appeared under miraculous circumstances, are less representational in style, stylizing and accentuating particular features and postures. Nevertheless, even these more abstract representations of the divine Krishna clearly emphasize his childish essence, and project a similar, childlike bliss. These popular conceptions of Krishna, inspired by medieval-era stories of Krishna's youth, delight in the natural capriciousness of childhood. But the Krishna theme stretches back before the medieval period and emphasizes in its older components not his youth but his adulthood, and some very adult characteristics. Consequently, identifying the essential and consistent element of the Krishna theme is problematic; ultimately, though, the attempt finds the adult and the child acting with a consistent disregard for social constraints and propriety.

THE KRISHNA THEME

The Child Krishna was born in a dungeon cell, in the dead of night, to the sister of a demon-king who had vowed to kill each of her offspring in order to protect himself from a curse. By supernatural means, Krishna's father Vasudeva carried him from the cell and across the river Yamuna, and there exchanged him with the child of a cowherd couple, stillborn the same night. Leaving Krishna to the care of Nanda and Yashoda,

Vasudeva returned to the cell of his wife and presented the king with the lifeless body of the cowherd couple's child. The king dashed the child on the stones of the courtyard, and from the smashed infant's body rose the Goddess Ninda to accuse the king and to confirm that his curse remained: in spite of the successive murders intended to avert his doom, he would yet be killed by his aunt's eighth son, Krishna Vasudeva. Krishna, then, the kshatriya prince and an incarnation of Vishnu, grew up a pastoral peasant among the cowherds on what we might call "the other side of the tracks." Apparently aware of his divine identity and mortal destiny from an early age, he nevertheless played the game appropriate to his setting, acting the part of cowherd. Though demonstrating his divine power on a number of occasions—in battle with various and sundry demons or in other extraordinary circumstances—he nevertheless made no attempt to rise above his cowherd station. Instead, Krishna grew up reveling in his commonness, playing as a child, and taking particular pleasure in his rural surroundings. Abruptly, he left it all. When of age, Krishna assumed his kshatriya status, leaving behind his cowherd life and land forever, and returned across the river. There, he killed the evil king, to live the remainder of his days.

Only, soon after freeing his homeland of Kamsa's rule and instituting a golden age in the land of his birth, Krishna again abruptly packed up and moved to Dwarka to live as a warlord. As an adult with a full compliment of soldiers under his command, Krishna participated in the battle between cousins, which forms the core of *The Mahabharata*, ceding, in classic Krishna style, his armies to one side of the fight while committing himself to the other. Krishna's revelation of his divine identity during the battle provides the theological moment of the *Bhagavad Gita*, and Krishna's participation in the battle otherwise is marked by lying and cheating. After the war, Krishna retired to Dwarka where his subjects annihilated each other and he himself was killed by happenstance.

Indeed, Krishna's story exhibits significant contradictions and discontinuity. The stories of his childhood luxuriate in his bucolic environment and the paradisiacal conditions in which he indulges his childish inclinations alongside his happy friends. The stories of his adulthood occur on very different terrain, and describe a character with little of the same impish joy, but rather one who is given to philosophical deliberation while engaging in cynical strategies of politics and war, and who finally dies a bleak death, alone. As a matter of textual history, furthermore, the primary literatures of Krishna's childhood and of his adulthood, which hardly acknowledge each other, are separated by six centuries, and, curiously, the adult appears and disappears first.

As indicated above, nowadays there is only the bucolic child Krishna who plays distractedly among the cows in Vrindavan's forests. In the fall of each year, India's state-sponsored television station, Doordarshan, broadcasts to all of India scenes from celebrations of Krishna's birth at festival sites all over India. The dancing, singing, storytelling, and general abandon that constitute these celebrations—the sermons, too, are punctuated with a whimsical sort of humor—indicate the kind of devotional worship the child Krishna inspires, which seems to have completely supplanted any older tradition that revered the adult. Today, no one worships the adult, Machiavellian Krishna of the *Mahabharata*. He does not appear in temples, nor in household shrines, not on calendars, posters, greeting cards, or other religious paraphernalia that celebrate his young alter ego. At most, the Krishna of contemporary worship appears at a rather smooth-cheeked twenty years of age. Even illustrated versions of the *Bhagavad Gita*, that small portion of the *Mahabharata* that continues to be an essential text to the understanding and practice of Krishna devotion, and in which Krishna exists ostensibly as an adult, present the adult-soldier Krishna holding the reins of a war-chariot while declaiming on the meaning of devotion and duty in the form of a rather willowy teenager.

Considering the historical and thematic distance between the two, the Adult and Child Krishna seem only to share a name. Indeed, the scholarly debate concerning the connection between the adult and the child Krishna continues. Some experts on the Krishna tradition, including Charlotte Vaudeville, accept that the two Krishna traditions—the adult warrior and the happy-go-lucky child—represent two distinct characters who merged during the first centuries of the Common Era.[2] Others, such as Alf Hiltebeitel, have argued for the unity of the Krishna figure, in spite of apparent discontinuity.[3] We may also add, of course, that mythological traditions may arise and evolve independent of each other even though demonstrably concerned with the same character.[4]

Hiltebeitel follows Madeleine Biardeau to develop a literary theory concerning disguise that may be useful for unifying the branches of the Krishna themes, since disguise of a mundane and a transcendent sort are recurring features of Krishna stories. The disguises that epic characters often assume, Hiltebeitel argues, are literary devices that "reveal [characters'] real character as much as they hide it."[5] Hiltebeitel points first to the *Pandavas*, the five, fraternal protagonists of the *Mahabharata* epic, composed between 600 BCE and 200 BCE. During the thirteenth year of a collective exile, and in order to avoid discovery by the scheming cousins responsible for their exile, the royal brothers enter the service of

King Virata in positions that appear quite other than their true, princely, *kshatriya* identities. Bhima serves as a cook, Nakula as a stable boy. The eldest, Yuddhisthira, serves as a Brahman counselor to the king. Given Bhima's legendary appetite and Yuddhisthira's renowned (if complicated) wisdom, these are not simply disguises, but true expressions of character. Similarly, Ram, the royal hero of the *Ramayana* plays a Hiltebeitelian role while living a Brahman hermit's lifestyle in exile—a role suited to Ram's sublimated, divine identity. For Hiltebeitel, such epic disguises do not shroud epic characters, but give readers very precise and accurate information about them.

But reading these disguises is not always so straightforward. While Bhima satisfied his true nature in the kitchen, Arjuna, the quintessential warrior, served as a eunuch in Virata's queen's entourage. A previous episode of the *Mahabharata*, which, somewhat literally, feminizes Arjuna, makes this role a rather suitable one for him. But, following Hiltebeitel, are we to read Arjuna as essentially female on account of this disguise? What to do with the superlative warrior who finds himself an emasculated dance instructor? And in the case of Krishna, what "revelation" of Krishna's true character is there in the cowherd disguise he assumes during his own exile from the royal court at Mathura? Or is it that Krishna's *kshatriya* birth in Mathura, his royal identity, is a disguise in the first place?

What the disguises might reveal about the "real" Krishna is contingent upon the use made of Krishna during the two periods that assert first the adult version of Krishna and then the child. The disguise the cosmic Krishna assumes is conditioned by the specific social circumstances that construct it. This understanding of the factors determining Krishna's adult and child personas follows Lauri Honko's theory of myth as an "integrating factor":

> In myths man is faced with fundamental problems of society, culture and nature. Myths offer opportunities of selecting different elements which satisfy both individual tendencies and social necessities. From these elements it is possible to create an individual, but at the same time traditional, way of viewing the world.[6]

In conjunction with Hiltebeitel, Honko provides a way of reconciling Krishna's two identities without necessarily entering the debate about one or two Krishnas. Variations of a theme develop, perhaps even independently, in response to immediate, unique conditions. Accordingly, whether one or two, or more, the adult Krishna and the child Krishna are manifestations of concerns of the times of their origin, and correspond with their own historical milieus; I would argue further that the circumstances that produced the child Krishna created a figure peculiarly suited to theatrical representation.

KRISHNA'S NONSENSE AS RESISTANCE TO AUTHORITY

Ralph Linton asserts: "Religion focuses upon sore spots, upon tense areas where people chafe and worry, scarcely able to cope. Advanced religions are not different. Their living forms arise where there is weakness and hurt."[7] Myth, the language of religion, creates what religion needs to address troubles as they arise.

In the time of the *Bhagavad Gita*, a portion of the epic Mahabharata dated usually c. 200, BCE, the sore spot of public discourse was mass exodus from the orthodox, Brahmanical religion associated with early Hinduism. The *Gita* partly arises to reinforce Brahmanical authority, which had, in W. J. Johnson's words, "established itself and its sacred body of knowledge, the Veda, as the arbiters of orthoprax and orthodox socio-religious conduct and values."[8] In the *Gita*, Krishna acts as spokesman for the Brahmanic order:

> O Scorcher of enemies (Arjuna), the duties of the Brahmanas, Ksatriyas, the Vaisyas and the Sudras are distinguished with reference to their respective dispositions, corresponding to their nature. Serenity, Self-control, austerity, purity, fortitude, on the one hand, and uprightness, knowledge, realization and faith, on the other, are the essential qualities of a Brahmana. The qualities of the Ksatriyas are valour, courage, firmness, skill, disinclination to flee from the battle, generosity and majesty. The duties of the Vaisyas comprise agriculture, cattle-breeding and trade, whereas the natural duty of the Sudras is service.[9]

At this point in the development of Hinduism, Krishna spoke to advocate conservative obeisance to Brahmanic authority, but particularly because some response was necessary to popular alternatives to Brahmanism. "A fact long acknowledged about the changes besetting Brahmanism during the opening centuries of the Christian era," writes Vijay Nath, "is that they were largely the result of sharpening of conflict amongst various religious systems fighting for space."[10] Norvin Hein contends that the *Gita* is in essence a call back to that old-time Brahmanic religion at a moment when the Brahmanic social structure was threatened by mass apostasy to the new heterodox/monastic orders led by Buddhism and Jainism. The *Gita*, to Hein, "is essentially a great sermon calling the alienated young back to their duties in the brahmanical social order."[11]

In the time of the *Harivamsa*, two or three hundred years into the Common Era, the situation had changed. The dissipation of the foreign Kusana empire and the founding of the basically Hindu Gupta empire restored old-time social order to the subcontinent. The Brahmanic order became fixed and thriving, providing freedom from foreign rule and the pressures that came with it, but inflicting its own repression in the form of the strict imposition of social roles. The revolutionary impulses of the days of foreign rule "were bound by belief that their own past acts were holding them justly in their bondage."[12] Caste structure became the new social anxiety and drove the old Krishna away in favor of a Krishna more suited to addressing the anxiety of the time. "Krsna the social moralist had done his work too well."[13] He made himself obsolete.

Enter the child. Krishna the infant/toddler/preadolescent emerged through the *Puranas* in the conservative Gupta period as a figure of freedom and vitality unknown in Gupta reality. The irrepressible individual who, in spite of warnings and punishments, does as he pleases became the icon of choice. But the attraction of this incarnation of God may come not only from the blessed anarchy he represents but from the peculiar creativity of that anarchy. As opposed to the adult Krishna of the *Gita* who, in defense of order, urges Arjuna to fight and to kill and to destroy, the Child Krishna inspires through his play the development of new modes of living.

Take, for instance, the *Govardhanadara* story, which seems to have iconographic and narrative roots in the oldest strata of the child Krishna cult. Told variously in the *Puranas* and elsewhere, it goes something like this: One day Krishna urges his fellow cowherds to cease from giving offerings to the God Indra, and instead to offer their gifts to a hill in northern Braj known locally by the name of Govardhan. The ever-amenable cowherds do as Krishna directs. Meanwhile, Krishna miraculously enters the hill and himself consumes all the offerings. Indra, furious, unleashes a downpour of epic proportions. The cowherd villagers are in grave peril from floodwaters and falling hail. Seeing their plight, Krishna hoists the hill Govardhan up on one of his fingers like an umbrella, under which the villagers take shelter for several days until Indra finally wears out. Ever after, the villagers worship Mount Govardhan as Krishna.

The nonsense of his existence manifests itself in other myths that concentrate on Krishna's person and behavior. To prevent him from stealing butter, so the story goes, his mother Yashoda ties the infant

Krishna to an enormous mortar. The infant dragged the mortar across the ground, uprooting trees as he went. His mother tried binding his hands, but no length of rope was long enough for the task. In the *râs lila* performance recorded by Hawley in *Krishna the Butter Thief*, a gopi tries to tie Krishna down. She finds herself tied, instead. So much for what happens to people who mess with him, but similar reversals of sense are manifest in Krishna's own behavior. Krishna's proclivity for thievery has been indicated, but in Krishna this antisocial inclination rises to the level of pathology. Krishna's friend Mansukha tries to reason with him about his practice of stealing. Hawley's record of this exchange reads:

> MANSUKHA: Look, your father has nine hundred thousand cows in his household, all of them giving milk, and there you go off taking bits of butter that the Braj gopis can come up with when there are literally hundreds of butter churns at work in your own home. So why go to the gopis' houses?[14]

At this, Krishna throws a terrible fit, literally kicking and screaming:

> KRISHNA: I don't care what happens. I'm not giving up this thieving.[15]

Krishna's behavior defies logic. He acts against all sense and without any apparent motivation. In so doing, Krishna is completely free. More so, perhaps, than his thievery and promiscuity *per se*, the aspect of Krishna that lends itself best to producing a sense of freedom within the *râs lila* is his absolute disregard for logic.

Herein is the continuity of the Krishna tradition. Whether as an adult in the *Mahabharata* Krishna urges Arjuna to kill and to destroy in order to preserve order, or whether as a child in the *Puranas* he defies convention and Indra's wrath for his own amusement, Krishna acts contrary to reason. In the present day, Brajwasis have grafted that antisensical character onto Braj itself, so as to infuse ideally the geographic area and its people with the same divinely irrational spirit. A full verse by the poet Megh Syam, employed in a *râs lila* performance recorded by Hawley, reads:

> Braj is where to cry is to laugh,
>   where hangmen's victims live and thrive,
> Where happiness spells sheer despair—
>   everything is upside down.
> Journey into Braj and watch
>   your curses turn to compliments,

> Where insults are the stuff of pride
> and crazy fools are seen as saints.[16]

As described here, Braj is the land of senselessness, where the land itself acts in emulation of the deity who presides over it, and the people who reside there are blessed by the nuttiness of it all. In *Journey Through the Twelve Forests*, David L. Haberman describes his experience as a participant in a *ban yatra*, a pilgrimage that ritually circumambulates the whole area of Braj, attending specific geographical sites now connected historically with the events of Krishna's life in the mythic Braj. Many of the experiences he reports describe the behavior of his companions, adults as himself, as apparently lacking the sense associated with "normal" behavior. Near Govardhan hill, he writes, "A woman approached a tree, wrapped it in her arms, and held it tight."[17] Later in the journey, struggling through a torrential downpour, a fellow pilgrim turned a broad smile to him and said, without dissembling, "Oh, David, what bliss this is!"[18] Describing what he saw at Khisalini Shila, the rock slide, he writes:

> Krishna and his friends enjoyed sliding down this rock, and the pilgrims did the same. They positioned themselves in the groove, let go, and squealed with delight as they slipped down the slide used by Krishna—a form of rump communion one might say. One by one, and in trains of three to five, they took turns sliding down the rock again and again.[19]

What seems senseless behavior is, in Braj, senseless, indeed. But Braj, as opposed to other places in the world, appreciates and encourages such behavior as divinely inspired.

Turning our attention now to the theatre that communicates Krishna to adherents in Braj, we find a fundamental emphasis on Krishna's defiant, subversive, and irrational character. Krishna's transformation from man to boy in the first centuries, CE, seems to have depended on a persistent Krishna-characteristic, which is explicit in his depiction in *rās lila* performances. Old or young, Krishna lies, cheats, steals, equivocates, and in other ways defies conventional morality. In this way, the Krishna theme seems always to have expressed some suspicion of social order as encapsulated in popular religion. The increasing interest in the child version of Krishna magnifies this persistent quality and adopts it as a spiritual ideal so that by the time of the *bhakti* revival of the sixteenth century, during which the contemporary *rās lila* form developed, this quality explicitly inspired the subversive, socially freewheeling ethos of *râs lila* performances. Krishna's historically rebellious nature suits him to the *râs lila*, and vice-versa.

NONSENSE AND FREEDOM IN *LILA*

The *râs lila* theatre in Braj, which brings Krishna to life on stage, dramatizes the variety of stories from the second, younger phase of the Krishna cycle—his miraculous birth, carefree youth, his inevitable triumph over his demon-uncle—and frames those stories in a context that is itself theatrically, interactively playful, so that he accords with modern, popular preferences for the impish child as opposed to the armored adult.

Lila, in the first place, means *play*, and from its first uses in South Asia the term has implied as many different things as its English counterpart. It is game, theatre, sport, pretense, pastime, and creativity—in general, any activity without a discrete material object—and it is especially important in the history of South Asian religion as a term for divine action. Although variations on monism dominate much of South Asian religion, many South Asian sects, such as those devoted to Krishna in Braj, conceive of God as personal and individual, with personality and passions. These sects often rationalize God's activity by an appeal to the *lila* concept, arguing that an omnipotent, omniscient, plenitude such as God might still act as a matter of play.

A personal God, goes the argument, who is all and has all may yet create without any particular motive. "Divine activity springs from absolute freedom (*svatantrya*), and in order to distinguish it from the limited human action, the metaphor of play is used to describe it."[20] Creation does not happen on account of the self-interest of the creator. Divine creation is *play*—completely unmotivated activity. Norvin Hein, who wrote the first definitive Western study of *râs lila*, explains that, consequently, God is free from the system of cause and effect to which the rest of us are subject. "His ever desireless acts entail no retribution. He is not the instrument of duty but duty's creator. The spontaneity and autonomy of his actions are absolute."[21] William Sax confirms this, commenting on Van Buitenen's treatment of the same subject. "Because God's cosmogonic *lila* is not motivated by desire, it generates no *karma*."[22] God's *lila* makes him ultimately free.

Clifford Hospital has identified several instances in which *play* is used to describe divine creative activity at least as far back as the epic *Mahabharata*, and certainly in the medieval *Puranas*. In the crucial period of the *Harivamsa*—an epic-style narrative of Krishna's youth from the first few centuries of the Common Era—the term *lila* came into use as a reference to divine playing.

> The first appearance of *lila* as a theological term is apparently a use of the word in the *Vedanta Sutra* of Badarayana (third century CE?). In 2.1.33 of that work the author defends the belief in a personal Creator against an objection that the God of monotheistic belief who is all and has all cannot be credited with creation, because persons create only in order to come into possession of something that they do not already have.[23]

Hospital asserts that, in fact, in the *Harivamsa* itself the term *krisnalila* first occurs to indicate both Krishna's divine play and the concept of mortal play in imitation of divine play.[24] In any case, the term *lila,* from an early point, has expressed a necessary freedom in divine action, and, rather naturally has been employed to characterize Krishna.

Writing of Shaivite concepts of *lila*, Bettina Baümer writes,

> Divine activity springs from absolute freedom (*svatantrya*), and in order to distinguish it from the limited human action, the metaphor of play (*lila, krida*, etc.) is used to describe it. This may be the general background of the idea of *lila* in Hindu religions, which becomes colored by the particular theology, spirituality, religious, and artistic practice of each tradition, whether Vaisnava or Saiva.[25]

Baümer goes on to assert strongly that a sense of *lila*, across the spectrum of South Asian religions, is consistent in at least one respect. "An action, even if it has the appearance of a game, that does not spring from freedom, cannot be called *lila*..."[26] The various dramatic forms of *lila* exist in part as an attempt to access that freedom for its participants—freedom from day-to-day responsibilities, freedom from the concerns of mortality, freedom from concern for forces beyond control. John B. Carman affirms this sense of *lila* with particular respect to South Asian dramatic traditions.

> *Lila* is drama portraying or imitating divine action or divine-human interaction. It is human action distinct from the normal human activity of work, it is "playacting." Such drama sometimes includes antinomian "games" or roughhouse, which suggest a temporary dissolution of the moral order.[27]

Just as God plays because he has no motivating concern, *lila*s provide people a place in which they can play because motivations, both internal and external, fade away, including the social structures that order and direct human lives.

Naturally, the motiveless activity of *lila*, and the freedom produced by it, often has the appearance of rebellion, since rebellion seeks out that essential *lila* quality. In many examples of theatrical *lila* in addition to *râs lila* there is a reversal of social roles. The boundaries of *lila* performances mark an area in which social roles, even if not entirely discarded, are extraordinarily fluid. William Sax describes the *pandav lila* of Himalayan India, which within its bounds gives special freedom to the local *kshatriya* castes. Within this performance honoring the five fraternal heroes of the *Mahabharata*, *kshatriyas* assume the status of Brahmans, and Brahmans take a supporting role. Even the boundaries traditionally circumscribing the social mobility of the lower castes are flexible (to a certain degree) within the context of the performance. Sax explains the freedom the *pandav lila* generates. "The atmosphere of *pandav lila* is, in short, one of playful abandon, where quotidian identities are abandoned and new ones assumed without fear of the *karmic* consequences."[28] In this case, identity confusion in the original myth provides the justification for the transgressions of the *lila*. In the epic, the five sons of Pandu are *kshatriyas* who often act like Brahmans, and the *pandav lila* works to provide for the same kind of boundary crossing within its own sphere of influence.

Similar reversals occur in the *lilakirtan* of Bengal, as described by Donna Wulff. Wulff agrees with Baümer that the notion of freedom is an essential part of the Indian concept of *lila*, and she emphasizes social freedom, pointing out that women not only participate in Bengali *kirtans*, but often direct and lead them. The mythology, says Wulff, justifies the contravention of convention, as the Gods themselves frequently disregard social norms.

> Although orthodox Vaishnava teaching has always asserted that the deities are not ethical models for human actions, the repeated dramatization of stories in which venerated deities defy social conventions may well have loosened the hold of Brahmanic strictures on Bengali society, if only in the realm of society.[29]

Shiva spends some time as a woman, and is frequently represented in art as a combination of male and female aspects. The Pandava brothers of the *Mahabharata* spend some time of their story in disguises at odds with their true status. The *Ramayana* similarly celebrates a *kshatriya* prince who spends much of his time living as a mendicant Brahman.

Krishna, too, defies the social order, not only as the *kshatriya* prince living as a cowherd, but in his popular conception as God in the form of a common cowherd. Furthermore, God's playing—his *lila*—as Krishna generally takes on socially unacceptable forms, as he steals from villagers, lies to his friends, and most notoriously as he frolics in the forest with women who are not only not married to him but are, in fact, married to other men. His very existence, let alone his behavior, epitomizes the disruption of social boundaries, and, consequently, we find in Krishna a rather natural, possibly inevitable, subject of *râs lila*.

NONSENSE AND FREEDOM IN *RÂS LILA*

At least, the paradoxical form of divinity and the *râs lila* form anticipate and reinforce each other. In *At Play with Krishna*, Hawley describes the activity preceding another *râs lila* performance in the central Braj town of Vrindavan.

> Sures Gosvami, the host, a lively, robust man in his twenties who has studied philosophy, breaks into the crowd that is waiting for him with huge leaps and shouts of gladness. He carries an enormous clay pot of yoghurt colored yellow with turmeric, and flings it about indiscriminately in a wild abandon of joy. Other pots mysteriously appear, and he himself is constantly going into the back rooms and coming out with more. The supply seems endless, and as more and more appear they are disposed of with greater and greater haste. Foreigners are not spared: I ended up with a huge one upside down over my head.[30]

Within the time and space of the *râs lila* all sorts of otherwise unacceptable behavior is acceptable and even desirable as an expression of one's appreciation for the divine game, and as a vehicle for one's participation in it.

In a social context as conservative as Braj, *râs lila* theatre would not emerge except through its connection with Krishna. Similarly, without a means of living expression, Krishna would not have accrued the kind of approbation given him in Braj. As we will see in the next chapter, the origins of *râs lila* theatre are intimately wrapped up with the development of *bhakti* (popular devotion) in Braj in the sixteenth century. In addition to its symbiotic relationship with *bhakti*, *râs lila* theatre's character also depends on Krishna's playful nature, an essential element of the theme that precedes and partly accounts for the sixteenth-century *bhakti* revival. Hawley reports that he witnessed one performance during which Krishna led the audience in chanting *lavar sant bhagavan ki jai*— "Hail God the crazy saint!"[31] Although aspects of the Krishna theme have changed considerably over time, this particular characteristic has remained fundamental. Krishna defies reason, and that quality both provides for the quality of Braj *râs lila* and suits Krishna to it.

Râs lila performances, then, are the preeminent escapism.[32] The aural and visual presentation of the collusion of Krishna's evil uncle with various demons to murder Krishna, of Krishna's clever and terrific counterblows to their attacks, of the schemes Krishna and his buddies hatch to disrupt order in their provincial community, of the pranks prepared by the local girls to stymie Krishna, of his delighted indulgence of their presumption, and of the games in which Krishna and his girlfriends engage, provide an effective diversion from mundane life. Furthermore, inasmuch as Vaishnava theology regards these episodes as exemplary, which is to say, as expressions of *play* as a divine principal, the *râs lila* provides a model for the way life should be lived. A possible reason for the popularity of *râs lila* performances is the message they deliver about living, which should be done with little seriousness, and with little attachment to mundane things and concerns, since the happiest people recognize that the stuff and complications around us ultimately resolve themselves in God's whimsy.

4. Origins of Child Performers in the *Râs Lila* ✑

THEORIES OF CHANGE DURING THE MUGHAL EMPIRE

The history of the Braj *râs lila*, as sketched by Western and South Asian scholars alike, dates its current form to the later part of the sixteenth century. Although performances of Krishna dramas were certainly taking place in Braj prior to this time, there is a general consensus that this period saw developments in *râs lila* presentational style sufficiently significant as to distinguish it from the form of prior practices. Developments of the time include, perhaps, the integration of classical *drupad* music with the play's dramatic action and the coordination of specific performances with the course of pilgrimage routes, by which the *râs lila* also at this time began to play a more formally liturgical role in Braj worship. Some also argue that the most significant development in the *râs lila* during the last half of the sixteenth century was the transfer of the chief *râs lila* roles, both male and female, to young boys, which is the way the roles are played today.

However, the textual history of the period is thin. We have convincing textual testimony from the time in question that Krishna dramas were taking place in Braj through the sixteenth century, but few documents survive that offer us any idea of the method of these performances. In sketching the history of the *râs lila*—especially with regard to child performers—scholars have to some extent been content to accept a lack of specific confirmation on this topic as evidence. The result of this resignation has been, I think, a misunderstanding of the role of children in the *râs lila* in the sixteenth century, a role that tells us something not only of the place of children in the contemporary art, but of the contemporary art's place in the practice of worship in contemporary Braj. A case can be made that children appeared in *râs lila* performances some time prior to other changes in the form that can be traced to the late sixteen hundreds; in fact, children may have been a long-standing feature of a local tradition within Braj, which, for theological reasons, found relatively sudden currency in the sixteenth-century rejuvenation of *bhakti* in the greater area of Braj.

Documentary evidence from outside the Vaishnava community establishes firmly that boys were playing the primary roles of *râs lila* performances by the end of the sixteenth century. In *The Miracle Plays of Mathura*, the first in-depth Western study of *râs lila*, Norvin Hein identifies in the 1597 court writings of a servant of the Muslim emperor Akbar, who at this time governed his kingdom from Agra, sixty miles south of Vrindavan, clear reference to the *râs lila* and an unmistakable description of the performers. Abul Fazl writes of *kirtaniya*s, Brahmans who "dress up smooth-faced boys as women and make them perform, singing the praises of Krishna and reciting his acts."[1] Although much about the origins of child actors on the *râs lila* stage is unclear, as we will see, Abul Fazl makes it certain that before the beginning of the seventeenth century, boys were employed in principal *râs lila* roles, including the female gopi roles, just as they are today.

Prior to Fazl, the certainties in *râs lila* productions give way to speculation as to when boys first appeared in the *râs lila* and why.[2] Norvin Hein argues that Fazl's description indicates a change in *râs lila* practice almost exactly contemporary with Fazl, and as a consequence of forces from outside the Vaishnava community itself. Hein writes:

> The use of males in the roles of women suggests that the kirttaniyas, despite their ancient instruments, developed their art in the special moral climate of the time of Muslim dominance. The use of child actors, which makes here its earliest sure appearance among Vaishnavas, sets this tradition apart from that of our known promoters of râslila of the middle of the sixteenth century [i.e. Ghamanddev]. These kirttaniyas represent a formative phase of the modern râslila, because we see in them, for the first time, the pattern of brahman teachers and child protégés that has since become dominant in the organization of the Braj theater.[3]

Hein here promotes the recognition of radical and sudden changes to *râs lila* method in quick succession. First, that men assumed places on the Vaishnava stage only in the sixteenth century, and, second, that boys on the Vaishnava stage followed this change only near the time of Fazl's writing. Though he does not here develop the idea, Hein's suggestion is strong that the artists involved in the early development of *râs lila* performance worked in an environment of religious repression. Ram Narayan Agrawal, the founder of the *Braj Kala Kendra* (Braj Art Center) and an affiliate of several research institutions in Mathura and elsewhere, seems to concur with Hein regarding the general period during which boys first appeared in the *râs lila*, and more directly identifies the political and social reasons for this occurrence:

> [Our] opinion is that the chief reason for giving permission to boys to take the parts of *svarup*s on the stage was the political situation of the time. Incidents of kidnapping and rape of Hindu women by the ruling class had become part of daily life. In such a situation, after hiding up women behind veils in their homes, the only option was to put boys on the stage in their place.... Therefore, in the re-establishment of the *râs*, religious leaders gave permission that brahmin boys be made *svarup*s on the stage so as to maintain the sanctity and spirituality of the *râs*...[4]

Hein and Agrawal suggest similar reasons for the sudden shift in *râs lila* performance practice: in the sixteenth century, Muslims were grossly mistreating Hindu women, or, at least, exerting a repressive force on Vaishnava religious practice so as to compel certain changes. Anti-Muslim sentiment still has currency among some residents of Vrindavan for explaining aspects of Vrindavan life, as I learned at a *kathak* dance concert in Vrindavan when I questioned a neighbor about the extreme infrequency of female performances there. My neighbor (a man) responded in cryptic English, "When the Muslims came, all they wanted to do was smash things." On another occasion, a local scholar explained to me why, even though no legal restrictions prohibit it, women do not take up the roles of *gopi*s in contemporary *râs lila* performances: "We want to keep women safe."[5] Although more moderate, refraining as it does from any direct accusation, his opinion nevertheless belies sentiments ascribed by Agrawal to the Vaishnava authorities of late sixteenth-century Braj.

Accordingly, we have to ask if the situation in North India in the sixteenth century was such as to justify the concerns to which Hein and Agrawal attribute this drastic alteration in the *râs lila*'s scheme. Historians customarily regard the rulers in the Delhi Sultanate and in the Mughal Empire (such as Akbar) as considerably more moderate than the Muslim conquerors of eleventh- and twelfth-century India. Indeed, Akbar, whose reign over the Braj area spanned 1556 to 1605, is generally regarded as one of the most liberal and enlightened of the Mughal rulers. The practices of the few rulers of the Delhi Sultanate, the empire that preceded the Mughal empire's control over the Braj area, may have been more religiously prejudicial than their immediate Mughal successors (at least, their successors until Aurangzeb). These practices included acts of temple desecration and iconoclasm—particularly in Mathura—as well as the imposition of laws restricting Vaishnava religious practices, such as bathing. These seem to have been acts of political repression rather than the religious zealotry implied by Hein or the moral licentiousness rehearsed by Agrawal.[6]

Hein supports his argument with references to additional writings—some older and some younger than Fazl's—including those of Nanak, the founder of Sikhism, and certain Vaishnava biographers of Braj. Each of these authors, Hein asserts, suggests an earlier form of the *râs lila* from which the version seen by Abul Fazl differed by including children. Guru Nanak, who had apparently traveled in the area around Vrindavan prior to composing certain hymns of the *Adi Granth* (c. 1500, CE) writes admonishingly in the *Asa ki Var* hymn about dramatic performances he saw. Hein translates the Punjabi slokas thus:

> 4. How many Krishna-tales there are, how many opinions on the Vedas!
> How many beggars dance and, twisting and falling, beat time with their hands!
> The mercenary fellows go into the market-place and draw out the market crowd.
> As kings and queens, they sing and utter fantastic stuff,
> Wearing rings and necklaces worth hundreds of thousands of rupees.
> The body on which they are worn will become ashes, O Nanak.
> 5. The disciples play instruments, the gurus dance,
> Shake their feet, roll their heads;
> The dust keeps flying and falls on their hair.
> People look on, laugh, and go home.
> It is for the sake of bread that they beat time and purposely fall on the ground,
> That the gopis and the Krishnas sing,
> That the Sitas and Royal Ramas sing.[7]

In some ways, the performances Nanak describes differ from the contemporary form of the *râs lila*, particularly in their marketplace venue and the rather wild falling about of their action that so captured Nanak's attention. However, we find in this verse from around 1500, CE, sufficient similarity to what happens today on Vrindavan stages, and to what happened in the performances seen by Abul Fazl, to conclude that what Nanak saw seems at least a genetic relative of today's *râs lila*, even if Hein's contention that these market shows are the "chronological limit of historical forms which can be called râslila" is not necessarily so.[8] In any case, Hein enlists this verse more for what it does not tell us than for what it does tell us, particularly that Nanak's verses do not explicitly mention child performers. Hein identifies the same lacuna in a few verses from Nabhaji's *Bhaktamal*, which reference the sixteenth-century theatrical activity of the Vaishnava saint Narayan Bhatt, who was active in the theatre of Braj shortly after the time of Abul Fazl. One of the three verses Hein mentions reads:

> The darling of Braj, the good Vallabh
> gave rare pleasure to the eyes.
> Clever in the virtues of dance and song,
> in the râs he makes sentiment rain down.
> Then in the lila, surrounded by Lalita and the others,
> he captivates the divine pair.
> Very liberal of salvation,
> his fame gleams in the Braj circle.
> He performs the Great Festival,
> giving great joy to all.
> The supreme love sentiment brought into subjection
> Narayan Bhatt, his master.
> The darling of Braj, Vallabh,
> gave rare pleasure to the eyes.[9]

This verse, composed in the seventeenth century, verifies that many of the elements we would expect of a *râs lila* performance were features of the very early seventeenth-century version, including song and dance in a circular formation, an abundance of sentiment, and the presence of divine characters. The last of the poetic biographies Hein cites in support of his argument against an early appearance of *râs lila* children is an early seventeenth-century verse by Dhruvdas that celebrates a certain Ghamanddev (Ghamandi), who was a figure central in the sixteenth-century development of the *râs lila*. The verse, as translated by Hein, reads thus:

> Ghamandi swam in sentiment ever
> In Vrindaban, his home.
> Performing the râs at Bansibat
> He served Syama and Syam.

Here, as Hein notes, is certainly "respectable evidence...which connects Ghamandi with the râslila."[10]

Considering Dhruvdas's lines, Nanak's verses, and Nabhaji's short poetical paean about Vallabh, Hein remarks, "we are struck by the lack of any reference to svarups, the child actors who are such a prominent feature of the modern performances."[11] For Hein, the absence of an unambiguous report of child performers in the few references to theatre in Braj in the extant pieces of sixteenth-century literature provides sufficient justification to theorize that at the time of these references the *râs lila* had not yet adopted child actors.

Hein pushes the evidence he supplies for his theory further, contending that the passages in question must have had adult performers as their subjects.

> Nanak's words referring to performers strongly suggest grown persons: beggars (*mangate*) who dance, *gurus* who dance, *celas* who play instruments, and mercenary fellows (*bajari*) who make a play for attention in the bazaars. The dancer Vallabh, celebrated in such concrete terms by Nabhaji, seems to be an adult since he is "clever in the virtues of dance and song." He is not a mere director of child actors, since he is praised directly for his pleasing action in the lila, among the gopis. Ghamandi, who bore a sannyasi's name and was given a sannyasi's burial, could scarcely have been a juvenile performer, and when Dhruvdas says that he performed the râs, he does not use a causative verb to indicate that he performed it indirectly through such children.[12]

According to Hein, then, the little evidence we have from the period that indicates a form of performance in Braj connected with Krishna worship tells us that adults alone were engaged in it.

Let us consider the degree to which these references must indicate adult performers, exclusively. Although Nanak most likely employed the terms *guru* and *bajari* to describe adults, there is no overwhelming linguistic reason we should regard the word *mangate* to refer exclusively to adults.[13] Nabhaji's dancer Vallabh may or may not have been an adult, but the simple fact of his cleverness does not conclude the matter. Nor can we positively conclude from a reading of Nabhaji's verse alone that Vallabh was not merely a director, since the precise nature of Vallabh's performing activity is not explicit in this verse. In the present day, *râs lila* directors are most often performers of some kind, as well. More often than not, the director himself acts as the lead singer and musician during a performance. Furthermore, from time to time, a director (particularly a younger one) may take up an adult's role in a performance, such as the role of Shiva. Since it appears in this verse that Vallabh was not performing the role of either Krishna or Radha—as his performance was enjoyed by the "divine pair"—it is entirely possible that Vallabh here plays a role appropriate for adults on a stage where children played roles reserved to themselves, as is the case in performances today where children play Krishna, Radha, and the *gopi*s while adults assume adult roles, including roles of mortals such as Krishna's mother and father, the semidivine sage Narada, and Gods such as Kama.

The stark similarities between contemporary performances and the sixteenth-century performance noted by Abu Fazl with respect to the function of children in *râs lila* suggest other elements, such as the involvement of directors, have been similarly enduring. The verse does seem to indicate a Vallabh who is more than a sideline musician; however, the verse fails to offer any conclusive evidence as to Vallabh's age. As for the allusions to *râs lila* theatre in Dhruvdas, Ghamandi had certainly become an adult by the time he was given a sannyasin's burial (as Hein calls it), but we need not conclude that he could never have been a juvenile performer at some time prior to his death.[14] In any case, there is some question as to whether the verse refers to *râs lila* performance at all. The verse as included in Mital's *Braj ki Râslila* differs considerably in its second line from the version translated by Hein. Mital's version reads:

Ghamandi ras mem ghumadi rahyau, vrndavan nij dham |
vamsivat tat vas kiy, gaye syama—syam ||[15]

In the second line here appears *vâs* (home) in the place of *râs*, eliminating entirely the *râs lila* reference Hein attributes to it. The additional variation in the second line—*gaye* (sang) in the place of *see* (served)—restores a small measure of the verse's reference to performance. Furthermore, *vrindavan nij dham* in the first line is more likely to be a reference to the spiritual aspect of Vrindavan from which Ghamandi's overwhelming sense of *ras* comes, and which provides a motivation for whatever kind of performing he may have been doing. A possible translation of this alternative of the verse reads:

Ghamandi was always dizzy from *ras* [as opposed to *râs*],[16] from the region of the true Vrindavan,
He made his home on the shore at Vamsivat, and sang of Krishna and Radha.

This rendering minimizes the "respectable evidence" Hein says this verse supplies to *râs lila* performances in Vrindavan in the middle of the sixteenth century. In his discussion of Dhruvdas's description of Ghamandi, Agrawal includes the same version of the verse as Mital.[17] Hein justifies his choice of versions by writing, "we shall have to assume that the critical edition has adopted its reading for a good reason."[18] Looking at both extant versions of the verse greatly diminishes the degree to which it conclusively characterizes Ghamandi as an early *râs lila* performer. Even so, in either reading is the suggestion that *performing*—be it by singing, dancing, or dramatic art—was a common element of the activity of worshiping Krishna's association with Radha in mid-sixteenth-century Vrindavan.

Given the age at which Krishna is supposed to have played in Braj with his similarly aged *gopi* girlfriends, would we not assume that these roles were originally and continuously adopted by child actors? Hein anticipates this objection to his argument while making a case for an undocumented tradition of Krishna performance in Braj prior to the sixteenth century. Directing his reader to a consideration of Sanskrit drama, which among dramatic traditions in South Asia rather exclusively provided texts, both dramatic, critical, and historical, from which to develop a sense of the nature of dramatic art in South Asia prior to the eighteenth century, Hein writes, "The impersonation of deities by children is not a convention of the Sanskrit stage…"[19] Citing a nineteenth-century article by A. V. W. Jackson, Hein concludes, "The theory that children were selected to play the roles of Krishna and the gopis, because Krishna and the gopis were children, only leads us to ask, 'Why and how, in the sixteenth century, did this natural fact become at last a compelling consideration?' "[20] Hein's question is partly a transition to his assertion that the "moral climate" of the sixteenth century necessitated a substitution of boys for women in Vaishnava plays, and is partly rhetorical, indicating his belief that prior to the period in question the most obvious means of dramatizing Krishna and the gopis on stage had not been adopted.

That the conventions of the Sanskrit stage, either in the sixteenth century or earlier, provide us with an understanding of conventions on vernacular (and essentially undocumented) stages in North India is dubious, if only because Sanskrit drama was suited to a specific, elite Indian audience through numerous, specific rules regarding every element of dramatic practice, while plays intended for specific functions in local communities, such as the semi-ritual dramatization of sacred history, would have been governed by more immediate requirements of the communities for which they played. Even so, if the conventions of Sanskrit drama might be taken as an indication of certain stage practices employed by performances apart from the Sanskrit dramas themselves, we still find a lack of evidence to conclude that characters such as Krishna would not have been played by suitably aged boys as a matter of course. Hein himself observes that "Krishna plays are lacking in Indian dramatic literature…"[21] As a consequence of this dearth of relevant scripts, we have no clear evidence, as Hein points out, that boys undertook the role of Krishna in performances that dramatized Krishna's life, even though doctrinal sources strongly imply such performances must have been occurring considerably earlier than the sixteenth century.[22]

However, considering the circumstantial evidence, and the weaknesses inherent in Norvin Hein's analysis of textual sources, we are equally inclined to conclude that children did occupy places of performance on the Vaishnava stages of Braj from early in the sixteenth century, or even earlier, as that they did not do so until near the beginning of the seventeenth century. Based upon his interpretation of these few sources, Hein contends that children did not take a place in *râs lila* performances until quite late in the sixteenth century. "We conclude," writes Hein, "that the râslila of the mid-sixteenth century was still usually an adult art."[23] This conclusion is more than the evidence will bear. As we have seen, Hein founds this assertion upon a lack of evidence to the contrary. And, indeed, given the paucity of solid historical sources on this subject, one is hard-pressed to lay any surer foundation. However, since neither Hein nor his counterparts in India have conclusively established the date at which children (particularly boys) first took to stages in Braj, the matter remains open; and given the thoroughness with which scholars have reviewed the historical testimony from the period, we apparently lack the historical material necessary to resolve the issue decisively. Given the inadequacy of the available evidence to settle the matter, any development of theories in this regard will necessarily rely on readings of sources less typical to scholarship.[24]

THE MYTHS OF *RÂS LILA* ORIGINS: PRINCIPAL PLAYERS AND PLACES

The religious literature of Braj includes a variety of legends that purport to describe the origins of *râs lila* theatre. Although many elements of these stories are undoubtedly fictitious, like other kinds of folktales, these tales may indicate a familiarity with the actual persons and practices they concern. At least, where the stories were developed or later employed as a means of justifying what is, we might suppose that the stories are aware of what is. In other words, the fanciful elements of the stories that are adopted to explain how things came about do not necessarily mar the extant material that needed to be explained. For example, whether or not Nanak emerged from under water after three days with the *Guru Granth Sahib* composed, there was a Guru Nanak and he did produce the *Guru Granth Sahib*; the story is not illegitimate with respect to its principal character and his principal accomplishment. Agrawal suggests that these myths, such as the *Râs-Sarvasva*'s miraculous *mukut* story—which is related below—were developed precisely to legitimize changing practices. Concluding his discussion of the substitution of boys for women in the *râs lila*, Agrawal writes, "Hence, in every available legend connected with the *râs* is some justification for making the Brahman boys of Braj into *svarups*."[25] In other words, the fabulous stories concerning *râs lila*'s divine origin, which today are regarded as gospel by many residents of Braj, coalesced after the fact of the *râs lila*'s existence, and with extant *râs lila* methods in mind. Consequently, we might consider that these stories reveal a familiarity with early *râs lila* practices, especially those that, at some time or another, may have required special justification.

The *râs lila*'s origin stories themselves vary greatly in their details, owing to sectarian differences regarding the participation (or lack thereof) of the principal figures. Commonly, however, a divine manifestation provides the impetus for the subsequent establishment of some kind of Krishna theatre featuring the employment of young boys in the lead roles.

One of these traditions places the beginning of the contemporary form of *râs lila* performances, in which boys are engaged as Krishna, Radha, and the gopis, in the time of important religious leaders in the middle of the sixteenth century at Mathura's Vishram Ghat. A text from the late nineteenth or early twentieth century titled *Râs-Sarvasva* (*The Essence of Râs*) provides a version of the story that exhibits these fundamental elements. Through Prabhudayal Mital's analysis of the story in his book *Braj Ki Râslila*, we find that in the sixteenth century a certain Swami Haridas and the actor-saint Ghamanddev went to Vishram (also Vishrant) Ghat in Mathura in order to meet with the revered religious leader named Vallabhacarya, recognized as the founder of one of the most significant *bhakti* sects of the present day. There they asked for Vallabhacarya's help in developing a means of making devotional feelings more tangibly apprehensible, and when Vallabhacarya exercised his supernatural power, there appeared in the sky a magnificent crown, which could be seen by fifty-two kings who had assembled there for a particular festival. The kings certified the event, Vallabhacarya chose eight Brahman boys to be actors, deputized Haridas and Ghamanddev, and the new troupe went to Vrindavan with authority to promote Krishna performances.[26] A slightly different version of the *Râs-Sarvasva* story is given by Agrawal. According to Agrawal, on the day in question, the Vaishnava saints Vallabhacarya and Haridas brought eight Caturvedi Brahman boys to Visram Ghat where a crown of peacock feathers (*mukut*) miraculously descended from the sky and settled on the head of the boy who was to play Krishna.²⁷ Vasant Yamadagni's account includes the paired mission of Haridas and Ghamanddev to Mathura, and Vallabha's supernatural manifestation of a crown.²⁸ The exception to these readings of the *Râs-Sarvasva* is Hein, who states that ten crowns appeared above the ghat.²⁹ In his later book, *Braj ka Râs Rangmanc*, Agrawal relates that Vallabhacarya appointed Haridas to do the first *râs lila*, and Haridas complied by choosing Brahman children to play the roles of Krishna and his girlfriends; but when the moment in the dramatic story came that Krishna was to disappear, the "boy who was acting Krishna really disappeared," and the children playing the *gopi*s who go frantically searching for Krishna "became themselves the object of a search."³⁰ When the parents of the missing children took the play's organizers to task, Vallabhacarya stepped in and told the parents to bathe in the Yamuna. When they had done so, the distraught parents saw their children playing happily in Krishna's divine bower, which settled that matter; but the brouhaha meant that that first performance failed. Subsequently, Vallabhacarya directed Ghamanddev to "adjust" or "oversee" the *râs lila* (*sambhâlnâ*), which Ghamanddev undertook to do by training Brahman boys in Karahla.³¹

The other strong tradition in this regard also emphasizes the importance of the small town of Karahla, near modern Barsana, over Mathura and Vrindavan. A strongly sectarian tradition holds that the Ghamanddev that accompanied Haridas to Mathura in the Vishram Ghat story above was directed in a vision of Krishna himself, who took his hand and enjoined him to institute the *râs lila* "on the spot of my original *râslila*." Ghamanddev then moved to Karahla, and within twelve years selected some local boys, instituted the first *râs lila*, and died.³²

The Karahla origin is developed in a different way by Karahlans, for whom Karahla is Ghamanddev's home town. In Karahla, they say, from an early time in his life, Ghamanddev pursued intense religious practice. In Agrawal's rehearsal of this story, in seeking to satisfy his deep longing for *real* experience of Krishna (*pratyaksh darshan*), Ghamanddev took to fashioning lumps of mud from a local lake into images of Krishna and the gopis. These figures he would dress accordingly, and arrange in scenes reminiscent of stories from Krishna lore, sinking the figures in the lake at the end of each day. One night, Krishna appeared to Ghamanddev in a dream, promising him that he would have the direct experience he wanted after getting some local boys dressed up and arranged as he had been doing with the mud figures. "At the time of the *râs*," said Krishna, "I will give you direct experience of me in the form of those boys." Accordingly, from that time, Ghamanddev began the *râs*, and in the *râs* dance realized Krishna as

Brahman boys (*Braj*, 94–95).³³ A further variation of this story appears in Agrawal's *Ras-Lila: Ek Paricay*, which lends to the *râs lila* itself some of the authority that the Vishram Ghat story gives to the saint Vallabha. Here, Ghamanddev's charge to integrate living boys in his imitation of Krishna's playing does not come from Krishna, but from Vallabha, to whom the yearning Ghamanddev goes for instruction.³⁴

PRINCIPAL PLAYERS: MANY GHAMANDDEVS?

Vallabha, Swami Haridas, and Ghamanddev vie in the minds of sectarian devotees for the place of father of the contemporary form of the *râs lila*, but there is no compelling need to undertake an examination of this dispute here.³⁵ It is clear that their lives in Braj overlapped to some degree, and that each was significant to the development of the *râs lila* form in the sixteenth century. However, among the various stories revolving around these three individuals, which concern the contemporary *râs lila*'s sixteenth-century origin, a "Ghamanddev" emerges as a constant. Even in those stories such as the *Râs-Sarvasva*'s, which place him in a subordinate chronological position to other figures such as Haridas, whose first arranged performance was in many ways a disaster, Ghamanddev is regarded as the early, established practitioner of *râs lila* art. Comparing the account of the *râs lila*'s origin in the *Râs-Sarvasva*, which emphasizes Vallabha's authority and Haridas's precedence, and the traditions that emphasize the town of Karahla as the place of *râs lila*'s origin, we find that Ghamanddev's endeavors in Krishna theatre over a period of time form the common element. "According to the *Râssarvasva*," writes Vasant Yamadagni, "...the *râs* appeared after Vallabhacarya made the crown appear at the urging of Swami Haridas, after which Ghamandev spread it in Braj under Vallabhacarya's mandate."³⁶ Furthermore, as we have seen, among these three founding figures, Ghamanddev is distinguished from the other figures of the origin stories by Dhruvdas's characterization of him as an actor-performer—a unique factor of his life that the extant tradition of the residents of Karahla confirms.³⁷ Consequently, Ghamanddev seems a reasonable focus of an examination of the development of actual *râs lila* practices in the sixteenth century.

However, having so settled on scrutinizing Ghamanddev, we now discover that, in addition to the various individuals that vying sects promote as founders of the *râs lila*, for similar reasons, parties in Vrindavan assert a variety of individual Ghamanddevs. Hein, who claims to have made a thorough investigation of documents with which to construct a timeline of the principal figures featured in the Vishram Ghat legend, concludes that Ghamanddev "was without a doubt a real person residing in Braj in the middle of the sixteenth century and that he was famous even in that century for some role in the performance of the râs."[38] However, Indian scholars continue to ask who and when this Ghamanddev was.[39] Agrawal determines there are three main branches of the Ghamanddev story, amounting to portraits of as many as three different individuals known as Ghamanddev. One of the Ghamanddevs whose fame has survived until now was the performing subject of Dhruvdas's verse included above. Agrawal identifies this Ghamanddev with a certain Ghamandiji who was involved with *râs lila* performances in Vrindavan. A second possible Ghamanddev was a disciple of the Nimbarkite saint Harivyas Devacarya by the name of Uddhav Ghamanddevacarya, who the Nimbark sect accordingly claims was responsible for the institution of the *râs lila*. The third Ghamanddev Agrawal identifies was the Ghamanddevji whose cremation site is now marked by a memorial in the village of Karahla. It may be that a reconciliation of these three versions of Ghamanddev, to the extent that such a reconciliation is possible, will produce an individual whose contributions to the *râs lila* will illuminate the character of the *râs lila* in its early days.

The task of reconciling the three possible Ghamanddevs is made easier by the general agreement that reason and the available evidence do not connect the Nimbarkite Uddhav Ghamanddevacarya with the practice or development of the *râs lila*.[40] In addition to laying claim to the Ghamanddev of the *Râs-Sarvasva*, who was present at Vishram Ghat at the appearance of the miraculous crown, the Nimbarkite tradition attributes Uddhav Ghamanddevacarya with his own divine vision commissioning him to institute the *râs lila*, after which he moved to Karahla, organized within twelve years a performing troupe of boys, and died.[41] The arguments against this version of Ghamanddev are generally reasoned from an inconsistency of time and locale. In the first place, Agrawal's analysis of the various Ghamanddevs determines that the Uddhav Ghamanddevacarya, whom Nimbarkites claim was responsible for the *râs lila*, must certainly be distinct from the other Ghamanddevs, to whom tradition gives specific roles in the development of the *râs lila*. Agrawal points out that Uddhav Ghamandevacarya must have lived considerably earlier than the alternative Ghamanddevs and the time during which the *râs lila* became a feature of Braj pilgrimage. The Nimbarkite lineage places Uddhav Ghamanddevacarya in the second generation of Harivyasdev's disciples, or three generations earlier than the one residing in Vrindavan at the time of

Vallabha's and Caitanya's arrival in the middle of the sixteenth century. If Uddhav Ghamanddevacarya had established *râs lila* performances, writes Agrawal, surely they would have been a well-established feature of Braj pilgrimage by the time Vallabha and Caitanya came on the scene, which pilgrimage accounts up to that time show was not the case.[42]

The catalogues of the prominent sixteenth-century devotees lend additional credence to the contention that Uddhav Ghamanddev's lifetime did not coincide with the other figures such as Vallabha and Haridas who were significant to the development of the *râs lila*. According to Mital, Uddhav Ghamanddevacarya's absence in these catalogues of the people who are important to the *bhakti* movement as it burgeoned in sixteenth century Vrindavan, as written by their contemporaries or near-contemporaries, is a substantial contradiction of the Nimbark sect's claim that Uddhav Ghamanddevacarya could have been involved with the *râs lila*, at least during this period. Furthermore, the chronicles do not connect anyone of that specific name with Karahla village, rather identifying a certain Ghamandi as some kind of performer or sadhu of Vrindavan, which undermines the Nimbark sect's claim.[43] Agrawal picks up this line of reasoning with reference to Dhruvdas, whose reference to Ghamandi noted earlier locates him in Vrindavan. The association of Ghamandi with Vrindavan accords with local traditions, there being a number of pilgrimage spots and temples associated with him in Vrindavan—though no such sites are associated with the Nimbark sect's Uddhav Ghamanddevacarya.[44]

Finally, there is a problem with the connection between Uddhav Ghamanddevacarya and Karahla village, a place commonly associated with the *râs lila*'s evolution in the sixteenth century. On the basis of finding a lack of evidence or motive for this Uddhav Ghamanddevacarya to have lived for any amount of time in Karahla, Agrawal decides this aspect of the Uddhav Ghamanddevacarya story as the Nimbarkite sect tells it is fabricated. In fact, sixteenth-century Nimbarkites had little to do with Karahla, which complicates the sect's claim that their Uddhav Ghamandevacarya took up residence in Karahla in order to promote *râs lila*. "The old strongholds in Braj of the Nimbark sect," writes Agrawal, "were Neech village and Mathura.... If the *râs anukaran* [*râs lila*] had been started by Uddhav Ghamanddevacarya, he certainly would have chosen his own and his sect's center of power for it, not Karahla" (*Braj*, 104). For these reasons, also, Mital concurs that the Nimbarkite association of Uddhav Ghamanddevacarya with the *râs lila* is greatly strained.[45] Agrawal notes that according to Karahlans, who point to the existing memorial in Karahla, the Ghamanddev who was significant to the sixteenth-century *râs lila* practice was a resident of Karahla in the first place, not an outsider who took up residence there late in life.[46] Agrawal concludes that owing to the similarity in names between their own saint and a possible factual individual from Karahla, the Nimbarkite sectarian writers simply "took him [Uddhav Ghamanddevacarya] to be the founder of the *râs*."[47]

The extreme difficulties inherent in considering Uddhav Ghamanddevacarya to be the Ghamanddev associated with the *râs lila* reduce our three Ghamanddev's to two. The two remaining are the performing Ghamandi who appears in the sixteenth-century chronicles of Braj, and the Ghamanddev linked to Karahla village. We have already seen Dhruvdas's description of Ghamandi, and noted how uncertain it is with regard to Ghamandi's identification with *râs lila* performing. Dhruvdas gives us a Ghamandi whose obsession with the metaphysical experience of the transcendent Vrindavan occupies his whole attention and all his time, and keeps him perpetually meditating in the environs of the material Vrindavan, which does not seem to be compatible with the characterization of Ghamanddev, in sources such as the *Râs-Sarvasva*, which give him credit for the spread of *râs lila* theater throughout Braj. Agrawal addresses Dhruvdas only in an attempt to show that the Ghamandi found there must be distinct from the Nimbarkite Uddhav Ghamanddevacarya; but in the process Agrawal describes a Ghamandi "who wandered around [Vrindavan] contemplating the spiritual world."[48] Nabhaji's *Bhaktamal* offers a brief description of an individual residing in Vrindavan named Ghamandi, but only tells us that this Ghamandi, a disciple of Jugalkishor, had a particular penchant for fasting, which seems much like Dhruvdas's Ghamandi, and little like the Ghamanddev we are looking for.[49] Mital's assessment of the biographical chronicles of the time is that "No one gives an account in any of them of a Ghamanddevji with a particular *râs* specialty."[50] It appears that a similarity between Ghamandi's and Ghamanddev's names, and, perhaps, the rough coincidence of their lifetimes, are the primary justification for identifying Ghamandi and Ghamanddev as a single person. Although inconclusive, an evaluation of the biographical notes concerning Ghamandi must leave us with a strong bias against identifying him as a founder of the modern *râs lila*. In fact, it seems that a blending of individuals on account of the similarity of their names may have occurred here, as Agrawal asserts occurred in the case of the Nimbarkite identification of Uddhav Ghamanddevacarya with the purported founder of the *râs lila*. Just as, according to Agrawal, that misidentification occurred unintentionally in the search for the subject of the oral tradition that called Ghamanddev the *râs lila* founder, but which provided little information as to his identity, the misidentification of Ghamandi with Ghamanddev may have happened for the same reason; that is, the Ghamandi of the Braj chronicles had a name sufficiently similar to suit him for the part.[51]

The Ghamanddev of Karahla is thus the only one of Agrawal's Ghamanddev trinity remaining. The primary text that asserts a connection between Ghamanddev and Karahla is the *Râs-Sarvasva*, whose account of the divine crown descending at Vishram Ghat in Mathura we have already examined. Although Hein suggests that the Nimbarkite sect uses this text as the "primary source of their information" by which to designate their Uddhav Ghamanddevacarya as the founder of the *râs lila*,[52] Mital points out that the author, Radhakrishna Das, and his family are associated with the Vallabhite sect.[53] More importantly, Radhakrishna Das was himself a *râs lila* director of Karahla; hence, his account seems to be an expression of the oral traditions of Karahla, which hold that the local Ghamanddev took the *râs lila* from Karahla to the rest of Braj. We have already noted some other accounts in Agrawal's *Braj ki Râs Rangmanc*, which apparently rely on the oral history of Karahla. Together, these accounts of the Karahlan Ghamanddev suggest that we adopt a considerably different approach to the problem of Ghamanddev's identity.

The significant elements of these Karahlan stories concerning Ghamanddev emphasize three things: (1) his own status as a performer, even prior to his involvement with the establishment of the *râs lila*, (2) his contribution to the introduction of child actors to the *râs lila*, and (3) his role as the proselyter of the reinvented theatrical form. We learn in these accounts that as a young man Ghamanddev sought to satisfy some religious desire by fashioning figures of Krishna, Radha, and the gopis from mud, costuming them, and arranging them in scenes invoking the action of Krishna mythology, a uniquely theatrical means of worship that seems to reveal a particularly dramatic sensibility in its practitioner. Even given the absence of an audience and, perhaps, dramatic action discernible in the movement and speech of the actors, the aspect of mimesis so strongly exhibited here insists we regard this activity as performance. If we understand this activity as performance, this story then offers us a Ghamanddev who was a principal performer in the theatre form he developed, responsible as he was for the scene that occurred (if only in his mind)—by which token he was the performance's director as well. The myth of Ghamanddev's early life indicates a scenario in which, originally, the performer himself is the principal innovator in the dramatic form—not so much a *founder* of a form as the developer of a rather uncomplicated idea that the mythology of Krishna's and Radha's association together might be more clearly brought to life for the devotee by dramatic representation.

The *Râs-Sarvasva* reserves for Vallabha and Haridas the credit for introducing children to the *râs lila* format, but the other Karahlan accounts give this distinction to Ghamanddev.[54] As Agrawal relates, Karahlan residents maintain that Ghamanddev received a personal mandate from Krishna to add living children to the performances he had been conducting.[55] Even in the *Râs-Sarvasva*, we see a vestige of this part of the legend in the way that Ghamanddev is commissioned by Vallabha to promote the *râs lila* in Braj.

Which brings us to Ghamanddev's role in the dissemination of this form of Krishna theatre in Braj. What did Ghamanddev do in this regard? The various accounts of the contemporary *râs lila*'s origins, especially as that origin involves the introduction of child actors, have in common, by way of the figure of Ghamanddev, the town of Karahla. Even the Nimbark sect's version of the appearance of children on the *râs lila* stage, which works very hard to privilege itself by associating the name *Ghamanddev* with one of its own important saints, returns us to Karahla, although the Nimbark sect itself has little or nothing to do with Karahla otherwise. Though the form of the *râs lila* for which he is said to be greatly responsible does expand beyond Karahla (and even beyond Braj), the stories consistently restrict Ghamanddev himself to Karahla. Although divinely commissioned—whether by Krishna himself or by the divinely authorized Vallabha, depending on the source—to widely disseminate this revealed form of theatre, Ghamanddev remains in Karahla, while his form of theatre develops around him.

The *Râs-Sarvasva* tells us that Vallabha directed Ghamanddev to gather students to continue the tradition, and that Ghamanddev subsequently set up shop in Karahla, assisted by two Brahmans named Udaykaran and Khemkaran. Udaykaran's son Vikram performed this *râs* form for the Mughal ruler Aurangzeb, and then for the Rajput ruler Jaisingh.[56] In which case we find that the descendents of the two other Karahlan practitioners named in the story seem to have taken Ghamanddev's theatre form furthest from Karahla and to the most distinguished audiences. The oral tradition of Karahla that Agrawal presents does not provide such detail, but Agrawal reasons that as the strength of the form and the support it received from religious leaders began to establish the *râs lila* beyond Karahla, "the name *Ghamanddev* came to be celebrated outside the limits of Karahla with *râs lila* directors."[57] At the very center (geographically and artistically) of what seem to be noteworthy changes to the dramatic representation of Krishna's *lila*, Ghamanddev becomes known outside of Karahla only in association with other directors carrying his contributions to the form to the rest of Braj. In this way, the oral tradition in Braj seems to favor a region as much as an individual as the father of the contemporary *râs lila*.

Which is to say, there was no Ghamanddev. Nor is it likely that any one individual can be credited with the appearance of children in the roles of the *râs lila*, in the sixteenth century or earlier, and not solely because the available evidence leaves us no other choice. Even when Ghamandi is accepted as the Ghamanddev of the *râs lila*, he is not identified as a *founder*.[58] Hein himself points out, "We know with fair certainty that the râslila tradition began before the time of Ghamandi..."[59] Guru Nanak's description of Krishna performances in Braj prior to 1500 makes this clear. There seems to be no compelling justification for regarding Ghamanddev as an individual who *invented* the *râs lila* we know today, or, even, something closely akin to it. Ghamanddev the individual seems to have germinated *post facto* in the lore surrounding the *râs lila* from the seeds of legend planted in a common understanding of the time that innovative theatrical practice in Karahla, evolving from a continuing tradition of Krishna performance, provided a model for staging the play of Krishna and the gopis, the distinctive characteristic of which was the use of young boys in the male and female roles. Ghamanddev seems to have become, thus, an amalgam of performers, directors, and saints whose combined activity over time produced a theatre scheme so appealing as to be eagerly adopted in its latest form by devotees throughout Braj—a figure not unlike epic poets such as Homer and Vyasa, who are often characterized as editors of disparate epic tales, or complete fictions altogether, representing instead the collective efforts of a number of individual poets.[60]

KARAHLA VILLAGE AND THE BRAJ PILGRIMAGE TRAIL

Considering the circumstantial evidence, the weaknesses inherent in Norvin Hein's analysis of textual sources, and the way in which Ghamanddev is linked to theatre in Braj tradition, I am more inclined to conclude that children did occupy places of performance on the Vaishnava stages of Karahla from early in the sixteenth century, or even earlier, than that they did not until near the beginning of the seventeenth century. It certainly may be that the widespread adoption of Karahla's *râs lila* in Braj did not begin until the middle of the sixteenth century—probably within the five-year framework suggested by Agrawal, from 1550 to 1555.[61] Agrawal arrives at his dates as a result of an analysis of sixteenth-century Braj pilgrimage journals. "Several accounts are available from before this time," writes Agrawal, "in which devotees on pilgrimage in Braj recount taking *darshan* and participating in *kirtan*s by either singing or listening, but only after this time are there accounts in which devotees saw this *lila* that was reconstituted by brahmans."[62]

However, rather than indicating the period during which the *râs lila* underwent a change as significant as the initial use of children on stage, the acknowledgment of *râs lila* performances on the Braj pilgrimage route by pilgrimage journals after 1550 suggests a new implementation of *râs lila* plays—one that facilitated a relatively quick distribution of the form around Braj. The dates at which *râs lila* performances began appearing on the Braj pilgrimage trail affirm the influence of the Caitanyaite saint Narayan Bhatt on the pilgrimage program after his arrival in Barsana, a Braj town near Karahla, around 1550. Bhatt's *Vrajabhaktivilâsa*, regarded as the oldest surviving programmatic itinerary for Braj pilgrimage, prescribes an extensive, sequential list of places travelers must visit, and practices they must engage in, in order to derive the full spiritual benefit of the pilgrimage. Among the prescribed activities of the tour is attendance at *râsa* festivals.[63] The text seems to have ridden the cusp of the popularization of the pilgrimage circuit and aided in its codification, as it not only outlines the course of the Braj pilgrimage as a whole but of newly conceived sub-passages centered around particular forests and towns.[64]

The biography of Bhatt written by a descendent in the late seventeenth century asserts that Bhatt introduced the practice of staging *râs lila* performances at various points along the pilgrimage trail.[65] The charge is substantiated to some degree by Narayan Bhatt's identification of new sites on the route with specific activities of Krishna.[66] I would suggest that shortly after 1550, when Bhatt took residence in Barsana, the coincidence in Braj of Vallabha, Haridas, and Narayan Bhatt, each of whom invested a particular interest in the *râs lila*, provided the spiritual and artistic legitimacy the *râs lila* needed to become a popular means of worship in Braj during the time at which Agrawal suggests the form went through its most important changes. Norvin Hein sets the "outside limits" within which Vallabha and Haridas might have "met together at Vrindavan" at 1530 to 1570 CE.[67] Agrawal corroborates these dates to some degree by placing Vallabhacarya's life in Braj from 1549, and dating Haridas's settlement in Vrindavan near 1560.[68] Where these dates coincide between 1550 and 1560, with Narayan Bhatt's appearance in Braj after 1550, makes plausible the notion that the middle decade of the sixteenth century saw the beginning of a widespread adoption of the *râs lila* as a legitimate artistic practice and orthodox mode of worship.[69] However, there is little to indicate that these individuals, let alone these significant five years, saw such a transformation of the *râs lila* as the introduction of children in the major roles.

The representation of God and his close friends by children in the Karahlan *râs lila* was a principal reason for its appeal to the pilgrims increasingly congregating in Braj in conjunction with the reinvigoration of *bhakti* modes of worship by the religious leaders who relocated to Braj in the sixteenth century (or otherwise concentrated their devotees' attention on Braj, as did Caitanya). The character of worship that these leaders brought to Vrindavan found its clearest expression and most direct means of consummation in the *râs* performances encountered in Karahla.

IMMIGRATION OF GAUDIYA PILGRIMS AND CAITANYAITE AESTHETICS

As noted in the previous chapter, Western scholars have commonly identified (though with varying degrees of enthusiasm) an interest in freedom as the kernel of Krishna *bhakti*—not an esoteric freedom common to South Asian religions, which denotes an anticipated liberation from the constraints of existence itself, but a liberation, even if only temporary, from the constraints of immediate social, political, and religious pressures.[70] In an article published in *History of Religions*, Norvin Hein suggests that the very inspiration for the origin of Krishna *bhakti* itself, as much as twelve hundred years prior to Caitanya and Vallabha, was the burden of Brahmanical oppression. "In the Gupta age...." Hein writes, "the Hindu caste order restricted with a thoroughness seldom seen in any system before or since."[71] Hein speculates that some of those upon whom the priestly class of the newly empowered Hindu Gupta dynasty imposed a strict system of *varnâsrama dharma* (the hierarchical social order sometimes, though perhaps erroneously, identified as the "caste system") found a kind of relief by proxy in religious practice that celebrated the insubordinate antics of the child Krishna.[72] Those in the system without much hope for temporal mitigation of their circumstances elevated to the level of a savior a child who complains, whines, breaks things, steals, makes messes of houses and people, and, in general, ignores everyone's loudly expressed behests. "It accords best with our historical information," Hein submits, "to believe that the religion of Gopâla [the child form of Krishna] is substantially a religion of people who suffer under extraordinary restraint, and that it came into prominence in the third and fourth centuries A.D. because India was experiencing at that time the culmination of the power of a resurgent Brahman leadership."[73] The earliest appearance of Krishna-Gopal *bhakti*, then, developed from an attitude of rebellion or resistance to highly repressive forms of authority, or, at least, escapism inspired by the same restrictive power.

The resurgence of devotional feeling in the fifteenth and sixteenth centuries may be attributed to similar circumstances, as Hindus of northern India at that time found themselves dominated by a variety of Muslim regimes. We have already encountered the charge that these Muslim kingdoms oversaw rampant abuse of Hindu peoples in an examination of Hein's theory that Muslim oppression was the impetus for removing women from Vaishnava stages. Although there was discord between Muslims and Hindus during the period in question, it does not appear that the dying Delhi Sultanate under Sikander and Ibrahim, nor the young Mughal empire under Babur and Akbar, made the oppression of Hindus a practiced expression of Muslim power. But we need not find such overt Muslim-Hindu contention to see how Krishna *bhakti* as imagined by Hein would find renewed appeal under Muslim sovereignty. Muslim political power in some ways threw established Hindu practice—which had previously identified itself with governmental authority—into question. David Haberman, in his examination of devotional literature, provides an example:

> [The] type of Vaisnavism expressed in the pre-Muslim *Visnudharmottara* reveals a religious structure dependent on an image and temple established only by the authority of a *cakravartin*, a king who had never been defeated in battle and was considered to be Visnu's representative on earth.[74]

Haberman attests that under such circumstances, the child Krishna reemerged as an attractive figure. The boy who plays aimlessly all day in the forest, who casually flouts the authority of the center of society, became an expression of religious practice that had necessarily withdrawn from its integration with the administration of public life.

Furthermore, as was the case with *bhakti*'s birth in the early centuries, CE, the revival of *bhakti* in the fifteenth and sixteenth centuries was characterized by a fairly radical approach to potentially oppressive social conventions of all sorts in Hindu society. The *bhakti* movement in sixteenth-century Bengal, writes Edward Dimock:

> ...had three discrete characteristics: its expression was through the vernacular languages, not through Sanskrit; it rejected the role of the Brahman as ritual intermediary between man and God, in some ways and times going further and rejecting caste entirely; and it propagated enthusiastic religion, with

singing and dancing as a part of the search for immediate and ecstatic communion with the divine.[75]

This way of reading Krishna *bhakti* over several centuries implies that the delight in a fantasy of social abandon is a *sine qua non* of the religion, and informs all subsequent manifestations of the worship of Krishna-Gopal.[76]

Stage actors nowadays know that there are two things to avoid scrupulously on stage. The first is an animal. Before a live audience, the unpredictability of an animal on stage is nothing less than a disaster that either has or hasn't yet befallen the play. The other is a child. Before a live audience, the unpredictability of a child on stage is nothing less than a disaster that either has or hasn't yet befallen the play. But the potential calamity inherent in child actors—made all the more likely by putting young children in leading roles—must have had great appeal for the *bhakti* religious movement of the sixteenth century as it sought expression for its spiritual rejection of the formality and customary prestige of civilization. Pursuing an argument similar to Hein's—that *râs lila* performances at one time relied on highly trained and disciplined female dancers—Agrawal speculates that the character of the *râs lila* necessarily shifted during the sixteenth century to better suit the character of *bhakti*.

> [It] is evident that to the time of *bhakti* [meaning the sixteenth century revival] the form of the *râs* which prevailed was very elaborate [*srṇgârik*: ornate in a way which emphasizes femininity], and the devotees, who had rushed to Braj and Vrindavan to be immersed in the ocean of feeling [*ras*, not *râs*] of devotion to a personal Krishna (*sagun krsna-bhakti*), could not satisfy their spiritual feelings through it.... For this particular reason, another restructuring of the *râs lila* was organized in Braj.[77]

Whatever the form of the *râs lila* preceding its mass popularity in Braj, Agrawal's opinion clearly associates the form—which, by featuring children actors, became popular in Braj—with the freewheeling nature of resurgent *bhakti*.

Agrawal parts from Hein here by contending that the "re-organization" of the *râs lila* occurred through the transmutation of the *rahas* dance dramas in the Lucknow court of Walid Ali Shah, for which boys were dressed as women.[78] Hein asserts, instead, that the *râs lila*'s practice of dressing boys as women came to Braj from related practices of dramatizing the twelfth-century devotional poem *Gitagovinda* by *shakta* cults in eastern India and Nepal.[79] Certainly, in Bengal and Orissa in the fifteenth and sixteenth centuries, the *Gitagovinda* enjoyed some kind of performance, in which adherents of the "new *bhakti*," such as Caitanya, found a space for delightful disorder.[80] This combination of dramatic performance with impulsive expression of devotion may, indeed, have found its way from the Bengali *shakta* cults into the Bengali practices of Krishna *bhakti*, and from there to Braj, as Hein suggests.[81]

Among the *shakta* cults, which were semi-tantric cults associating divine creativity with female power (*shakti*), the *Sahajiya* sect is especially relevant. This version of shaktism, antedating Caitanya's movement, substituted Krishna and Radha for the typical male/female unity-in-duality of Shiva and Shakti, and emphasized the expression of devotion through spontaneity (*sahaja*). These cults seem to have influenced the type of *bhakti* made orthodox in Bengal by Caitanya, and advanced in Braj by his disciples. Edward Dimock argues that there was a relationship of mutual influence in Bengal between the Sahajiya and Caitanyaite doctrines.[82] The roots of the transformative effort Haberman identifies in *râgânugâ bhakti sâdhana*, as it was formulated in Vrindavan in the sixteenth century by Rupa Goswami, may have developed from the love of spontaneity evident among the Bengali Sahajiyas.[83] "The Sahajiya doctrines," according to Entwistle, "were presumably known to Rup Goswami and other theologians of the Gaudiya Sampraday, and probably influenced their conception of the love of Krishna and Radha as something abstracted from the physical that could lead the devotee to experience a purely emotional and psychological transmutation."[84] The transmutation suggested here by Entwistle corresponds directly with the adoption of the nature of one of the characters of the divine *lila*, both through *sâdhana*, as Haberman argues, and through less structured means of imagining. "Constant thought, remembrance, reflection, and action," writes Dimock, "lead to becoming. This is also the essence of the Sahajiyâ idea of transformation, though it is termed by them *âropa*."[85] To the degree that Rupa's writings regarding *sâdhana* reflect a common yearning in Sahajiya and Vaishnava thought, the child actors of the Karahlan *râs lila* stage must have had enormous appeal to the transient Bengali devotees massing in Braj to encounter the freewheeling, which is to say, *spontaneous*, child Krishna as a focus of potentially transformative meditation.

TENTATIVE CONCLUSIONS

Certainly, this characterizes the appeal of the *râs lila* today, in which the young (sometimes very young) actors do little on stage but act as themselves. Contemporary audiences manifest a palpable delight in the *playing* of the children in the *play*, which contemporary troupe directors appreciate and encourage by giving their actors wide freedom to do as they wish during a performance. There is a common sense that Krishna is more manifest in such playing than otherwise—since Krishna would most certainly act with the same spontaneity under the same circumstances. John S. Hawley judges from his experience with *râs lila* performances, "the best Krishna is the one who acts most like himself, a child unbridled."[86] The same sentiment is confirmed by a variety of Indian sources. A director performing today in Vrindavan parried with some impatience my own focus on the lack of discipline evident among his cast members: "Whatever the child does, that is Krishna!"[87] Vasant Yamadagni told me that any mistake the child actor makes on stage is *prâbhu icchâ*—God's own inclination—further elaborating that "Krishna wanted to do things that way, so there it is."[88] The reasoning is delightfully circular: the child is Krishna, the evidence of which is that he acts just like Krishna.

A further significant influence of Sahajiya doctrine on Caitanyaism was the conception of man as inherently male and female. The physical form of a man masks a spiritual identity that partakes of the essence of both Krishna and Radha. "Man is a sort of hermaphroditic creature, and the two sides of his nature, in terms borrowed from ancient views of the dualism of matter and spirit, are called *prakrti* (female) and *purusa* (male): in the self is *prakrti* and in the self is *purusa*."[89] Consequently, given his capacity to balance these two aspects of himself, a man is perfectly capable of existing as a woman, and of perceiving spiritual reality (that is, Krishna) as a woman. This notion of the individual has obvious implications with respect to Rupa's formulation of *sâdhana*, and with respect to the way in which early Caitanyaites—those entering Braj prior to Rupa's theologizing—may have apprehended and reacted to Braj culture. For a Caitanyaite Vaishnava traveling in Braj in the earliest days of the movement, a dramatic tradition that included the portrayal of Krishna's pastimes would potentially have satisfied the deepest of spiritual longings.

However, such a dramatic tradition may have run afoul of a general—if paradoxical—prejudice against women in early Caitanyaism. Caitanya's own feelings regarding women are quite clear. The *Caitanya Caritâmrta* records Caitanya as saying, "I can never again look upon the face of an ascetic who has had anything to do with a woman. The senses are weak, and are attracted toward worldly things.... One who consorts with women is immoral, and opposed to Krsna-bhakti."[90] According to Dimock, Caitanya pressed the same views upon his followers, perhaps even refusing to look again at one of his disciples who had accepted alms from a woman.[91]

With such an attitude so strongly in place at the top of a movement that had a significant presence in Braj after 1500, we need not chalk up the disappearance of women from the Braj stage to Islamic persecution. Nor is it necessary to look as far as Nepal for a prototype of the Braj practice of all-male casting, as Hein does. A much simpler line of reasoning recognizes the affinity for effusive worship and spiritual role-playing that the Caitanya cult brought to Braj and the misogyny of the young movement that would have necessitated alterations in the appealing, but incompatible, stage practices already existing in Braj. Agrawal implies as much with his already noted reasoning that the sixteenth-century devotees rushing into Braj found the extant form of *râs lila* too *elaborate* [*srngârik*] to satisfy their spiritual feelings, which may be as much as to say that the Krishna theatre these devotees found in Braj was too *feminine* to satisfy their spiritual feelings.[92]

I would argue that, in the first place, prior to the sixteenth century, child actors—both boys and girls—occupied appropriate roles in Krishna performances. They were inheritors of a long-standing tradition of Krishna theatre—perhaps as old as *bhakti* itself, as Hein argues—in which actors, especially the girls, could be highly skilled dancers, their relative youth notwithstanding. At the beginning of the sixteenth century, the Braj village of Karahla seems to have been the main repository of this tradition, which had waned in prominence in conjunction with the ebbing of *bhakti* in general. The resurgence of *bhakti* in the early sixteenth century, and the consequent influx of pilgrims seeking spiritual fulfillment in Braj, gave this dramatic tradition new life, as it provided an incarnation of the transcendent play of God the pilgrims sought. However, the presence of girls on the stage could not withstand the sensibilities of a significant percentage of pilgrims for whom femininity was anathema, or at least suspect. Subsequently, in response to the prejudices of Caitanyaism, girls gave way to all-male casting—a transformation that Caitanyaism not only required, but facilitated, since its intercourse with Bengali Sahajiyism had already theologically adjusted it to recognize female-ness in male presence, and its particular appreciation for spiritual anarchy had adjusted it to relish theatrical immaturity. Tuned in this way to the sensibilities of its patrons, the *râs lila* appealed to the minds of prominent saints working to codify *bhakti* theology as well as programs of devotional activity in Braj, such as the routes and exercises of intra-Braj pilgrimages. Thus, by the middle of the sixteenth century, the *râs lila* had become a fixture of the *Braj-yatra*, and began to become an integral component of worship and meditation. Then, by the beginning of the seventeenth century, myths had already begun to develop concerning the *râs lila*'s divine origins, accounting for all-male casts as a divine institution as revealed through the founding figures of particular *bhakti* sects. These revelations also accounted for the *râs lila*'s surviving cartographic connection with Karahla by constructing a sectarian figure by the name of Ghamanddev, who individually bore responsibility for the appeal of Karahlan theatre, and through whom individual sects might yet claim theatrical authority they did not have by geography.

Children have been the defining characteristic of Krishna theatre in the age of *bhakti*, just as Krishna's essential nature is childish. The changes in *râs lila* casting that may have occurred in the sixteenth century, while greatly altering the superficial appearance of the *râs lila*, did not change the fundamental affinity in *bhakti* for child performers. Indeed, the haphazardness introduced to the form with its sudden shift to untrained boys perhaps suited it better to the sixteenth century's reinvention of *bhakti*, as the new form of the *râs lila* made it more closely resemble the freewheeling, even chaotic, celebrations of devotional feeling that characterized newly popular modes of worship.

5. Acting in the *Râs Lila* and Real Realism[1]

PLAUSIBILITY EAST AND WEST

This was one of those performances that troubles a person for days, tainting every mundane experience and thought with a flavor of misery. Even removed from it by years, a slightly sickening aura lingers. *Trojan Women* never was a play to inspire glee, but the suffering in this performance was particularly bald, or, rather, the suffering of the actress playing Andromache was particularly bald. This actress's raging grief, employed in the portrayal of Andromache's lament over her son's death, made my skin shrink, even at a time before I had children of my own, which may have better equipped me to identify with the tragedy of it all. It was a horrifically physical performance, exhibiting a violence of body and mind that stabs itself at the hearts of feeling people, and demands pity.

On another stage, for another audience, a twelve-year-old actor playing Krishna in a *râs lila* stood on a rickety platform behind a painted curtain drawn up waste-high to show he was on a boat in the middle of the Yamuna River. Other boys playing Krishna's girlfriends stood downstage at a short distance, nearly in the laps of the audience seated on the floor that served as the playing space. The young players shifted back and forth, nudging each other and snickering as in turn they shouted insults at Krishna in a stylized falsetto vaguely reminiscent of the voice of the muppet Prairie Dawn; and when an elderly woman collided with an upstage pillar while trying to cross the playing space behind the set, the boys on stage laughed hysterically, some of them doubling over, as Krishna returned their insults from his curtain boat.

The actress's performance in *Trojan Women* struck me as a terrifically *real* performance, partly because of the emotional investment it derived or compelled from me, which felt in every way *real* at the time. Furthermore, to the extent that *real* means *plausible* in the physical world we live in, my evaluation of her performance as *real* was borne out in the *real* world when I later saw television news footage of a woman, behaving in every way similarly, who had to be forcibly removed from the trial of a relative's murderer. On the other hand, *râs lila* performances, of which this episode with the boat was typical, have never seemed to me very *realistic*, even though patrons of the plays who are also Krishna devotees regard them as quintessentially *real*. In my eyes, which are accustomed to seeing only one, physical reality, the way in which the *râs lila* lives comfortably and simultaneously both in the world of its own sacred mythology and in the world of its audiences' mundane experience makes it fall short of the plausibility necessary to oblige my identification of it as *real*.

A few days after seeing the production of *Trojan Women*, I learned from friends involved in the performance that the actress playing Andromache had herself lost a son—her only one at the time—when he was very young. After discharging her onstage role each night, she spent long periods of time backstage in a state of incapacitating grief. Apparently, the action of the stage mythology so intensely evoked the memory of her own experience, and her memory evoked the mythology of the stage action, that the line between her role's onstage grief and her own offstage grief—her *real* grief—blurred considerably during the play. I do not know what technique, if any, she may have used so as to join her own emotional experience with her character's. Perhaps her own experience was so acute and fresh, and so similar to her character's, that she needed no means of attaching it to her stage action. But, even if the specific process in this case is unclear, this association of offstage experience with the requirements of a stage role provides a convenient model of the product of a means, common in Western acting traditions of the twentieth century, of making a stage role *real*, which is to say, plausible for an audience with respect to the role's expression of emotion. The acting "System" of Stanislavsky is the flagship technique by which actors (particularly, though not exclusively, Western actors) employ emotional memory as a means of developing the stage representation of characters in such a way as to make their characters credible when measured against the emotional experience of their audiences. To whatever degree such techniques accomplish their aims, this kind of acting has come to dominate performance in the West, especially because of the success of subscribing actors in film and television.

Râs lila actors seem to be far removed from any such technique. Indeed, to the degree that *râs lila* actors employ any acting technique at all, it seems to be characterized by the rote imitation of troupe directors, who demonstrate for their actors piece-by-piece the physical and vocal style accepted as appropriate for the representation of Krishna, Radha, and the *gopis*. The *râs lila*'s acting style, consequently, can seem very wooden, and not only to the Western eye. In his book *Folk Theater of India*, Balwant Gargi refers to *râs lila* performance as *poor*, and not in the Grotowskian sense with which the term is used to describe an intentionally unfinished theatrical aesthetic. "Theatrically, Raslila is poor," he writes. "It offers the actor very little scope.... There is no opportunity for training in a system of acting. Even the *Kathak* style dance and the classical melodies, essential elements in the performance, are flatly executed."[2] A similar sentiment informs the evaluation of *râs lila* by Daya Prakash Sinha. "It might be wrong to classify *RaasLila* as drama because one cannot expect boys of 12 to 14 years of age to emote and do effective *abhinaya* (acting)."[3] As is evident in the performance scenario briefly described above, the emotional investment in a character on the part of *râs lila* actors is extremely limited. Nor do the actors make any apparent attempt to draw on their own emotional experience in order to invest their characters with an increased emotional plausibility. As one might expect, the identification of the audience with the stage illusion (that is, with the action of the drama as distinct from the action of life) is also limited. The audience members at Sudama Kutir that afternoon laughed as readily as the actors at the poor woman trapped by the set, and just as readily redirected their amusement back to the stage action in which Krishna humorously taunts his friends, as though it were all part of the same funny play. Every immediate element of a *râs lila* performance suggests that an aesthetic rules here, which is far different from that which underpins the success of System acting in the West.

However, the degree to which the *râs lila* audience identifies the stage action as *real* is similar to the desired effect of System acting. Depending on the type of story being dramatized in a given performance, audience members will shed real tears, or bristle and shout with real anger, fully revealing that, in spite of the ostensibly unrealistic manner of *râs lila* presentation, they regard the stage action as just as real (which is to say, plausible) as any play staged under System auspices. Even more so. Any given audience member chosen at random at a *râs lila* performance is bound to affirm that the characters on stage are not representations but incarnated beings, and will bear this out at the conclusion of the performance—just as they did shortly after the old woman above was helped out of her predicament—by worshiping at the feet of the actors on the stage.

Which is not to say that the effect the *râs lila* has on its audiences indicates the *râs lila* has come to understand something that System acting, and other techniques, have failed to grasp. Quite the opposite. The superficial differences between *râs lila*'s manner of staging and Western theories of acting mask some curious affinities. Consequently, Western systems of training may be useful models for an explanation of the theological and aesthetic elements that combine in the *râs lila*'s expression of *reality*. At this point, however, we should acknowledge that such comparisons are fraught with complications, the ignorance of which does injustice to Western theories and South Asian practices alike. I would contend that, in spite of potential pitfalls (a few of which I will address, directly), we might say something about the connection between life in Vrindavan and Stanislavsky's System, as well as with other Western theories of acting. In doing so, however, we must be careful to avoid mischaracterizing both the acting theories here introduced and the unfamiliar aspects of Vrindavan living that we hope better to understand by way of comparison with the familiar. As the present discussion concerns a theory of acting in the context of *râs lila* performances, a comparison with Western theories of acting should not be considered inappropriate per se.

My goal here is twofold. First, I hope to communicate my experience of Vrindavan as a site for performance to a reader who may be more familiar with Western acting theory than with South Asian aesthetics. Consequently, I propose to reference Western theory as a potential analogy for what may occur beneath the obvious in Vrindavan with respect to theatre. Second, I think Vrindavan may be able to tell us something about relationships between audiences and performances, especially about the way in which audience members are trained in acting (indirectly, perhaps), as much as *râs lila* actors themselves. To some extent, the temptation to make these kinds of connections between so apparently distinct theatrical traditions is irresistible. A Vrindavan religious scholar, responding to my explanation of Strasberg's acting Method, proclaimed that *râs lila* actors are Method actors. This may or may not be, and I do not intend to push this issue. However, those of us who approach the conundrum of *râs lila* acting from an inescapably Western point of view might better understand *râs lila* acting by acknowledging certain tantalizing likenesses, even if only for the sake of argument. Ultimately, I hope to show that elements of Vrindavan life do correspond to elements of Western acting methods (small "m"), principally Stanislavsky's System (big "S"), so as to render less opaque the way in which the *râs lila* achieves its profound emotional and spiritual effect.

In short, *râs lila* actors are sort-of-System-atic Actors. They are invariably born and raised in or very near Vrindavan, and Vrindavan itself is a great and infinitely complicated acting exercise, which churns up a communal memory and associates that memory with every seemingly insignificant activity of living, such that the feelings associated with that memory become part of the actors'—and other Vrindavan residents'—every day lives. In fact, the sort-of-System-atic actor training Vrindavan gives to *râs lila* audience members, as opposed to the actors, may be more significant to the *reality* of a given performance than any onstage technique employed (or not) by the actors themselves. And this may tell us something about dramatic performance in general. Having compared and contrasted the ways in which the techniques of Stanislavsky's System and *râs lila* acting conventions work to similar effects with respect to particular audiences, we are likely to find that the effectiveness of an acting technique may depend more on audience than on actors, and on the degree to which the audience members invest themselves in a particular technique.

STANISLAVSKY

Constantin Stanislavsky began to develop his acting "System" in the early days of the twentieth century while associated with the Moscow Art Theatre in Russia. The type of acting he encouraged challenged prevailing Western acting styles, which emphasized oratorical vocal technique in conjunction with fixed physical gestures as a means of representing character and action.[4] Stanislavsky sought after a kind of acting that would more convincingly resemble "real" life by replacing such formulaic practices with the expression of "real" emotion and psychologically motivated stage action. The philosophical underpinning of Stanislavsky's theory was nineteenth-century Humanism, a basic tenet of which is that human beings are all, at a fundamental level, similar; that is, our common human feelings and physical senses are qualitatively the same. As a consequence, as humans we experience the same world in the same way, and one person's emotional and physical tenor in the presence of any given combination of stimuli will be essentially similar to the tone of another person's experience of the same. Thus, because emotional and psychological qualities are common to humanity, we identify and sympathize with each other, and an actor can presume to be able to represent a character in a "realistic" manner.[5] The actor can trust that his own familiarity with sorrow, joy, anger, and the like, is qualitatively the same as his character's; therefore, he can rely on his own experience as a foundation for understanding and expressing the nature of the character before him. "The broader your memory of emotions," Stanislavsky can therefore say, "the richer your material for inner creativity."⁶ The capacity of an actor to "remember" the emotional, psychological, and physical quality of his experiences becomes very important then, as his breadth of experience and his ability to tap into it constitute the variety of the experiential repertoire with which he can identify with various characters and dramatic situations—the component of the System known as *emotion memory*.⁷ But Stanislavsky became suspicious of an undue emphasis on emotion memory, which proved itself somewhat inconsistent as a method, and a little disturbing to him personally. Accordingly, Stanislavsky worked to find coherent procedures, both physical and intellectual, which might generate in actors a psychological affinity with their characters and also reproduce convincing states of emotion. The integrated use of a number of physical exercises and intellectual applications that Stanislavsky developed to accomplish his kind of stage realism has come to be known as the System.

Two of these intellectual exercises bear mentioning. First, Stanislavsky directed his actors to invest their imaginations in filling in the gaps a playwright leaves in a character's life. Too often, for Stanislavsky, a playwright would deliver a character with the least of possible descriptions, leaving the actor without sufficient familiarity with the details of the character's life to generate an affinity with it. To supplement this deficit, Stanislavsky had his actors develop a "running score" for a character, a sort of mental movie providing the absent details of a character's life and a vivid expression—for the actor—of the character's circumstances. The second significant intellectual component of the System was the identification of a character's "motives" (or "objectives") and the comprehension of these objectives within their own discrete periods of dramatic action, identified as "units." As they functioned in the System, motives and units provided for an actor the psychological justification for stage actions, which, Stanislavsky reasoned, would make stage actions more plausibly resemble the action of real life (which was itself, so goes the theory, psychologically justified).

THE SYSTEM AND *RÂGÂNUGÂ BHAKTI SÂDHANA*

David L. Haberman has already proposed a connection between Vaishnava life in Braj and Stanislavsky's actor training in his 1988 book *Acting as a Way of Salvation*. Haberman was not concerned here with the *râs lila* theatre of Vrindavan, but with particularly formal meditative disciplines of Krishna devotees (*sâdhana*), especially those associated with the Bengali or *Gaudiya* schools of devotion. Explaining *râgânugâ bhakti sâdhana* as a devotional practice whereby a devotee seeks to transform his inner self into a self coinciding with a character of Vrindavan's mythic history—Krishna's mother or father, a cowherd acquaintance, or, especially, one of Krishna's bucolic girlfriends—Haberman made a serious attempt to identify *râgânugâ bhakti sâdhana* with the philosophical and practical substance of Stanislavsky's acting System. The attempt makes some sense, on account of what appear to be similarities of motivation and product between the two practices. Both are concerned with role-playing, and propose to offer a means of more effectively inhabiting a role. Likewise, both practices profess they offer to practitioners a special relationship with *reality* (though this relationship is variably understood, by Haberman and others: a means of transforming an inner reality, a means of accessing an external but imperceptible reality, a means of making a convincing reality of fiction, and so forth). Haberman made much of these apparent similarities, likening the psychological theories that informed Stanislavsky's physical exercises to the theological reasoning of *bhakti* saints interested in role-playing as religious activity and proposing ways in which the apparent effects of Stanislavkian practice illuminate the effects of meditation in the context of *bhakti*.

Haberman's justification for this comparison seems to rest on the convenience with which Stanislavskian concepts and terminology suit themselves to a discussion of well-focused role-playing activities. Stanislavsky proposed a discipline by which actors might cast a role at an audience with a greater degree of emotional plausibility. His discipline developed from humanistic philosophy and behavioral psychology, adopting such terms as "emotion memory," "motivation," "subtext," and "inner pictures" to elucidate ideas intended to bring actors and characters into closer psychological proximity. The System aspired to culminate in the personal identification of an actor with his or her role such that on stage a character was more apparent, or, at least, more plausible, than the actor. For these reasons, the System makes itself a convenient model for role-playing of all sorts. "Accordingly," Haberman proposes, "Stanislavsky's insights lend themselves to an understanding of how dramatics might be used in an intentional process of identity transformation."[8] In this way, Haberman makes Stanislavsky a touchstone for the analysis of practices that have to do with role-playing in the context of *bhakti*.

Haberman's connection between Stanislavksy and *bhakti* meditation is strained, however, not because there is nothing to learn by comparing the two ways of thinking, but by fundamental misunderstandings of Stanislavsky, which mischaracterize his System, and, hence, put into question the conclusions Haberman reaches with regard to the way in which Stanislavskian acting illuminates our understanding of *bhakti* meditation. In the first place, Haberman consistently depicts the objective of Stanislavsky's System as the literal, if internal, transformation of an actor into a dramatic character.

> The goal of such imitative action [Stanislavkian exercises] is to "live the role," that is, to completely enter into the world of the character one is imitating.... Stanislavsky believed that the actor, through perfected acting technique, could totally identify with the character being portrayed, and for the time of the performance, could "become" that character and experience his or her world.[9]

This interpretation of Stanislavsky's program makes it seem very much like the *bhakti* meditation about which Haberman writes, the purported goal of which is the spiritual transformation of a devotee into an inhabitant of the spiritual version of Vrindavan.[10] But Stanislavsky made a special effort to resist this interpretation of his program. The inner transformation of an actor does not mean, Stanislavsky maintains, "that the actor must surrender himself on the stage to some such hallucination as that when playing he should lose the sense of reality around him, to take scenery for real trees, etc."[11] In fact, Stanislavsky insisted to his actors, "always [to] act in your own person."[12] Haberman seems to acknowledge this difference when he admits, "...the ordinary actor does not completely forget he or she is an actor....A dual consciousness is required of the actor. Actors never lose sight of their ordinary identities (social selves?)"[13] But the degree to which Haberman believes this characterization of the System is unclear, since he, nevertheless, persists in his characterization of the objective of Stanislavskian acting as a loss of self identity. "The result of true acting for Stanislavsky," writes Haberman, "is to live the role, to experience the world of the character being enacted.... For Stanislavsky, the successful actor was the one who could momentarily leave the socially constructed reality and enter into that of the character in the play."[14] We do not find in Stanislavsky the intent to convert an actor's identity, either permanently or temporarily; rather, Stanislavsky asserted that an actor's own feelings, own emotions, own personal experience could provide plausible material for the construction of a dramatic character. As noted above, the eighteenth- and nineteenth-century Humanism that informed Stanislavsky's thinking regarded people as essentially similar, so that the feelings of one would be qualitatively the same as the feelings of another. Based upon this evaluation of people, Stanislavsky encouraged actors to rely on their own feelings in the building of a character, since their own feelings in the circumstances of a character would inevitably be similar to the character's feelings, and it would be convincingly plausible. *Living the part*, according to Stanislavsky himself, meant "actually experiencing feelings that are *analogous* to it..."[15] The goal of Stanislavsky's System is the development of a convincing stage plausibility, as opposed to the goal of *bhakti* meditation as represented by Haberman: a spiritually meaningful transformation of personal identity.

There is also a discrepancy between Stanislavskian process and the process of *bhakti* meditation. Stanislavskian method, according to Haberman, concentrates on the adoption of the physical characteristics of a character such that their imitation and repetition transforms the psychological nature of an actor. "The whole of Stanislavsky's research demonstrates," according to Haberman, "that the actor can actually experience the inner world of a character (present only through a literary script) by imitating that character's physical actions (as expressed in the literary script)."[16] This, again, accords nicely with Haberman's understanding of *bhakti* meditation. Summarizing the writings of the medieval saint Rupa Goswami on this topic, Haberman writes, "If the *bhakta* [devotee] could somehow take on or imitate the *anubhâva*s [actions] of the exemplary Vrajaloka [associates of Krishna], he could obtain the salvific emotions of that character and come to inhabit the world in which that character resides—Vraja [Braj]. This imitation of the ways of the Vrajaloka is the Râgânugâ Bhakti Sâdhana."[17] The fundamental principal of this form of meditation, according to Haberman, is plain, physical imitation, the practice of which causes the desired inner transformation; and he is convinced that Stanislavskian acting works in the same way. Thus Haberman writes, "...we return to the insight shared in kind by Stanislavsky; the inner emotional world of the Vrajaloka is reached by taking on their physical expressions (*anubhâvas*)."[18] Both *Bhakti* meditation and Stanislavskian acting for Haberman can be summed up thus: acting like a character makes you feel like the character.

The process of Stanislavsky's System is quite different, however. Stanislavsky, in the first place, opposed the styles of acting that dominated the Russian stage at the end of the nineteenth century, which, in one way or another, fundamentally relied on physical imitation. "Mechanical" styles that utilized a catalogue of conventional gestures, and "naturalistic" acting that concentrated on a detailed reproduction of physical appearances failed for Stanislavsky because they depended on "theatrical effect in place of expressiveness."[19] Instead, Stanislavsky promoted a new approach to acting that was to replace plain imitation as the basis of representation with a concentration in the beginning on the interior state of the actor. Rather than starting with the physical emulation of a character (of the sort that Haberman suggests would bring about an internal transformation), Stanislavsky encouraged actors to begin with an internal adjustment, which would in turn unaffectedly produce the physical manifestations required by a part. Colin Counsell assesses Stanislavsky's approach in this way:

> Once the right internal states have been established, Stanislavsky maintains, these will shape the physical performance automatically; just as in everyday life our thoughts and feelings automatically appear as words and actions, so the "physical materialisation of a character to be created emerges of its own accord once the right inner values have been established…"[20]

What we see in Stanislavsky's System, then, is precisely the opposite of Haberman's interpretation of it. Acting like the character does not make you feel like the character; rather, feeling like the character makes you act like the character.

Two components of the System seem to have inspired Haberman's misinterpretation. The first may have been Stanislavsky's "Psycho Technique," the method by which an actor might generate feeling. Drawing on the work of behavioral scientists such as Pavlov, Stanislavsky reasoned that emotional states might be artificially induced by proper physical conditioning. A Stanislavskian actor relies on his or her own emotional reservoir for producing a plausible representation of a character, but not every actor has a natural capacity for calling up a dormant emotional state. Stanislavsky's solution to this problem was not to have the actor simply act as if he were the character, with the expectation the character's emotional state would follow, but, in training to attach his or her own useful emotional states to particular, detached stimuli, in the pattern of Pavlovian conditioning. A needed emotional state would then follow a given stimulus in performance. But this is not the same as saying that acting as a character produces the character's feeling.[21] The stimuli that Stanislavsky sought for this effect were not to be drawn from characterization, or even to be logically associated with the intended emotional states themselves, so as to have a more spontaneous, which is to say, natural, effect. Colin Counsell's description of the connection between Pavlovian Behaviorism and System acting emphasizes this:

> Just as Behaviourism asserts that stimuli can evoke physical responses directly via the nervous system, without willful choice, so the Psycho-Technique is presumed to enable emotions to find physical expression not consciously but

precisely by *bypassing* consciousness. Moreover, emotions are to be evoked using a false stimulus...actors must provide their own trick stimuli, consciously fabricate lures for their unconscious selves in order to induce emotional responses....[22]

Hence, the so-called Psycho Technique does not provide the actor with a means of inner transformation, but with a conduit through which significant aspects of the actor's self can find their way to the manifest world.

The second component of the System that confuses Stanislavskian actor training and *bhakti* meditation's method of self-transformation is the "Method of Physical Action." Haberman points to this element of the System, with which Stanislavsky began experimenting only two years before he died, as that which has physical imitation of character as its starting point. "The anger of a particular character, for example, is realized by imitating the physical expressions of that particular character's anger—e.g., pounding fists on the table. This [Stanislavsky] called the 'Method of Physical Actions.'"[23] I would argue, however, that the Method of Physical Actions is not concerned with manifesting the feelings or personal identity of a character in an actor, but with providing for an actor an environment in which *motives* are more clear. Stanislavsky provides an example of the method in *Creating a Role*, in which the director tells an actor to begin a scene without having read it. The student objects that he does not know what to do. To this protest the director responds, "Don't you know how to go into a room...?"[24] According to David Allen, jumping into the physical environment of a character in this way "puts you in the middle of the *given circumstances*. It makes you ask yourself: what would you do if you were in this situation?... Entering a room, moreover, immediately evokes the question: what is your objective?"[25] Contrary to Haberman's interpretation, the Method of Physical Actions is less concerned with generating emotion (a feature of a character's identity), and more concerned with finding motivation (a feature of an actor's intellectual stimulus). The central principal of Stanislavskian acting—that the process of "becoming" a character does not work from the outside in—still informs this component of the System. To justify the Method of Physical Action with respect to the System as it has developed to this point, Stanislavsky writes:

> Whatever part an actor plays he must always act in his own right, on his own responsibility. If he does not find himself in his part he will kill off the imaginary character because he will have deprived him of live feelings. Those live feelings can be given to the character he has created only by the actor himself. So play every part in your own right in the circumstances given you by the

playwright. In this manner you will first of all feel yourself in the part. When that is once done it is not difficult to enlarge the whole role in yourself.[26]

Even in this last phase of the development of the System, a phase that places more initial emphasis on physical exercises, Stanislavsky does not seek to transform an actor's identity, but to provide a coherent intellectual means whereby an actor might effectively employ himself.

What appears here is not the simple line between physical imitation of character and personal identification with character, which Haberman identifies as the agreement between *bhakti* meditation and Stanislavsky, but a meandering path from an actor's developed stimuli to the generation of an actor's own emotional state to the physical manifestation of emotion that, it is presumed, is plausibly in accord with a character. The two systems seem to coincide where the practitioner encounters the physical characteristics of a role. But where Haberman's meditator makes this encounter the means of producing a sympathetic feeling, the Stanislavskian actor expects to reach the encounter by way of his own feelings as inspired by a combination of intellectual and physical exercises designed to arouse it.

There is a further potential here to confuse Stanislavsky's adaptation of Pavlovian conditioning with the process of *bhakti* meditation. Both systems make some use of an actor's or a devotee's capacity to imagine the circumstances of a character. Haberman seizes upon their apparent similarities with respect to calling for practitioners to mentally realize the details of imaginary worlds:

> It is important to add, as Stanislavsky also points out, that circumstances shape an emotion; thus the actors must know the circumstances of the emotional roles they are enacting. Likewise, Rûpa would have the *bhakta*s not only follow the *anubhâva*s of a particular character of Vraja, but also surround themselves with the given circumstances (*vibhâva*s) of the emotional role of that Vrajaloka. In this manner, the entire set of dramatic components of a particular Vrajaloka [spiritual character]...are to be known and incorporated into the imitative activity.[27]

There appears in this interpretation of Stanislavsky a direct correlation between System acting and *bhakti* meditation, which is convenient for Haberman's argument. The devotee, we learn from Haberman, like the System actor can more effectively assume a transformative physical semblance of a spiritual character by conceiving in meditation all the appropriate contextual details of the spiritual character's environment, which work together to reinforce the role-playing effort. But this interpretation depends upon the fundamental mischaracterization of System acting as primarily concerned with the physical imitation of a character. Stanislavsky certainly endorsed the imagination of sensory circumstances in the service of acting, but his objective in this respect was consistent with his opposition to acting that began with physical representation. Rather than enjoining actors to imagine the physical circumstances of their characters as a means of more effectively emulating their characters, Stanislavsky directed actors first to the recollection of specific emotional experiences of *their own*, with a special focus on remembering in detail the physical circumstances associated with them. There were two intents to this practice. First, to identify the milieu of an actor's own feelings that would be analogous to a character's (Humanism, again), and, second, to develop Pavlovian triggers by which actors might access their own emotion memory as necessary on stage. Where Pavlov famously provided a stimulus for the salivation of his dogs, Stanislavsky insisted an actor must condition herself by developing her own stimulus. The "inner pictures" or "running score" subsequently produced by such imaginative staging could be "called to mind to add depth and substance to a role,"[28] and could act to elicit an actor's own feelings by conditioned response. Colin Counsell summarizes the theoretical mechanism of the process:

> By imagining a series of 'inner circumstances' that correspond to the role, Stanislavsky asserts, the actor provides baits to 'lure' out their subconscious. The imaginary details are to act as 'challenges to action,' stimuli which provoke genuine responses. At the same time the actor's concentration on these imaginary 'facts' is to focus attention away from emotion itself, so that it is not drawn into conscious consideration and remains automatic, 'subconscious.' In effect, the actor must recreate something resembling the conditions of everyday life, wherein thoughts and emotions are born non-consciously in response to situations, so that the Psycho-Technique seeks what amounts to a reproduction of behavior onstage.[29]

Although this practice seems much like a method of meditation by which the vivid imagined details of an unmanifest world lay a new identity on the practitioner, Counsell here indicates that the end result is a "reproduction of behavior"; which is to say, a scenario in which an actor's physical expression arises naturally from the actor's inner state, in accordance with the way, Stanislavsky assumed, people acted in life.

For Stanislavsky, the "running score" utilizes an actor's intellectual imagination to provide necessary motivation for the actor's every action. The actor increases the plausibility of the stage environment by giving her body, in idle and active moments, a context in accord with the dramatic scene. The direction of the actor's physical expression continues to be from the inside out, and the source of the expression remains the actor's own identity. The "running score" may, indeed, provide some degree of the inspiration for an actor's emotional state. The actor's imagination of the variety of elements of a staged environment (time, temperature, altitude, airspeed, surface material, aroma, what have you) in a humanistic way can help an actor in tapping the memory of his or her personal experience of such things. Whereas, for Haberman, the sensory details of the spiritual world into which a devotee might enter should determinatively affect the devotee's apprehension of personal identity. "The world of mental images or imagination is taken much more seriously in India than it is typically in the West. If one could somehow hold in mind (*smarana*) a mental image harmonious with Ultimate Reality, one would live in or participate in (*bhakti*) that reality. One becomes what one 'holds in mind.'"[30] We will subsequently take up an examination of the compelling correlation between Stanislavsky's "running score" and the South Asian concept of *smarana*, which Haberman introduces here. The confusion to avoid at this point in comparing Stanislavskian acting with *bhakti* meditation, however, is the identification of Stanislavsky's "running score" with imagination of the sensory details of the spiritual world conjured up by the *bhakti* devotee in which an adopted spiritual character is lived.

Identifying the discrepancies in Haberman's correlation of Stanislavsky's System and *bhakti* meditation is not to say there is no correlation at all, only that the comparison is not as straightforward as it may seem, and, in any case, is difficult to justify. The rationale behind pointing out apparent similarities between the two practices—deriving from a common interest in earnest role-playing—seems to assume that the similarities themselves are sufficient reason for the comparison, taking for granted Stanislavsky's authority in the realm of acting theory, and neglecting to acknowledge the ways in which the flaws inherent in Stanislavsky's theories moderate its usefulness as an accessible model for South Asian meditative disciplines. Haberman banks on the literally transformative nature of Stanislavskian acting to compliment his assessment of *bhakti* meditation in positing that such role-playing can, indeed, transform. In his introduction, Haberman writes, "The ability of dramatic role-taking to transform identity, and thus to carry an actor into the world of that role, has been thoroughly explored by Russian director and philosopher Constantin Stanislavsky. Stanislasvky drew critical attention to the powerful affectivity of dramatic acting, to the ability of dramatic acting to change the life of an actor."[31] As we have seen, however, Stanislavsky's System does not intend to so transform an actor; consequently, there seems no justification for introducing Stanislavsky to the issue at all.

In tying *râgânugâ bhakti sâdhana* to the System, Haberman attempts to span a gap between performance practice and meditative practice. The personal nature of the latter practice, in which the only audience is the performer himself, excludes the bystanding appreciation essential to the former, which has as its *raison d'etre* an appeal to the sympathetic feelings of an audience of observers, whose involvement in the action of the performance is never more than indirect. The connection between the two can never quite close across the audience gap.

The South Asian concept of *rasa*, which, in spite of being terrifically complicated, has been the central idea in South Asian aesthetics for upward of sixteen hundred years, clarifies the nature of this gap and emphasizes its significance in South Asian thought. The medieval philosopher Abhinavagupta, whose commentary on the *Natyashastra* provides the philosophical basis of subsequent South Asian aesthetics—including Rupa Goswami's—insisted that *rasa*, the most sublime "sense" (the South Asian commentators more often prefer "taste") of beauty arising from drama/literature, cannot be experienced by an actor. Masson and Patwardhan proclaim clearly: "Abhinava is clear in his refusal to grant aesthetic experiences to the actor."[32] Such a pronouncement invites resistance. Why shouldn't actors experience the culmination of aesthetic sense during a performance? After all, actors are people too. Masson and Patwardhan elaborate on Abhinavagupta's thinking on this subject: "The actor, in the opinion of Abhinavagupta and most later writers, does not experience *rasa*, nor does the original character, nor even the author. For *rasa* implies distance. Without this aesthetic distance, there cannot exist literature, only the primary world."[33] An actor's direct involvement in a performance prevents him from transcending the immediate circumstances and feelings of the performance's action. Abhinavagupta's reasoning in this regard is illuminated and reinforced by the distinction—residing in the audience—that is evident between performance and meditation.

The more an actor is transformed into the role she plays, the more her feeling becomes the feeling of her character, and then the less able she is to experience the aesthetic force of the role—a force that is a quality of an action only perceptible as distinct from that action. If it were not so, we would not regard artistic action as in any way different from any other kind of action, like changing a tire. Although some observers could perceive aesthetic force in the changing of a tire on the roadside, they would undoubtedly be appreciating particular qualities of the process—speed, agility, coordination—which are essentially superfluous to the practical matter of getting the tire changed. The more the happenstance mechanic's own sympathies are invested in changing the tire, the less they can regard the art in it. The more an ad hoc audience appreciates the *beauty* of the changing of the tire, the less it regards the action as a matter of getting the car back on the road. "The spectators do not fall in love with Sîtâ," says Abhinavagupta.[34] Even if they sympathetically *feel*, they do not appreciate the flat tire in the same way as the stalled driver. "Untroubled by the responses which naturally accompany actual emotions, [the spectator] can allow himself to enter the make-believe world of art with an unsullied and untroubled mind. He can then rise above conflict, doubts and anxieties."[35] Hence, the highest appreciation of the *art* in a role—of *acting*, as such—in a theatrical performance only appears in an audience, for which the dramatic action of a play exists.

Given this assessment of the actor's condition, the degree to which we should identify actors with meditators is greatly limited, regardless of the natural affinities of role-playing. The devotee involved in meditation, such as *râgânugâ bhakti sâdhana*, must fully identify with his character, even to the point, if we follow Haberman, of *becoming* the character. The meditative role exists in and for the meditator himself. For this reason, *bhakti* meditation is irremediably distinct from theatre (and irremediably distinct from Stanislavsky).

THE SYSTEM AND *RÂS LILA* PRACTICE

The same gap does not stand between System acting and *râs lila* acting. Both theatrical practices exist for the sympathy of and consumption by an audience. *Râs lila* is a theatrical activity that may exhibit some of the characteristics of meditation, not a meditative practice that exhibits some affinities with acting. *Râs lila* audience members laugh, cry, shout, and cheer, and are in every way emotionally wrapped up in a performance as a performance, while nevertheless regarding that performance as the expression of something ultimately "real"—more real than they themselves. In fact, it seems that *râs lila* performances succeed—in spite of a disregard for psychological plausibility—in generating a stage reality to a degree that matches (or even outdoes) the best efforts of Stanislavskian methods. Consequently, a comparison of the *râs lila* with Western theatrical traditions such as Stanislavsky's acting System not only makes sense, but, considering the way they both strive to manifest some "reality" on stage and the methods they employ to this end, the comparison asserts itself.

There is no established program of training common to *râs lila* troupes, in the way that System Acting is a proper noun—a coherent program whose elements are more or less consistent and which identify each other by way of their cooperation as characteristics of an orthodox scheme. *Râs lila* actors are much less *trained* in acting than they are *taught* what to do on stage. Nevertheless, there are some vaguely consistent training practices.[36] In the first place, a *râs lila* actor learns the matter of his role—the lines, the songs, the dances, the physical gestures that correspond with emotional states—by rote. In the beginning of a child actors' career, he must meet daily with his troupe's director for instruction in his part. These training sessions for actors as young as four years old can begin as early as four in the morning, and may extend for a few hours at a time (figure 5.1).

The sessions are characterized by a purely mechanical imitation of the director's speech and movement, in the way that artistic training, particularly in music performance, is commonly done throughout India. Apart

Figure 5.1 Young *râs lila* actors preparing for a performance (Photo by D. V. Mason).

from these training sessions with a director, an actor's means of rehearsal are performances themselves. A troupe director, sitting with the musicians to the side of the stage, commonly becomes a part of the stage action by feeding lines to young actors, or to older actors who have assumed new roles (most often the director knows the lines by heart, but can sometimes be seen using a prompt book). With respect to functioning in stage dances, a young actor reinforces the rote training he has received from a director by following his older companions on stage. In fact, nervous glances from actor to actor, sheepish grins at wrong turns, and even an actor or two dropping out of a dance momentarily (until they can again pick up their part in it) are features of typical *râs lila*s.

The *râs lila* actor's training does not have much to do with learning *characterization* as such, and does not coincide with Stanislavskian acting in this respect. The *râs lila* training regimen, as it is today, exhibits little or no interest in plumbing the psychological depths either of the actor or of the *râs lila*'s characters. A psychological investigation of the *râs lila* character would be pointless anyway, even if the actors were to approach the matter from the point of view of Stanislavskian training. Because it concerns divine characters, the *râs lila* does not rest on the humanistic foundation that underlies the theory of internal identification in Stanislavskian acting. The transcendent characters of the *râs lila* are far beyond the reach of any psychological or emotional affinity.[37]

SMARANA AS A TRAINING MECHANISM

The intersection of the two acting traditions appears to be through a similarly genetic dependence on *memory*. Although, of course, the concept of memory does not necessarily cross cultural boundaries in one piece, we can identify a sufficiently wide overlap of ideas on this subject between these two otherwise culturally distinct situations.

Emotion memory is a concept of the psychology of the subconscious that took root in Europe as the nineteenth century became the twentieth. Posited by psychologist Théodule Ribot, whose work Stanislavsky read, the term "emotion memory" refers to an individual's capacity and inclination to stow away physical and emotional experience in the subconscious such that the same sensations might express themselves later in their original character, given the appropriate circumstances. Stanislavsky found in this idea the mechanism actors could exploit to reproduce emotion that would be in essence *real*, having been derived in the first place from common human experience. Colin Counsell describes the relationship between Ribot's theory and Stanislavsky's System thus:

> According to Ribot, individuals retain a subconscious record of emotional experiences accumulated over the span of their lives. These are not stored in isolation, however, but are always associated with the physical and sensory circumstances that accompanied their first occurrence. In Stanislavsky's view, by re-evoking these circumstances imaginatively with the Psycho-Technique the actor is able to summon the associated feelings.[38]

Stanislavsky charged his actors to draw upon the material available in their own emotion memory to generate an "internal state" appropriate to a given character. A suitable "physical state," or the manifestation of the character an audience must see and hear, Stanislavsky asserted, would naturally follow such an adjustment of the actor's inner self.

Stanislavsky, following Russian Behaviorists such as Pavlov, accordingly devised, as part of the System, a physical discipline designed to suture psychologically the valuable emotional states identified in an actor's emotion memory to physical stimuli, so as to assist actors in accessing these authentic states under artificial circumstances. Through specific repetitive physical exercises, an actor could be conditioned, Stanislavsky reasoned from his familiarity with Pavlov, to associate a particular physical stimuli with a particular emotional state—even if the stimuli itself had apparently little or nothing to do with the emotional state with which it was joined. All the better if the relationship between stimulus and state was not, in fact, natural, in order to facilitate a more mechanical connection between the two. Such superimposed stimuli could then effectively be employed by an actor in reproducing an inner state with a greater degree of spontaneity.

The *memory* with which *râs lila* performances have to do is *smarana*, from the Sanskrit root *smr* meaning "to remember, recollect, bear in mind, call to mind, think of, be mindful of."[39] We have already encountered this term in David Haberman's explanation of the role of imagination in *bhakti* meditation. A preferred translation for the term among some Western scholars is *remembrance*. Vaishnava scholars in Vrindavan aver that *smarana* is the very thing without which there is no Vaishnavism. The saint Ramanuja, whose eleventh-century writings on *bhakti* provided the philosophical basis for the *bhakti* revival in Braj in the sixteenth century, regarded *smarana* as the essence of *bhakti*. "Râmânuja declares that *smarana*, this constant remembrance... is what is meant by the term *bhakti*."[40] In popular *bhakti* ideology, the Sanskrit term indicates a kind of memory through which factual knowledge renews itself—a "recollection" or "re-assemblage" of pieces of the past, or of knowledge hidden away for a time. On one hand, this seems to indicate a process by which knowledge is transmitted from one generation to the next, and on the other, it appears to indicate the self-recovery of an individual's own latent knowledge.

The content of *smarana* in the context of Vrindavan is the historical reality of Krishna's manifestation as a child in Vrindavan thousands of years ago. The memory of Krishna's historical presence in Vrindavan has traversed the millennia from the firsthand observation of Krishna's own associates to the present day through the process of *smarana*. Srivatsa Goswami compares this aspect of *smarana* with an individual's concept of personal heritage. How do you come to have a knowledge of your great-great grandfather?, he asks. Through the firsthand experience of him as passed on to you from the recollection of succeeding generations of your family. "His reality comes to you by way of memory."[41] In this way, *smarana* indicates the preservation of knowledge through time, the movement of knowledge from past to present, which reinforces a tradition of scriptural texts and lineages of gurus.

In another way, *smarana* is an individual's revivification of a reality with the elements inherited from history. This kind of *re-membrance* inherent in the meaning of *smarana* presupposes the sense of the word just noted, and further accounts for the potential of a devotee to muster and polish the elements descended to him or her through history to make the past a living present. Your imaginative faculties, continues Srivatsa Goswami, make living pictures of the stories you hear (or read) of your great-great grandfather, such that he becomes a living person on the stage of your mind; not that you have *imagined* him in the sense of *inventing* him, but that your creative capacity has fused the pieces of history handed to you and infused them with a vivid life. Accordingly, David Shulman considers a range of meanings of the root *smr* as "...connected to modes of making someone or something present."[42] In this way, *smarana* is a "memory" that is both a repository for and a conjurer of reality.

The way in which these two aspects of *smarana* coexist and compliment each other may be seen in a brief consideration of the Shroud of Turin, which, according to tradition, bears an imprint of the face of Jesus. In the early 1980s, artist Curtis Hooper produced a painting that aspired to be a realistic portrait of the head and face that left the imprint on the shroud.[43] The piece of cloth on which appears the imprint (in combination with the tradition that identifies the source of the imprint), passed down for some time as a relic of Jesus, is an example of the first aspect of *smarana*. The use of the cloth to generate more "realistic" images of Jesus's face is an example of the second aspect of *smarana*. The painted portrait is not itself an authentic—which is to say, original—representation of Jesus, which is exclusively, if at all, the domain of the historical relic; rather, the painting is a contemporary "recovery" or "re-assemblage" of the historical memory that has descended through time, and which invests the relic and the memorial it bears with a new life.

A more personal example involves the Malik family of Vrindavan, in whose *haveli* my family and I lived for several months. The core of the family, the two parents and three teenage children, developed a special relationship with my two-year-old son David. Through their daily play together, they developed a personal system of communication based upon phrases my son could speak, the most popular of which was the interminable exchange of "Why?" and "Because." They also developed between them preferred pastimes, particularly including vehicles. My son could sit for an hour at a time on the Malik's scooter, imagining, we suppose, that he was driving, and the Malik children were only too happy to hop on the back and imagine with him. We subsequently purchased a "cycle-bike" for him—the Vrindavan vehicle that combines the whimsy of the American Big Wheel with the imbalance of a tricycle. The "cycle-bike" was immediately David's favorite thing.

When I returned alone to Vrindavan after seeing my family off at the Delhi airport for their trip back to the United States, the Maliks immediately regaled me with an account of how they all missed David terribly, and how their pain in separation was assuaged to some degree when Bitu, the twelve-year-old, squatted down on the "cycle-bike" and tooled around the *haveli* courtyard shouting, "Look at me, I'm David!" A few days later they asked me for pictures of David, which I did not have in print; when I pulled up photographs of David on my computer, Mrs. Malik began an astonishing interchange with the computer screen, beginning with, "Hello, David!" and continuing to roll out all the pet phrases she and David shared. ("Why?" she asked the computer. "Because," she answered.)

The Malik family here exercised *smarana* in distinctively Vrindavan fashion. Separated from David, they made efforts to recall him by assuming his role in the *haveli*. To the degree that these recollecting acts brought David clearly and closely to mind, David was, in fact, present again in our common courtyard, riding the cycle-bike and blabbering.

In Vrindavan, the efforts to take advantage of the power of *smarana* in recollecting Krishna are elaborate. The day is organized in eight successive periods, during each of which Krishna engages in distinct pastimes upon which devotees can focus their attention (sleeping and eating, of course, but also bathing, tending cows, frolicking with the village girls, preparing to frolic with the village girls, and so forth). The schedule governs ritual activity in Vrindavan's many temples: when to feed Krishna, what to feed him, when to put him down for a nap, whom to ask over after school to play with him, and so on. The fixed schedule, as the temples follow it, spills over into Vrindavan streets and homes, whose residents and pilgrims determine their schedules according to the temples' schedule. "The devotee not only participates in Krishna's activities," writes A. Whitney Sanford, "but also patterns his or her daily life on this model."[44] Haberman gives us a glimpse of the complexity and inclusiveness of Krishna's schedule in the lives of *bhakti* meditators:

> The daily cycle commences with the beginning of night's end, a point which coincides with a moment called *brahma-muhûrta*. *Brahma-muhûrta* occurs three *muhûrta*s before sunrise (a *muhûrta* is a period of forty-eight minutes).... The meditative cycle follows each of the eight periods in order, until the cycle is completed and the day begins again. Each period has a particular *lîlâ*-event associated with it, and the practitioner is to visualize the appropriate event in the proper period.[45]

In minute detail, the cycle accounts for every minute of Krishna's day. This fact, and the way in which Krishna's ritual schedule penetrates Vrindavan's "secular" life, makes of the schedule something similar to a ready-made "running score" such as Stanislavsky charged his actors to imagine. The details, which are a part of the cycle, work to call from the memory of those minding it the mythic world of Vrindavan in which Krishna is eternally at play. "By replicating elements of Krishna's existence," Sanford adds while analyzing the influence on devotees of living in accordance with Krishna's eight-period day, "the devotee can physically experience many of the sensations described in the poetry; for example, the aroma of Krishna's meals, the dust of Vraja under one's bare feet, the shade of the Kadamba tree, and so forth."[46] In this way practicing devotees—even non-practicing devotees, by virtue of all that occurs around them—access in a very Stanislavskian way the physical stimuli of the world they wish to inhabit. Krishna's daily cycle, as it has become codified in scripture and ritual, also provides a dramatic script already divided into discrete "units," as Stanislavsky employed the term, which clearly delineates the beginnings and endings of actions.

Haberman shows us that *smarana* can become a disciplined practice as employed in the meditative system of *râgânugâ bhakti sâdhana*. Devotees engaged in this method, in accordance with the codified directions Rupa

Goswami wrote in the sixteenth century, make *smarana* the sum and substance of their daily activity, following elaborate and complex descriptions of Krishna's remembered schedule as a sort of "daily planner" of their own. Thus ritualized, *smarana* occupies each minute of the devotee's waking day with an imagined stream of references to Krishna's divine world, governed by a daily cycle that is at the same time both mythic and temporal.

However, not everyone in Vrindavan enjoys the economic circumstances that permit such single-minded devotion, nor, in any case, is everyone inclined to it, and yet, *smarana* pervades Vrindavan culture. *Râgânugâ bhakti sâdhana*'s formally structured application of *smarana* need not be regarded as exclusive. Considering the significance given *smarana* in *bhakti* theology from the time of Ramanuja to the present day, and considering the relatively few number of people formally engaged in *râgânugâ bhakti sâdhana*, we should expect to find evidence of *smarana* in more mundane Vrindavan circumstances.

We do, in fact, see an active recollection of Krishna at every level of activity in Vrindavan, to the extent that Donna Wulff characterizes Braj in the Vaishnava imagination as "a giant stage."[47] This fact of Vrindavan's dramatic character suggests that the actors who live there engage daily in a kind of Stanislavskian acting exercise through which, as a matter of course, they make more vivid for themselves the spiritual world of Krishna the *râs lila* aspires to express. Since Vrindavan was "identified" as Krishna's home in the sixteenth century, it has existed as a town only in response to the increasing number of pilgrims visiting the area in order to find experience of Krishna's divine play. Consequently, day-to-day life in Vrindavan has to do almost exclusively with imagining the presence of Krishna and the favorite of his girlfriends, Radha (who also enjoys her own divine status), and efforts to call their memory to mind permeate every activity from formal worship in the town's many temples, to shopping in the bazaar, to morning chores.

The number of temples now standing in Vrindavan is customarily numbered by residents at four thousand. In a town of forty or fifty thousand, this means there could be a temple for every ten people. This estimate may be a little high, but temples of some grandeur and shrines no larger than a suitcase are all over Vrindavan, and even if the local estimate is an exaggeration, what appears to the eye as one walks through Vrindavan suggests that more temples per capita are located there than in any other Indian city. With a few exceptions, each of the temples offers daily programs of worship, interrupted periodically to accommodate Krishna's patterns of eating and napping (even the breaks call Krishna to mind).

In addition to the seasonal ritual celebrations that emphasize Krishna's connection with temporal conditions in Braj, temples also often sponsor special events such as recitations of the entire *Bhagavata Purana*, or *katha* performances, which combine recitations of portions of the *Bhagavata Purana* especially concerned with Krishna's childhood with devotional song and doctrinal commentary. Something big—something which imposes a recollection of Krishna in a highly sensory way—is always happening in one temple or another. One temple even sponsors a daily *râs lila* performance by various troupes.

One also sees in Vrindavan an unending stream of pilgrims, rich and poor, who take temporary residence in Vrindavan's many ashrams and guest houses. The pilgrims spend their few days in Braj following a vaguely programmatic itinerary from temple to temple and from sacred site to sacred site, and from spiritual event to spiritual event, singing and chanting much of the way, and pausing perhaps only to take food at any of the "pure veg" food stalls (the consumption of meat is summarily forbidden in Vrindavan), or briefly in the bazaar to purchase devotional items—books, clothing, ritual objects, and such—which provide the material base of Vrindavan's economy. The pilgrimage program even includes the circumambulation of Vrindavan itself. The walk takes around three hours, which pilgrims and residents alike fill with songs of Krishna's pastimes, beauty, and love for Radha. On festival occasions—which occur frequently; while living there I often thought to myself, "Every day's a holiday in Vrindavan"—pilgrims join in very loud processions through Vrindavan's narrow lanes, chanting, singing, and dancing with gusto while following after an elaborately decorated wagon bearing a local temple image, or the picture of a popular saint, and accompanied by a cart toting electronic equipment to amplify prerecorded devotional music to dangerous levels (figure 5.2).

Other sounds of worship in Vrindavan are incessant. Chanting is omnipresent, both on a macro and a micro level, as the names of God are recited by groups and individuals in all situations and at all times of the day. Even when the sound of chanting is not immediately present, Vrindavan residents and visitors use phrases made of certain of God's names, especially "Radhe-Radhe," in almost every personal encounter to mean everything from "Hello, how are you" to "Get out of the way!" Standard doctrine holds that the sound of God's name manifests God himself; in which case, God is ever-present in Vrindavan. The persistent echoing of the names of God, and the regard given to the sound of God's name in Vaishnava theology, makes for an environment in which—according

Figure 5.2 Vrindavan pilgrims (Photo by D. V. Mason).

to one Vrindavan pilgrim—"it is impossible not to worship" (which is to say, *re-member*). To be certain that this worship is, indeed, continuous, some ashrams have arranged twenty-four-hours-a-day schedules of chanting carried out in shifts by local devotees, the maintenance of which can be verified by a 3 AM walk through Vrindavan's otherwise dark lanes. Additionally, temple bells ring at all hours of the day and night, drawing one's attention to God's own daily routine (I was regularly woken at four in the morning—the most auspicious time of day—by the bell of the temple next door). The markets, also, are filled with the sound of devotion, as shops blast snippets of the latest devotional cassettes loudly enough to be heard above the sound of scooters and bicycle bells, hawking and bartering, dogs barking, cows mooing, and the other miscellaneous noises of semirural India.

In addition to the sights and sounds of Vrindavan, we might further discuss the expression of devotion in Vrindavan with respect to smell, taste, and touch. But it may be sufficient at this point to say that Krishna-*smarana* hangs suspended in the air of Vrindavan. No particular part of Vrindavan, material or immaterial, evades its touch, so that the most mundane element unavoidably alludes to Krishna. The principal event inspiring Margaret Case's discussion of spiritual sight in Vrindavan

Vaishnavism in her book *Seeing Krishna* involves the chance passing of a beetle near *bhramar ghat*—the "bee steps," which devotees seized upon as the appearance of Krishna in the form of a bee, for which there is scriptural precedent.[48] Neither the happenstance of the event, nor the fact that a beetle is not a bee, are relevant objections. *Smarana* makes reality from the simplest of referents. In the introduction to her translation of Kalidasa's play *Abhijnanasakuntala*, which has memory as its central concern, Barbara Stoller Miller writes:

> In Mammata's *Kâvyaprakâśa* (10.199), *smarana* is an *alamkâra*, defined as the recollection of an object as it was experienced, when a similar object is seen.... Viśvanâtha modified the definition, replacing Mammata's restricted relation between visual perception (*drsta*) and recollection with a more general concept of perception (*anubhâva*) as the source of recollection, so that a recollection of an object arising from the perception of something like it is termed *smarana*...[49]

The piercing insight of Vrindavan-*smarana* saw the spiritual nature in the passing of a beetle—a revelation of Krishna's infinite life in Vrindavan. *Smarana* creates from the least august things the world of Krishna's *lila*.

This environment in which every stimulus is somehow connected to recollecting and reimagining the presence of God, from worship at a variety of temples, to passing twelve shrines and hearing seventy widows chanting the name of God on your way to get pure veg food from the local *bhojanalaya*, to telling someone to move out of the way, is one thing for pilgrims who choose to make Vrindavan a temporary place of worship apart from their lives in the real world, and who may well appreciate the intense concentration of attention on Krishna and Radha for the short time they are able to devote exclusively to such things. But imagine a boy born and raised in Vrindavan, whose access to elsewhere—including cities like Delhi, even though it is relatively close—is limited to travel as part of a *ras lila* troupe. Even satellite television, which is ubiquitous throughout India, is only a small window on what are, for the most part, lands so distant and unattainable as to be the stuff of fantasy. An eight-year-old boy in this environment may very well perceive life itself as uninterrupted *smarana*, a persistent revelation of Krishna in all daily activities—at least in all he does in his waking hours, and, perhaps, in everything that happens around him while he sleeps.

In addition, the actor in Vrindavan finds his very own existence to be the site of Krishna *smarana*. In the first place, the boy grows up as a child of India, the religious significance of which is magnified under the lens of Krishna devotion. Hawley notes that, "the 'worship' of children...is a general feature of Indian life."[50] Children in general enjoy a much favored place in Indian society, being allowed an unusual freedom and receiving unusual regard. Considering a number of sociological studies on the phenomenon, Norvin Hein writes:

> The child is waited upon with devotion and patience. Toilet training, which is effected without reproaches, comes very late. Children go to bed when they are ready, they play in any state of dress or undress, they are seldom coerced or thwarted. The mother's protection and support are unconditional. The child's grandparents and adult maternal relatives make its indulgence complete.[51]

My experience with children of my own in India bears out the extraordinary adoration they receive. My own children are treated regally in India, and with much more sincere delight by people from all walks of life than one encounters under day-to-day circumstances in the United States. When the old *sadhus* living along the banks of the Ganges in Rishikesh would see my wife and I coming with our six-month-old daughter strapped to one or the other of us, they would clap their hands and call out with laughter, "Mother Ganges!" As we ate in restaurants from time to time, elsewhere in India, waiters would customarily take our daughter to meet the entire staff. Often she would disappear for the length of our meals, and we would finally discover her playing with the cooks in the kitchen. Customarily, most of the other restaurant patrons would also insist on holding her before we could leave.[52] When we visited the Taj Mahal with her—and this was typical when we visited tourist sites—we were asked thirty or forty times to pose her for photographs by Indian nationals (later, when I had occasion to visit the Taj without my children, I wasn't asked to stand for a single photograph).

In this special regard India gives its children, boys typically have a higher place, and in Vrindavan the place boys hold takes on religious significance. Sociologist David Mandelbaum has noted the exceptional degree of deference afforded the young boy in India. "Even when a woman has several sons, she cherishes and protects and indulges them all to a degree not usually known in the western world."[53] In Vrindavan, this regard, which comes from more than familial affection, conflates boy children with Krishna, the premier child. As Hawley reads the Vrindavan environment, "It would be hard to think of a place where children are more shamelessly indulged and idolized, particularly the boys."[54] More than once Vrindavan residents flatly told me that boy children are God (*bhagvan*). An adult *râs lila* actor made clear to me that this was not an empty statement when I saw him touch his forehead to his baby son's feet, an act normally reserved for the ritual worship of a temple image, or a guru (who also holds a divine status for his adherents). The boy actor receives a special dose of this regard, as *râs lila* directors try to drum into their actors (more often than not, their sons) from the beginning of their training the thought, "I am Krishna."[55] On another extended stay in India, seven years after I had paraded my infant daughter through a variety of Indian restaurants' kitchens, residents of Vrindavan generally referred to my two-year-old son as Gopal, one of Krishna's names with special reference to his toddler years. Some suggested with full sincerity that I really should change his name.[56] The association of children with Krishna makes small boys themselves into living sites of *smarana*, which suits them naturally to take the *râs lila*'s divine roles.

BHÂV AS A QUALITY OF ACTING

Given how hard the environment in Vrindavan works to set up these boys for their roles, it sometimes seems that the young *râs lila* actors do nothing, but are only put into their roles by context, much like props. But there is, in fact, an inner, inherent quality of these child performers that contributes to their competence as performers, in addition to the way in which Vrindavan's various mechanisms of memory transform them from the outside. Among devotees, at least, the inclination to associate children with Krishna derives from the popular understanding of spirituality known as *bhâv*, a quality also essential to the audience experience, as I will explore in the next chapter. For the actors, *bhâv* is a fundamental quality and an important piece in the correlation of *râs lila* acting and Stanislavskian theory.

The term derives from classical Sanskrit dramatic theory going back to the *Natyashastra*, which codifies several distinct but interconnected kinds of *bhâv—anubhâv, sthâyibhâv, vyabhicâribhâv*, and so on. The distinctions are very important to an understanding of classical dramaturgy, but of little consequence to the contemporary concept of *bhâv* in popular worship. Its connection to classical theatre, however, has characterized *bhâv* as a fundamentally theatrical thing, across sectarian lines in India today. Most simply, *bhâv* is emotion. Discussing the devotional activity of Vallabhite devotees in Vrindavan, Jeffrey R. Timm defines *bhâv* first as "any intense personal emotion."[57] However, in devotional practice in Vrindavan and elsewhere, *bhâv* takes on other, more specific, more theatrical, meanings. For certain Ram devotees, for example, *bhâv* refers not only to devotional emotion or feeling, but to one's peculiar character, either natural or developed. Peter van der Veer writes of Ramanandi monks for whom *bhâv* is "basic human emotion" and also "the attitude a devotee adopts when trying to refine this emotion in order to experience a certain relation with the beloved God. For example, a paternal feeling can be evoked by considering oneself as Dashrath..."[58] For the Ram devotees with whom van der Veer is concerned, *bhâv* refers to the character a person plays in what van der Veer calls a "ritual theater of devotion."[59] Even across sectarian lines, then, *bhâv* in popular understanding retains a distinctly dramatic element. A person feels *bhâv*, and cultivates *bhâv* as a mechanism of personal transformation.

Swami Fateh Krishna Sharma tells a story of a *râs lila* performance in Jaipur in which, as an adult, he played the role of a cowherd distraught by Krishna's absence. Following the performance, Swami-ji was called out by a man identifying himself as a Bollywood filmmaker.[60] This director offered his appreciation for Swami-ji's performance, and added that he could pay crores of rupees to his film actors and would not get the kind of convincing emotion out of them that he had just seen in Swami-ji. For his part, Swami-ji is quick to attribute his acting ability to *bhâv*, bestowed on him as a "blessing" (*krpa*).[61] In this case, as in the other common cases of performances in which a character's sincere attachment and devotion to Krishna is evident, the actor essentially expresses his own attachment and devotion, which, as the Hindi film director perceived, money cannot buy. In fact, in such cases the degree to which actors *act* is in question. In Jaipur, Swami-ji did not express the sadness of a distant, perhaps fictional, cowherd for whom Krishna's departure from Vrindavan caused sorrow, but expressed his own deep sadness in the gulf estranging him from Krishna, the object of his own, exquisite yearning.[62] Hence, his stage tears were his own tears as much as his cowherd character's. In some ways this scenario resembles the plight of the actress playing Andromache I saw years ago. And it may not be unreasonable to suggest that that actress was not acting, either, but giving way to her own, very intense *bhâv*.

For *râs lila* actors, *bhâv* is the final Stanislavskian contingency and the ultimate justification. In the same way that a Stanislavskian actor relies upon access to his own feelings as the basis for a character, the *râs lila* actor relies on the *bhâv* he finds alive in himself. A devotee actor, one whose devotional living has nurtured and refined his own *bhâv*, has no need to develop through an additional acting "system" the means of plausibly expressing the nature of his character, since his own feelings in the devotional stage situation are more than adequate. But because actors rely on their own spiritual nature, their own *bhâv*, in building their characters, their acting process—such as it is—does, actually, resemble Stanislavskian discipline, which similarly recognizes that that inherent feeling cannot be artificially generated or manufactured, only nurtured and channeled into service. Without *bhâv*, any transformation of *râs lila* participants—actors and audience alike—is impossible. Indeed, the nurture of that unmade quality makes spiritual experience in *râs lila* theatre possible.

In fact, it is precisely this understanding of *bhâv* that justifies the use of often undisciplined children as actors in the *râs lila*. *Bhâv*, Vrindavan residents say, is most pure in children. In fact, the younger the child, the purer his *bhâv*. Vasant Yamadagni suggested to me that "pure *bhâv*" (*shudh bhâv*) exists in the child in the absence of worldly passions and vices such as greed, jealousy, cruelty, and so forth, and he provided this example: You buy a toy for one thousand rupees and give it to your child. He breaks it. You go through the roof because of your attachment to the monetary value of that toy, disturbed that you may as well have dropped the money in the trash can. But the child has no sense of this value. The younger the child is, the less the monetary loss disturbs him—and the more likely he would just as happily drop that money in the trash can in the first place as break the expensive toy (or flush the car keys down the toilet).[63] The child's concerns are not worldly, but are entirely consumed in play, and this is the evidence of the purity of his *bhâv*, which exists naturally in him in the beginning. The child, then, is not only more "ritually appropriate" for playing Krishna, but also, at a basic, internal—shall we say, *Stanislavskian*—level, most like Krishna the character: playful, imperturbable, carefree. That Krishna nature, of course, wanes with age, making necessary the adoption of devotional life as a means of preserving and nurturing it.

CONCLUSION

Considering the pervasive religious environment in which an eight-year-old Vrindavan boy is enveloped on a daily basis, and the way in which, from minute to minute, a boy finds himself to be one of Vrindavan's limitless mementos of Krishna, I would suggest that by default *râs lila* actors are well-trained in the principal psychological aspects of Stanislavskian acting. They know what it means to "live" through a part, how to imagine themselves as if they were someone else, how to regard their environmental circumstances as manifestations of another time and place, and they know how to transform those circumstances imaginatively into a tangible reality. Although Krishna and Radha do not have "objectives" and "motivation" in the way mundane characters do, *râs lila* actors know through the simultaneously single-minded and aimless life of Vrindavan the essential nature of their roles, and by daily exposure to the ritual program governing Vrindavan's motion, based on the regularity of Krishna's minutely timed pastimes, they know the "units," or discrete activities, that comprise Krishna's eternal play. It is no wonder that Krishna actors profess to feel a very Stanislavskian identification with their characters in spite of what seems a fixed and broad disconnect on stage. As an object and function of the world of Vrindavan, the *râs lila* actor does "live his part." Swami Amicand Sharma's son, who played Krishna in his father's troupe for ten years, told me that at every moment during a performance his mind was occupied with the thought, "I am Krishna."[64]

6. Theatre Is Religion: The Acting Audience[1]

I have argued that young *râs lila* actors, though they lack formal acting training as we understand it in the West, grow up in an environment that trains them—inadvertently, perhaps—to act. Vrindavan *is* a stage, a big theatre constructed for dramatizing God, and its temples and markets, riverbanks and fields, its temple rituals and its business transactions, all cooperate and conspire as parts of the divine play. The child who grows up in Vrindavan grows up an actor. But the same theatrical environment surrounds everyone else too. To the extent that Vrindavan inevitably trains its young boys to be actors, it also trains its young girls and its old men and its housewives and its retired generals and college professors. As I have suggested, the acting competence of these audience members may be more important to the efficacy of the *râs lila* than the skill (or lack thereof) of its actors. In taking advantage of performances as mechanisms of meditation and other kinds of devotion, *râs lila* audience members tend to be explicitly active in their involvement with performances, and this involvement both resembles acting and surely contributes to the audience members' experience. What is explicit here may be implicit in other theatre moments. The kind of overt activity in which *râs lila* audiences engage may be going on furtively among other audiences.

"THE EWW-EFFECT" IN ART AND RELIGION

In 2004, I attended a college production of a period play involving swords.[2] In a climax building to the sigh of intermission, two characters took up arms against each other, and, after a series of lunges, feints, and parries, one of them dealt a deadly thrust and the other followed with a quick stage death. Before the tension of the moment dissipated, however, the triumphant character bent to the stage corpse of his theatrical foe, placed a finger in the stage wound, and with a dramatic flourish jammed the befouled finger into his own mouth. Immediately, a sound rose like a signal to the house lights and the obligatory fifteen-minute break—a signal not from the stage but from a cluster of undergraduate students seated together close to the stage and center, who in perfect unison and stunning phonetic agreement said, "Eww!"

From the standpoint of any one of the historical understandings of theatrical mimesis, this "Eww-Effect" is a problem. It is one thing to acknowledge that theatrical activity inevitably imitates things outside the space and time of the theatre. It is something of a different order to confront the evidence that theatrical activity can take on a real, living life of its own, effectively existing as an ontological reality in the experience of the audience. Perhaps a degree of verisimilitude in theatre sometimes fools our conscious thoughts into a state of mistake; but in this case, the stage grotesquerie did not even include fake blood.

Reasoning from this one case, a production's naturalist aims, the psychological authenticity of its actors, the realism of its set, apparently have little to do with this Eww-Effect. Apparently, whatever the degree of realistic illusion intended by a production, the trappings of the theatre experience, from paid-parking to poorly upholstered seats to velour curtains, impose on an audience an uninterrupted discourse of fabrication; and yet, not only might we cringe at blood-sucking on a stage, but we might weep at Astyanax's death, grit our teeth at Stanley's abuse of Stella, and laugh at Bottom's disfigurement, as though all these things really happen while we watch. The philosophical term *Paradox of Fiction* denotes the problem of reacting to stories—as presented in novels, in cinema, in painting, and so on—as though to immediately real events. The theatrical variation on this paradox is that staged action can affect us as though it is not pretense, even while it *demonstrates* its pretense. Cort Webb, our college classmate, is never dead and bleeding on stage, and while the presence of his familiar, not-character body makes the pretense explicit, while we know in a very conscious way that he's neither dead nor bleeding, we nevertheless see Brad Bergeron eat his blood, which, momentarily, grosses us out.

As suggested in the previous chapter, a similar conundrum is apparent in *râs lila* performances, which, though often rather lackadaisically produced, nevertheless deeply affect their devotee audiences, who cry, laugh, cringe, shout, and otherwise react to the staged action as though it has an ontological authenticity of its own. There is no escaping the plain fact that *râs lila* productions defy every naturalist convention developed in the last century and a half for the purpose of more effectively affecting an audience. Audience members sit on the stage, scenes are set with garish, two-dimensional backdrops, music persistently interrupts the action, as does song and dance, costumes are gaudy and often ill-fitting, and the *actors*—the boys who *are* divine persons appearing for the graceful benefit of the audience—they declaim in a tedious singsong, assume stylized postures iconographically representing emotional states, interact directly with audience members, forget their lines, forget their blocking, visibly tire of the action, and direct their attention everywhere, anywhere but the story in which they play (figure 6.1). Nevertheless, these productions affect audiences at an emotional level as deep and as sincere as any naturalist production featuring Kachalov, Olivier, or Brando. Donna Wulff reports that a *râs lila* performance she attended had to be stopped prematurely. "Afterwards," she relates, "I was informed that the *gosvâmî* presiding over the occasion feared that the devotees watching the *lîlâ*, who had been weeping profusely throughout, would not be able to bear any more grief."[3] At least for outsiders to the tradition, the paradox of fiction is a central feature of the *râs lila*. In spite of every cue otherwise, how can devotee audiences react to the *râs lila* as though it were fully, empirically, real? Similarly, in spite of their uncomfortable seats, the glowing, green exit sign to the

Figure 6.1 Krishna adjusts his costume during a worship ceremony (Photo by Celia Mason).

left of the stage, the velour curtains, and their plain recognition of their school chums in costume, the undergraduates at that cloak-and-sword play reacted to a bald pretense as though it were fully, empirically real.

Of course, the *râs lila* operates in an environment in which explicit religious forces are at work, which may distinguish it from whatever happens on the main stage at Georgia College and State University. Devotee audiences are, after all, *devotee* audiences. Spiritual life in Vrindavan prepares audience members for their roles at a play in the same way that it prepares actors. The aesthetics of *râs lila* theatre are not distinct from its spirituality, nor is the aesthetic effect on audiences distinct from their religious experience. In fact, in the worldview of *bhakti*, staged action does, indeed, have an ontological authenticity of its own, affirmed in the religious practice of the audience. *Bhakti* in Braj reconciles stage pretense and spiritual reality by expecting audience members to *act* every bit as much as the *râs lila*'s designated actors (or even more so), and the role-playing participation of the audience in this case generates a condition in which, as in other religious circumstances, separate realities coexist with equal legitimacy.

But the explicit spiritual forces in Vrindavan that set up audiences to experience theatre in a particular way may be implicit in other—even secular—theatrical circumstances. Like devotees, theatre audiences may adopt roles, and the degree to which they do may mean more to the aesthetic and emotional effects of performances than the efforts of the performances themselves. At least, paradoxes such as the Eww-Effect seem to occur where audience members enter into a mutually-affirming relationship with a performance, like the religious experience that results from a person's active complicity with spiritual worldviews. The *râs lila* audience—as strange as that audience can appear at first glance—models the way all theatre audiences, like devotees, construct and resolve multiple realities, and indicates the overlap, generally, between aesthetic and religious experience.

In *The Varieties of Religious Experience*, William James includes the anecdote of one of the "keenest intellects" of his acquaintance, which reads, in part:

> On the previous night I had had, after getting into bed at my rooms in College, a vivid tactile hallucination of being grasped by the arm, which made me get up and search the room for an intruder; but the sense of presence so called came on the next night. After I had got into bed and blown out the candle, I lay awake awhile thinking on the previous night's experience, when suddenly I

felt something come into the room and stay close to my bed. It remained only a minute or two. I did not recognize it by any ordinary sense, and yet there was a horribly unpleasant "sensation" connected with it.[4]

It is hard not to note certain compelling similarities between the experience of James's acquaintance and the Eww-Effect. In both cases the subjects suffer a physical experience or reaction, and in both cases that reaction is predicated on a stimulus that appears in all respects to be imaginary. That is, both experiences are of the type that art theory has considered paradoxical. As though throwing their arms in the air when confronted by a man with a banana, the subjects' physical/emotional response overlooks the actual, physical stimulus in favor of seeing and reacting according to a constructed, or imagined, stimulus. The kinds of experiences Aesthetics has dubbed paradox of fiction, Religious Studies seems to know only as religious experience.[5]

William James points out the essential perplexity of religious experience. Because their nature is not communicated or validated through sense content, he notes, following Kant, terms like *god, soul,* and *immortality* have no real significance. "Yet strangely enough," writes James, "they have a definite meaning *for our practice*. We can act *as if* there were a God; feel *as if* we were free; consider Nature *as if* she were full of special designs; lay plans *as if* we were to be immortal..."[6] In other words, the religious person acts (and reacts) as though things were much different than all the evidence suggests. In fact, a dogged disregard for the divide between the empirical world and the unverifiable seems to characterize religious experience. The experience of theatre can be much the same, as we act or react, like the undergraduates at GC&SU, not *because* of our senses, but *in spite* of them. To some degree, perhaps, the *râs lila* as a case study of the paradox of fiction is not appropriate, since our Eww-Effect undergraduates do not believe in the blood onstage in the same way Vrindavan devotees believe in Krishna; hence, perhaps, the same paradox that is evident in the Eww-Effect does not arise in Vrindavan. However, *Eww!,* to the extent that it comes from a circumstance that has no empirical basis, resembles the development of a religious worldview, which similarly develops without an empirical foundation. The only difference may be duration. If there is a difference between *Eww!* and spirituality, it is one of degree, not of kind. *Eww!* is momentary. Religiosity may last a lifetime.

The theatre-goer who experiences staged fiction as though real may be engaged in a creative activity analogous to the spirituality of the devotee, who imaginatively affirms a world that does not manifest itself empirically.

To some degree, this correlation of religious and aesthetic experience only recapitulates the postulations of some extant theories about the paradox of fiction, such as those elucidated recently as *make-believe* by Kendall Walton *et al.*, as discussed below. What seems to be less well articulated in philosophical approaches to the paradox of fiction, including Walton's, is the specific activity—the method, so to speak—by which an audience member comes to respond to what is empirically absent as though objectively real. A theory about the way individuals arrive at religious experiences may productively supplement aesthetic philosophy with a sense of the human activity—both mental and physical—that lays the foundation of cognition.

THE PARADOX OF FICTION

The philosophical argument about the paradox of fiction has swung in recent decades between an insistence on its inscrutability, the assertion that it's all in our heads, and the contention that there is no paradox in the first place. Colin Radford took up the paradox with fascination thirty years ago. "What is worrying," he writes, "is that we are moved by the death of Mercutio and we weep while knowing that no one has really died, that no young man has been cut off in the flower of his youth."[7] And while Radford is never content with any of the several possible solutions he considers, he does identify a few points significant to the present discussion. Particularly relevant here is his contention that we cannot resolve the paradox by resorting to argument by suspension-of-disbelief.[8] We do not, Radford argues, ever not disbelieve. If we *did* suspend our disbelief, he reasons, we would be forced by the theatrical circumstances in which we, consequently, *do* believe to confront our own immediate relationship to the action. "Do we shout and try to get on the stage when...we see that Tybalt is going to kill Mercutio? We do not."[9] Our approach to a play and its content is always, and foremost, as an audience member at a play. This is an important point to keep in mind as a link between theatrical experience and religious experience, in which, whatever the degree of reality ascribed to a spiritual world, distinctions between material present and spiritual present are consciously maintained.[10] Decades later, Radford concedes that the paradox continues to defy resolution. "[We] are irrational, inconsistent, and incoherent in being moved to pity for fictional characters," he concludes, "and we are nonetheless moved (of course)."[11]

The competing proposals attempting to resolve the paradox of fiction are consistently audience-centric. We seem to have satisfied ourselves that the work of fiction itself does not mandate an emotional response; or, if it does, that the paradox of an audience's emotion in the face of its consciousness of a work's fictionality does not arise. We also seem to accept that an author does not elicit by fiat an emotional response to or through her work. The audience's own activity, the way it meets and engages with fiction, recurs as a fundamental piece of aesthetic theory dealing with the paradox.

In recent work addressing the paradox of fiction, theorists such as Murray Smith and Noël Carroll have attempted to account for the persistence of our unbelief by challenging the premise that emotion always requires belief. Instead, they propose separate mental mechanisms through which an audience member supplements fiction's cognitive deficiency. Smith's mechanism is a particular kind of *imagination*, while Carroll's mechanism is a specific understanding of *thought*. Both theories indirectly, and perhaps unintentionally, elevate the role the audience itself plays in developing the condition in which real emotion arises in response to an apparent fiction.

Noël Carroll's approach to the paradox of fiction, for instance, hinges on *thought*, a mental faculty by which an audience elevates fiction to a cognitively legitimate status. In many cases, argues Carroll, *thought* is a sufficient cognitive component to produce legitimate feeling, and what he calls "unasserted propositions"—thoughts about the truth, of which we maintain neutrality—if entertained imaginatively inspire feeling as if true propositions.

> You do not need to believe that you are going to put the knife into your eye. Indeed, you know you are not going to do this. Yet merely entertaining the thought, or the propositional content of the thought (that I am putting this knife into my eye), can be sufficient for playing a role in causing a tremor of terror. For emotions may rest on thoughts and not merely upon beliefs.[12]

By insisting on the "unasserted" nature of the thought of a knife in one's eye, Carroll accounts for overt fiction that foments feeling, while proposing a mechanism by which the fiction affects.[13]

Writing of the paradox as evident in audience reactions to cinema, Malcolm Turvey argues that the mental mechanism that Carroll postulates, upon which our emotional response to fiction rests, is unnecessary, even if it operates as Carroll asserts in certain circumstances. Turvey points out that if its principles are legitimate (and exclusively so), Carroll's Thought Theory suggests that thought or imagination alone, divorced from any particular medium, should be sufficient to inspire emotional reaction. If a mental mechanism mediates between an inadequate stimulus (such as the fictional content of a movie) and emotion by supplying the cognitive foundation for real feeling, a person ought to have the same reaction whether he "views the hypothetical fiction film or reads the shooting script upon which it is based."[14] Rather, says Turvey, the cinematic medium is sufficient in itself to affect us emotionally.

Following Turvey's critique in *Beyond Aesthetics*, Carroll offers a very useful adjustment in the form of a connection between the activity of authors and audiences. To account for the increased emotional efficacy of a finished film, as opposed to the screenplay that expresses the same fictional content, Carroll suggests that artistry serves to direct and shape the attention audiences give to the unasserted propositions or thoughts that arise from fictional content. Additionally, and most importantly, Carroll reasons, an audience reciprocates. The authors of fictions, Carroll tells us, offer us unasserted propositions that attract our attention, and then manipulate our attention through artistry so as to focus our anticipation as an emotional expectation, which we seek to sustain and satisfy in the work of fiction.[15] Carroll sees that the kind of fictional objects that inspire feelings must be of a special, augmented sort. Under the scrutiny that an author sculpts, fictional objects, writes Carroll, "are lit, in a manner of speaking, in a special phenomenological glow...apposite to the emotional state we are in..."[16] That is, Carroll suggests, we the audience invest fictional objects with the peculiar characteristic that enables them reflexively to draw emotional responses from us.

This element of Carroll's model is useful, identifying as it does a way in which an audience actively contributes to the way in which fictions affect them; but its applicability to specific examples, such as the *râs lila*, is limited. The emotional force of *râs lila* performances certainly depends upon the emotional state of their audience, otherwise they would either appeal in the same way to all audiences—devotees and unbelievers alike—or not at all to any. However, devotee audiences in Vrindavan do not respond to unequivocally *unasserted* propositions. Although their lives in Braj or as devotee pilgrims may have begun by entertaining unasserted propositions such as "Krishna is here," by the moment of the performance itself, many devotees attending a given *râs lila*—especially those most emotionally responsive to the performance—would aver that the proposition is true that Krishna is, in real, ontological fact, present in the production, and this orientation toward the truth content of the play surely contributes to their emotional response. Because the development of devotional spirituality may depend in its early stages on the entertainment of unasserted propositions, Carroll's theory seems to me a useful starting point for an examination of the devotee's life *prior to* the performance, rather than during it.

Thought Theory's usefulness to discussions of emotional responses in more secular circumstances may be limited to understanding what we might call the "back story" of emotional responses to fiction. The "emotional state" of an audience member, upon which the "phenomenological glow" of Carroll's theory depends is, most often, well developed before the audience member's encounter with a fictional work, and is very often founded upon both unasserted and asserted propositions the audience member has already come to regard as equally true. The audience member's emotional state largely preexists her experience of a play, whether in the short term, say, an argument with a cab driver on the way to the theatre, or in the long term, such as the accumulated emotional and psychological weight of a life of poverty or ill-health or the never-simple relationships of any never-typical family; and the emotional content of those experiences for the audience member is largely shaped by both asserted and unasserted propositions the audience member has come to regard as equally true (or, at least, valid), including conventions of courtesy that govern driver-passenger interactions, economic theory, medical ethics, and religious doctrines that contextualize such things as family relationships. The audience member's emotional state may itself be a product resulting paradoxically from entertaining unasserted propositions; in which case, attention to the way an individual's emotional state phenomenologically lights a work of fiction is the beginning of the discussion, rather than the end.

In a response to Colin Radford, Michael Weston suggests that what we might call the audience's "back story," such as the *râs lila* audience's religious environment, plays a significant part in its emotional response to fiction. Although Weston denies that a real paradox exists in the paradox of fiction, he nevertheless must construct an explanation of the phenomenon—an explanation that relies on recognizing how significant an audience member's own context is to the emotional viability of a fictional object. Citing social anthropologist Peter Winch, Weston notes that humans, as opposed to animals, do not only live but have a "conception of life," which imbues things with particular values, and develops meaningful associations between them. Consequently, Weston writes, "[the] importance of art to us is one way this concern to make sense of our lives appears. The possibility of our being moved by works of art must be made intelligible within the context of such a concern."[17] Weston here supplies Carroll's theory with an important supplement. Fictional objects, taking Weston and Carroll together, develop emotional significance depending upon the part they play in an individual audience member's worldview, and, consequently, have a real emotional force to the same extent that the audience member's own "conception of life" (or worldview) is "real." The unasserted thought "Manhattan is made of pizza" produces no emotional response because we cannot to any degree maintain neutrality about its truth content, and cannot find a place for it in our worldview. However, "Astyanax is dead" can produce an emotional response in us; for, even though we remain non-neutral with respect to the truth of this specific thought, we nevertheless find a place in our worldview in which is assigned a value to children, to their relationships with their mothers, and to their untimely deaths, and this mechanism of location injects the thought of Astyanax's death with real emotional force. To some degree this is only a reiteration of Factualism. But in his critique of Thought Theory, Weston articulates how our sociocultural environment provides the premise for the imaginative role-playing that others regard as essential to understanding the paradox.

Following Kendall Walton, Gregory Currie, Richard Wollheim, and others, in developing a theory of "imagining 'from the inside,'" Murray Smith offers an approach to the paradox of fiction that dwells more on an audience member's activity during the encounter with the work of fiction.[18] For Smith, whose preferred medium, like Carroll's, is film, a spectator's emotional response to fiction comes from her capacity to imagine the experience of a character as presented by a work of fiction. Smith argues that, while watching a movie, audience members engage in a variety of simulative activities, imitating, in a way, what they can imagine is the emotional, affective, and autonomic experiences of the movie's characters. In this way, they imaginatively enter the movie, and their own responses to the movie's circumstances are the product of more or less successfully inhabiting in a make-believe way one or another of the movie's characters (or, even, many of them at once). In Smith's terms, the undergraduate reaction in the case of the Eww-Effect described above results from their vivid imagination of what it must be like to be Clindor, sucking fresh blood off the end of his finger. Following Smith, we might further theorize that the audience member who weeps at Krishna's absence during a *rās līlā* play must be vividly imagining what the experience of Krishna's absence must be like.

However, it seems clear that a good number of devotee audience members in Vrindavan lament Krishna's absence during a performance along with the *gopi* characters, not from viewing the experience from inside the play, in empathy with the *gopi*s, but on account of how the material of the play coincides with their own, real-life, outside-the-play experience of Krishna's absence. Smith's direction of imaginative movement is reversed in the *râs lila*. The audience member, in this case, does not enter into the world of the fiction as much as the fiction enters into the world of the audience member. The fact that the audience member's world may itself be largely fictional—in the sense of being imaginatively constructed without an empirical foundation—is the principal point of intersection between the world of art and the world of religion, as we will discuss in greater detail later in this chapter.

The immediate point is that the Eww-Effect may arise not from the audience entering into the play, but from the play spilling off the stage into the laps of the audience. Our groaning undergraduates do not respond in accord with Clindor's—the character's—experience, which is characterized by barbaric ferocity rather than by squeamishness, but in accord with their own real-life aversion to the experience of fresh blood in their mouths. Which is to say that in the *Eww!* moment, they are not so much inside the play as the play is inside them. Smith partly accounts for this discrepancy by proposing different kinds of inside imagining. Acentral imagining, he asserts, involves "imagining the scenario 'outside' any [particular] character's perspective."[19] As an example of acentral imagining, Smith directs our attention to a scene from the film *Homicide*, in which we see a homicide investigator insult a murder victim and slur her ethnicity, unwittingly within earshot of the victim's granddaughter. Smith argues that our visceral reaction to this scenario arises not from imagining the experience of a character in the scene, but from a much broader, more omniscient perspective than any one character in the scene could have.

Smith contends that acentral imagining is, like central imagining, a kind of imagining "from the inside" of the world of fiction. But the omniscience necessary to acentral imagining prevents us from inhabiting the inside of the fictional world, as much as it prevents us from inhabiting the experience of a particular character.[20] Like the uncomfortable seats and velour curtains in a theatre, an omniscient or multi-perspective view reminds us perpetually of our position as viewers, outside the events of the fiction, so that whatever reactions the audience has as omniscient viewers are necessarily rooted in their own world of the theatre house. The play, or the movie, or the novel seems to produce emotional and other kinds of reactions to its content by infiltrating the audience's world, as much as the other way around.

Murray Smith's approach lays more explicit emphasis than Carroll's on the active input of an audience. Like Carroll's "phenomenological glow," Smith's conception of the mechanism of "imagining," either centrally or acentrally, depends largely on the audience's own "back story," but focuses on the mental activity of the audience rather than on its emotional state. By promoting *make-believe* as the foundation of our paradoxical feelings for fiction, Kendall Walton takes an additional, crucial step, and one that unmistakably characterizes the audience experience as analogous (at least) to religious experience.

Walton draws our attention to the imaginative playing of children, and asserts, "We appreciators [of fiction] also participate in games of make-believe..."[21] The salient element of Walton's theory is "personality," which "activates psychological mechanisms" in the face of fiction so as to bring on "genuine distress."[22] Walton describes at some length a scenario in which a person goes caving: crouching, crawling and, eventually, wriggling deep into an ever-narrowing and lightless tunnel until the passageway is so attenuated as to prevent turning of any sort—and then the caver's lamp fails. Following this story, Walton concludes, "My imagining of the spelunking expedition taps into my actual personality and character. This, I am sure, is why it affects me as it does. It is because of my (dispositional) claustrophobia that I find it distressing to imagine slithering on my belly through the cramped passages of a cave."[23] An individual, continues Walton, awakes her dispositional nature through an active process of make-believe, or, more philosophically stated, through mental simulation. The claustrophobic anxiety paradoxically felt in the comfort of an easy chair on the back patio arises naturally, and in a real way (or, at least, a manner that is really felt) from the way her active, mental simulation of the caving scenario awakens, directs, and focuses her own inherent phobia of dark, oppressive spaces. The real feeling, such as it is, is not created by the scenario, but "is a standing (or dispositional) condition which I had all along and which is merely activated and revealed by my imaginative experience."[24]

Walton's "dispositional condition" sounds very much like the Vrindavan devotee's understanding of *bhâv*, which provides the cognitive foundation for emotional experiences of *râs lila* performances. Recall from the previous chapter Swami Fateh Krishna Sharma's discussion of his encounter as a *râs lila* actor with a Bollywood film director. The intense and (apparently) fully-felt emotion in Swami-ji's performance that so impressed the Bollywood director arose, according to Swami-ji, from his own *bhâv*—that is, from his own devotional inclination, which in a real way regarded Krishna's absence as a sorrowful thing. The acting activity in which Swami-ji engaged—the mental simulation or make-believe or what-have-you—stimulated his own dispositional condition so as to produce a real lament with real tears. Perhaps we could similarly discuss the actress playing Andromache who had lost a son of her own, as described in the previous chapter.

What I am reaching for here, however, is not a recapitulation of arguments about Acting, per se, but of Audiencing, especially to suggest that there might not be a reason to distinguish too clearly between the two. Like *râs lila* actors, *râs lila* audiences work rather explicitly to cultivate *bhâv*. Life in Vrindavan and moments of theatre offer devotees opportunities to mentally simulate, in Walton's terms, the *gopis*' experience of Krishna, which provokes devotees' real feelings and, indeed, accounts for their reaction to theatrical performance as real. Audiences in general may be engaged in much the same acting exercise, as is more or less explicit depending upon the degree and quality of the affective experience they manifest. Like *râs lila* audiences, theatre audiences in general approach plays as something in which they can *play*, something which they, too, can experience as participants, even if the play offers no empirical feedback. This relationship between playgoers and plays resembles the interaction between devotees and religious life.

ROLE THEORY OF RELIGIOUS EXPERIENCE

Religious experience is a phenomenon similarly dependent on a particular cultural worldview and the degree to which an individual plays within that worldview. Because of the way in which religious experience may be said to arise from the manner in which individuals order and value what they encounter, often in open disregard of their apparent, physical circumstances, religious experience provides a very useful model for the kind of theatrical experience in which emotional response to fiction arises. Proceeding from William James's premise that religious experience is fundamentally irrational, we can identify a similar paradox in religious experience: whereas with fiction we wonder how we can feel while recognizing pretense, we might wonder, at least from the point of view of an empirical theory of knowledge, how religious experience is at all possible.

One way of approaching the paradox of religious experience is Role Theory, a psychological theory developed by Hjalmar Sundén, once a professor of the Psychology of Religion at the Uppsala University in Sweden. Role Theory understands religious experience as a combination of social and environmental forces with an individuals own propensity for role-playing. The theory that Sundén developed beginning in the late 1950s is not only theatrical in its own terminology and conception, but provides a way of productively reconsidering what theatre audiences undergo. Refocused on theatrical experience itself, Sundén's theory offers a compelling resolution to the Paradox of Fiction by describing in psychological terms the way in which audience members actively contribute to their experience of art.

Sundén's theory, in the first place, rests on the same premise as Weston's argument concerning the paradox of fiction, which is that individuals inevitably seek out ways of making sense of their lives. Weston postulates that this search for sense or meaning accounts for our emotional experience of fiction. Similarly, Sundén suggests that an individual's search for meaning accounts for his or her religious experience, and he conceives a specific psychological mechanism by which the individual proceeds from search to experience.

According to Sundén's Role Theory, individuals attain to religious experiences by way of preparation and participation. Myths—broadly understood as history, legend, scripture, theology, philosophy, and so forth—repeated in the context of religious life provide models and patterns of meaning that individuals may adopt for themselves by identifying with the roles in the myths. As a consequence of this role-playing, individuals prime themselves to experience what their mythical prototypes experience. "If one has therefore learned the narrative [myth] in question…" writes Holm, "one is in possession of a set for specific religious experience. One then carries a latent psychological propensity to experience the world in a religious manner."[25] The myth, then, provides a meaning-generating structure for an individual's experience of life. "If, from the individual's own perspective," continues Holm, "there is a similarity between his own situation and a particular narrative in the holy tradition, the myth, a restructuring phenomenon can occur in that person, so that the mythological reality also becomes reality for the individual in question."[26] Given effective stimuli—present circumstances that seem to correspond with the circumstances of mythic paradigms—the individual who has incorporated those paradigms into his or her worldview responds in the character of an appropriate model, conflating his or her immediate experience with the experience of the mythic role, such that the individual and the role blend.

The effect of the process Sundén proposes is that the individual upon whom such a pattern works comes to order his or her perception of reality in a particular way, and not, necessarily, in accord with an empirical view. What is "real" to the religious individual is that which corresponds to and reinforces the mythic models, as well as the individual's correspondence to the models. At some length, Sundén offers the example of Max Dauthendey, a German national interned by the Dutch on Java at the start of World War I, in whose Bible was found the following note:

> Tosari—Saturday June 30, 1917. In the morning this day when I read the Psalms of David numbers 50 and 60 and insight flashed upon me. I understood that there is a personal God. Three weeks before my fiftieth anniversary I got this revelation.—What a splendid certitude about the goal entered today into my heart, into my spirit, into my body.—God lives, He is a person, and everything lives through Him.[27]

With reference to Dauthendey's journal, Sundén proceeds to interpret the experience in the following way:

> From his diary we learn that Dauthendey was very anxious about his native country, which on June 30th, 1917 had been engaged in a great war for three years. When he came to Psalm 60, which in the Luther-Bible has the heading *Gebet in Kriegszeiten* (or "prayer in times of war"), he found words that he could easily make his own. Doing so, the reading may have changed into a real prayer.... Dauthendey had in fact been in real trouble. He could therefore experience God's "I will come to your rescue" statement as addressed especially to him, and the words he found in Psalm 60 made it easy for him to take the role of the praying man who approached God in this way. What then happened seems to be that God... suddenly enters his perceptual field as a personal presence that gives it new structure.[28]

Dauthendey, then, serves as an example of the way an individual, through his perception of a similarity of circumstances (war), identifies himself with a sanctified model (the Psalmist), and restructures his worldview so as to accommodate the correspondence between himself and the mythic model. The Psalmist experienced a revelation of God, and Dauthendey, by entering into the role of the Psalmist, does too.

We must note, however, that Dauthendey does not come to think of himself as the Psalmist. His perceptual field does not change in such a way that he loses his sense of distance between himself and the writer of the Psalms. For Dauthendey, the Psalmist is still dead, his written words still on the page (even if sacred), the biblical moment still an event removed by history from Dauthendey's immediate circumstances. Dauthendey's experience, then, coexists with a clear and conscious awareness that he has not entered into the Psalmist's relationship with God in any literal way; rather, the experience he has through an association with the Psalmist is distinctly his own.

The individual's anticipation of a particular experience associated with an adopted role tunes the individual to find that experience in his or her own circumstances. This kind of anticipation fulfillment operates in secular as well as spiritual ways. Holm summarizes a decidedly secular example, frequently cited by Sundén.

> In Northern Sweden the criminal police received knowledge of a criminal league from Finland which was wreaking havoc on the Swedish coast. A search party set out. It was discovered that a wrecked cottage had been broken into and that the thieves had stolen a couple of rifles, together with ammunition. A rowing boat had also disappeared. The latter was discovered on an island. Therefore the thieves were also probably present on the island. The search party disembarked and moved forward over the open countryside. Suddenly the commander leapt behind a rock for shelter. He had seen a man pointing a gun at him. He waited for the whistle of bullets, but nothing happened. Finally, he got up and searched carefully over the terrain. He found a beer-bottle lying on the ground, with the neck pointed toward him, and this shape corresponded to an element in the preparedness that the commander had built up: the gun barrel which he had been expecting to see.[29]

Here, the commander's training as a police officer, his experience in the profession, the circumstances of this case, cooperated to fuel a specific anticipation that his immediate environment easily fulfilled. And we find in this particular case something not unlike the Eww-Effect, as the commander reacted to a beer bottle as though it had been a rifle.

Of course, this commander's fear for his own, real life, such as theatrical audience members never experience, contributed in a unique and significant way to the misperception; nor was the commander simultaneously faced with explicit frames of fabrication, such as theatrical audiences generally face. If applied to theatre and audiences simply to say that, by entering roles that correspond with stage characters, audience members anticipate stage action in such a way that finding the means of fulfilling those expectations is almost inevitable, Role Theory does not contribute to the discussion of the paradox of fiction beyond the conventional understanding of "suspension of disbelief."

But by further distinguishing between "role-taking" and "role-adopting," Sundén provides an additional way of thinking about what audiences do, and, consequently, about the nature of their experience. For Sundén, not only does the religious individual *take* the role of a counterpart in myth (thus anticipating the role's experience), but the same individual also *adopts* the role of God, which is to say that the individual incorporates the perspective of that figure to which is attributed the power to fulfill the expectations of the mythic role. This understanding of the dual aspects of roles develops from the interactionist model of sociology and psychology, which reasons that identity is partly constructed through an individual's understanding of how others perceive him or her. According to this model, an individual role-plays especially as a mechanism of self-examination. "Through role-play, the child for example is able to enter into the experience of how others perceive it," Holm explains. "The child can be both child and mother in one and the same game. By means of such games, the child learns to internalize other people's evaluations of itself. The child, in other words, acquires its conscious knowledge of generalized others."[30] What this means for Sundén's theory is that dual perceptions characterize religious experience.

> [The] individual *takes the role* of the human party in a mythical role play, and simultaneously *adopts* God's role, which unconsciously structures perception so that what happens around the individual is actually experienced as the action of God. For a brief instant, the person can quite concretely experience the action of God. A *phase shift* has taken place, and the individual field of perception has become structured by a mythical role.[31]

In this way, the individual's perception of the ontological reality of God is partly a consequence of inhabiting God's point of view with respect to the mythic model at the same time as inhabiting the mythic model itself, which the individual has identified with his or her situation. Wikström describes the process in this way: "[When] someone *takes* the role of a human in a text, he *adopts* or anticipates the role of 'the Other.' He will expect that God will act towards him in his actual situation in the same manner as God acted towards the figure he identified with in the text.... When the religious frame of reference is active, there is a readiness to perceive reality in an alternative way."[32] Not only does the police commander take the role of "target" while searching the countryside, but he adopts the role of "sniper," a point of view that restructures his perception. Not only does Dauthendey take the role of the Psalmist, he adopts the role of God in response to his own dire circumstances and pleas, and doing so reconfigures his reality.

Margaret Case's account of the Vrindavan event in which Krishna appeared in the form of a black beetle, detailed in a previous chapter, may also be read in the terms of role theory. The familiarity with scriptural precedent had, by those present at the event and their eagerness to enter into the world of scriptural pattern, facilitated a fluid shift of perception, so that, in this occasion of communal worship, Krishna appeared very literally in the form of a wayward beetle. The same Vaishnava community makes a similar shift on occasions of theatre. There is no paradox in the experience of devotees, for whom the stage action is both theatre and reality at the same time. As I have argued earlier, the environment of Vrindavan is a scriptural paradigm, and it very overtly trains residents—actors and audience alike—to inhabit the paradigm as suitable characters. Attending *râs lila* theatre, devoted patrons very actively seek to align their *bhâv*, their attitude, their consciousness with the *bhâv* of Krishna's childhood friends, so as to see Krishna as scripture avers they saw him.

One of the important stories in the *râs lila* repertoire concerns Shiva's interest in Krishna. At one time, Shiva developed a consuming interest in seeing Krishna's late-night carousing with his girlfriends, but could not transgress the cosmic law that grants access to Krishna's roistering to women alone. So Shiva turned himself into a woman. In one dramatization of this story I saw at Jaipur Mandir in November, 2001, a slightly heavy-set actor as Shiva, the divine manifestation of destructive cosmic energy, strode onstage sporting a full, black beard, holding a rather menacing trident, and wrapped in a sari. In myth, Shiva's transformation goes much deeper. Emerging from the river Yamuna, Shiva became, in fact, a woman; and only on account of this literal transformation did he gain direct vision of Krishna's nighttime rowdydow.[33]

Devotees regard Shiva's self-transformation in this myth as a model for the kind of inner transformation that devotion requires. Vasant Yamadagni connects Shiva's transformation with an audience member's development of *bhâv*. "The audience takes on the *bhâv* of the *gopi*s, not their physical form," he says, "and this is no less than what Shiva did."[34] A person can watch the play, and see actors stumbling through a story, in which case one's feeling is not affected and the paradox of fiction does not arise. Or a devotee can see Krishna and his girlfriends revealing supernal truth, and enter into that world with all the feeling appropriate to it. The latter circumstance depends on a transformation of self on the same order as Shiva's. The play affects the devotee through the mechanism of the character he or she has adopted and brought to the performance. The orientation of a devotee's consciousness that allows for the perception of the stage action as a manifestation of Krishna's divine *lila* depends upon his identification with a character approved in tradition as a witness, the *gopi*s being chief among them.

An adaptation of the *astayama lila* ("Play of Eight Periods") makes clear just how much a *râs lila* audience actively contributes to a performance. In October, 2001, Purushottam and Srivatsa Goswami staged at Jaisingh Ghera an eight-day dramatization of the eight periods of Krishna's typical day, presenting in roughly three-hour blocks—one per day—Krishna's ritual cycle of waking, eating, washing, bathing, and so on. Each of the eight periods coincided on stage with its corresponding time of day, one each day, until after eight days the twenty-four-hour cycle was complete. The first installment, then, concerned the period of sleep until morning, and the curtain rose around 2 AM. Swami Fateh Krishna Sharma and his *râs lila* troupe's musicians provided the musical accompaniment for the performance, which displayed extravagant sets of flowers and greenery designed especially by Purushottam's son Srivatsa. In these respects there was nothing particularly unusual about this *astayama lila*.[35]

But there were no actors. While Swami-ji musically narrated the scene, describing through a combination of devotional poetry and classical music the transcendent qualities of Krishna and the world around him, Krishna and Radha became evident among the flora of the set. Swami-ji narrated the action between Krishna and Radha, but both alike remained stock still. Swami-ji provided dialogue between the two, but the characters themselves were mute. In this eight-day celebration of Krishna's daily cycle, the lead roles were assumed by Krishna and Radha themselves: the images from Purushottam's household shrine. As their movement from one part of the stage to another was necessary, male members of the Goswami family—acting in the capacity of temple priests—moved them, and fulfilled other functions essential to each individual daily period, such as providing food. Altogether, the cyclic performance took on the character of an elaborate ritual. The ashram's official publicity took the position that this version replicated the "original" *râs lila* form, which is not likely in light of the available evidence.[36] The significant thing in this performance was the emphasis it placed on the audience to construct Krishna's and Radha's immanence on stage. Without the slightest "acting" cue on the part of the lead characters, the audience of the *astayama lila* nevertheless saw in them the actual presence of Krishna and Radha, no less real for not moving nor speaking for themselves.

Thus, we see in this *astayama lila* the way a *râs lila* audience assumes its own role in a *lila* performance. Perhaps a few audience members engage in some form of formal meditation like *râgânugâ bhakti sâdhana*, such as David Haberman analyses in *Acting as a Way of Salvation*, and take advantage of a *râs lila* performance like this *âstâyama lila* in the course of their meditation,[37] but the majority of *râs lila* patrons are simply devotees, who, nevertheless, become actors for the course of a *râs lila* on account of the *bhâv* they have developed in devotional living. Whatever gaps exist in a *râs lila* actor's characterization will be filled by the audience's own spiritual proclivities to complete the transformation of stage action into otherworldly action. The audience must themselves be characters in the drama in order to perceive the divine drama through the staged scene.

Donna Wulff, writing of the way in which Rupa Goswami characterizes ideal devotion, describes the theatricality of Krishna devotion in this way:

> In his [Rupa's] works the devotee is represented not only as witnessing the eternal drama of Kṛṣṇa and Râdhâ, but also assuming universalized roles in relation to the Lord. On this basis one might characterize Gauḍîya Vaiṣṇava religious life as essentially play-acting.... For Gauḍîya Vaiṣṇavas, the *lîlâ* of Kṛṣṇa with Râdhâ and the others is metaphysically real: what appears to be play-acting from the perspective of the ordinary mundane world is from a different vantage point participation in the eternal drama that is ultimate reality.... Correspondingly, the Gauḍîya Vaiṣṇava ideal for the religious life is perpetual absorption in the divine *lîlâ*. As we have seen, the *bhakta*'s consciousness of that *lîlâ* is enhanced through participation in group practices...especially through drama, whether enacted physically or envisioned mentally.[38]

When audience members attend *râs lila* performances, they are already living in an explicit condition, which conflates their own circumstances with the stage action. So, a twelve-year-old boy, as easily as a black beetle, *is* Krishna, and what happens to him on the stage really happens. In this way, a *râs lila* audience assumes the bulk of the responsibility for the effectiveness of a performance, which seems to distinguish the *râs lila*'s interaction of play and audience from the interaction in typical Western theatre.

Generally speaking, Western dramatic performance, at least of the last century, expects the actor to generate (by skill, training, talent, inspiration, or whatever means at his or her disposal) the world of the play, and to dynamically draw the audience into that world.[39] The degree to which Olivier *is* Hamlet is a function of the deportment of Olivier. The Stanislavskian System developed precisely to better equip actors to assume this responsibility. And not only the so-called realistic forms of Western theatre rely on the actor as their means of cogency. Artaud, Brecht, Grotowski, and Bogart all put actors at the center of their theories of performance. The degree to which Weigel's scream directs our attention to the crime of human inconstancy is a function of Weigel's own asserted aspect. The dependency of theatrical performance on actors is not unreasonable. Since the actor is the medium by which dramatic narrative generally occurs, he therefore seems the natural instrument to vivify that narrative.

However, as we have seen, the development of character in Stanislavskian acting depends upon the actor's self. In performance, the basis of an actor's characterization—the substance of her *acting*—must reveal itself ultimately as an authentic part of what her audience regards as their own, audience-perspective existence. Consequently, the truest performances—or, perhaps better said, the most effective even according to the terms set by Stanislavskian acting itself—are those in which the acting, as such, is most deftly cracked so as to reveal something that transcends the acting.

Given this understanding of Stanislavskian acting in practice, acting in the *râs lila* theatre is not so different, drawing out as it does the System's dependence on an actor's self to its logical conclusion. The stage actors who convey the dramatic narrative of the performance do not also bear the responsibility to quicken that narrative. The degree to which Uma-ji *is* Krishna in a *râs lila* performance is not a function of Uma-ji's acting, but of the audience's. Which is not to say that *râs lila* actors do not *perform* to any degree. As I have shown, *râs lila* actors do perform, and do train for their performing in ways similar to adherents of Stanislavskian programs, albeit somewhat inadvertently. But the actors' training is of the same sort as that of any *râs lila* audience member, just as the actors' acting during the moments of performance is of the same order as the audience's. Thus, the actor and the audience member at a *râs lila* performance are of one sort, oriented at the same angle with respect to the action of the play.

ROLE THEORY BEYOND RELIGION

When applied to the paradox of fiction as manifest in theatre, Role Theory may suggest that what is explicit in the theatre of Braj may be unavoidably implicit in other theatre traditions. We can read dramatic literature as scripturally paradigmatic and fictional characters, dramatic characters, as enjoying an ontological status similar to the roles of Sundén's theory. An audience member takes and adopts roles relevant to stage action in a way similar to the subjects of religious experience. Certainly, for the believer, the biblical Abraham is more real than Mercutio. But historical existence is not the issue here. The act of reading the Bible itself does not bring Abraham to immediate and tangible life for the reader, whatever his or her position with regard to Abraham's historicity. For the reader, Abraham is absent, removed from perception. Nor, as Sundén conceives it, is a religious experience that arises from reading Genesis even conceptually an experience of Abraham's existence, but it is an experience of God through the model of Abraham's experience of God, as available solely through the text and the cultural tradition of the text. Consequently, since none of them is any more present than another in the reader's or the spectator's experience, Krishna, Abraham, and Mercutio enjoy a similar status, and we can interpret each as a facilitator of Sundén's theoretical process. When we do, we see that the audience may similarly identify with Mercutio and his dramatic circumstances so as to associate them with the audience member's own circumstances.

Taking, in the first place, Mercutio's role, the audience member enters into a condition of anticipation, expecting the pattern to come to a conclusion and associating the pattern with his or her own circumstances in such a way as to develop meaning both for the stage action and for his or her personal situation. Simultaneously, the audience member adopts a role that the pattern suggests stands in a transcendent position enabling it to fulfill the pattern's expectations. Given the audience member's consciousness of the fabrication of the dramatic circumstances, this role inevitably emerges as the forces of the playhouse itself, embodied in the playwright, the director, the actors—those involved in the artistry of the production—so that the audience member's emotional experience arises, à la Sundén's religious experience, from the audience member's dual identity as a subject of circumstances (a Mercutio type) and as a creator of circumstances (an artist). By integrating the model with a sense of power over the model, the audience member unifies the fictional world and his or her empirical world so as to enter a "phase shift" in which "the individual field of perception has become structured by a mythical role."[40] At this point, the reality of the play and the reality of the theatre are blended. Insofar as the audience member believes his or her own living circumstances to be *real*, when those circumstances mingle with the circumstances of the play there is, in fact, a cognitive basis for the audience member's tearful belief, just as religious experience develops from the blending of empirical and spiritual realities.[41] Art and spirituality occupy similar positions in both types of experience, as the individual subject actively constructs (even if only on a temporary basis) a legitimate understanding of what is happening in his or her field of perception.

What Sundén's Role Theory gives us is a sense of how actively an audience contributes to a theatrical production. The individual comes to religious experience as the object of cultural conditioning, to be sure, but ultimately only as a consequence of his or her propensity for playing with—and *in*—that conditioning. Certain activities such as scripture reading, prayer, and ritual explicitly assist the individual's play and provide reflexive reinforcement for the individual's sense of a role's legitimacy, so as to facilitate the phase shift by which the individual, as the protagonist, plays out a mythic pattern. Theatre (usually) does not offer such explicit assistance to audience members. But theatre audiences similarly approach productions from a position of cultural conditioning (to which theatre itself contributes), and, in their uncomfortable seats beneath the exit signs, enter into play that combines both the world inside the production and the world of the theatre. In this way, theatrical experience *is* religious experience. Both seem to defy reason, and both develop through the same mechanism, which is the audience's creative activity. Emotional experience of theatre, the kind that seems to be at odds with a production's explicit fabrication, is, thus, less the consequence of the production itself—its realism, style, expression, the peculiar power of its *artistry*—than it is the result of the production's harmony with an individual audience member's worldview and that individual's peculiar propensity for play.

ROLES AND REAL PLAY

The way in which *râs lila* performances affect their audiences depends much more on their audiences than on their haphazard, and entirely unrealistic, performance style. *Râs lila* performances are a function of the uninterrupted life of devotion in Braj, the essential nature of which is itself dramatic, as shown in the previous chapter. The *real* play going on in Vrindavan is Vrindavan itself, framed as such from *real* life outside Vrindavan by the peculiarities of Vrindavan devotion, exhibiting a wholly congruous internal consistency, of which the *râs lila*, with all its fits and starts, is a part. The lapses in focus on the part of the *râs lila* child actors and the other characteristic clumsiness, which seem inconsistent with an audience's capacity for emotional identification, foil only those whose "dispositional condition" is not tuned to the eternal play of Krishna that Braj manifests. Vrindavan audiences, like other religious groups, not only regard divine activity as theatrical, but see the mundane, physical world as a play within that play. Consequently, devotees see physical life and its problems and paradoxes from a perspective resembling that of a theatre audience that watches a play apart from and transcending the mundane details, and in which the contradictions and paradoxes of mundane life are reconciled.

Consider Bottom in Shakespeare's *A Midsummer Night's Dream*. In this play, Bottom the character assumes the role of an actor himself playing a character in a play. During the performance of this meta-play in *Midsummer*'s fifth act, Bottom proves himself a comically undisciplined actor by insistently breaking from his adopted performance role to explain the action of his play to his play's audience, composed of characters in *Midsummer* like himself. Bottom's micro-audience of *Midsummer* characters, the nobility of Athens, point out his failings as an actor, mercilessly. And yet, Bottom's lack of Stanislavskian concentration in his role, his apparent inability to keep his own Bottom identity channeled into a plausible and unbroken representation of Pyramus, which causes such consternation among the Athenian nobles, is not regarded by the macro-audience of *Midsummer* as any such thing. The macro-audience for whom Bottom and the Athenian spectators alike are "characters" of an order similar to Pyramus do not perceive in Bottom's haphazard performance as Pyramus any break in the consistency of the *Midsummer* world itself. *Midsummer*'s macro-audience understands Bottom's thespian shortcomings to be a coherent piece of *Midsummer*'s internal action: the play's *play*. If Theseus, Lysander, Hermea, and the remaining members of *Pyramus and Thisbe*'s Athenian micro-audience were to reorient their perception of Bottom's performance so that they appreciated it from the point of view of George, Herbert, Susan, and other members of the Utah Shakespeare Festival's macro-audience, they would find themselves much less disturbed by the inconsistencies of Bottom's behavior.

In fact, so reoriented, Theseus and his retinue might find Bottom's performance particularly effective. As a sixth-grader, I played a root-beer pitch man in a school play. The school's principal was drafted to play himself, as the skeptical consumer for whom the television-style spiel was beneath consideration. He was a poor actor; though he was required only to be himself on stage, he was unable to play straight or consistently. But his bit elicited the most direct and appreciative in-performance response from the audience, who recognized that Mr. Maag was an outsider to the performance, knew that he was only playing himself, and saw in the cracks in Mr. Maag's acting the *real* Mr. Maag—that is, the categorical

Mr. Maag who inhabited the audience's own reality. In a high school production of *A Funny Thing Happened on the Way to the Forum* I attended, a pillar that detached from the upper floor of one of the set's Roman houses nearly smashed Marcus Lycus, alone on stage, and in full view of the audience. The actor elicited an uproarious response by looking at the cardboard pillar at his feet, looking up at the balcony from which it fell, and looking to his audience in deadpan and shrugging his shoulders. In this case, the audience took delight in seeing the *real* actor—that poor schmuck who lived in the audience's world in which rehearsals could not prevent disaster—cracking through the persona of Marcus Lycus. In these two cases, what the audience seemed to appreciate was a sort of metaphysical orientation toward the stage action that the actors and audience held in common.

So well for comedy, in which such breaks of character are at least excusable if not laudable. But even ponderous drama can be an instrument through which audience and performers together transcend the circumstances of the play. In the case of the actress playing Andromache, mentioned in the previous chapter, the *real* actress and her own grief over her own lost child apparently cracked her performance. Since what showed through those cracks fit the tenor of the performance, the cracking did not reveal itself to the audience as the *real* actress; however, the cracks nevertheless provided the avenue by which the actress's *real* emotion could inform the performance and directly engage the audience as a quality transcending the always obviously fraudulent action of the play. The actor in these cases joins the audience as players observing a play.

Of course, this kind of cracking does not necessarily support the intent of a production. Marvin Carlson notes the way Spalding Gray's own persona affected a 1988 Lincoln Center production of *Our Town*. According to Carlson, the way Gray himself cracked through his character in delivering Wilder's line *Nice town, y'know what I mean?* "converted [the line] into a modern, ironic, cynical put-down, and the sentimental nostalgia that drives the play was constantly disrupted."[42] As a case in point, what apparently most affected the audience here, most *truly* spoke to it, was Gray the actor cracking through the Stage Manager's line. Bottom's asides are not in the service of *Pyramus and Thisbe*, but are Shakespeare's omnipotent reach toward the *Midsummer* audience; and Gray's cynicism (intended or not) may not serve a traditional rendering of *Our Town*, but speaks truly to an audience observing the action of *Our Town* as the plainly fabricated action it is. Gray and Bottom both reveal something that transcends the small environment of the play on the stage.

If we reorient our own audience-perspective, we can regard the apparently undisciplined performances of *râs lila* actors in the same way. When viewed from the macro-viewpoint of Krishna's eternal play, rather than from the micro-viewpoint of individuals at a show, the missed cues, the clumsy dancing, the giggling and fidgeting, even the old woman trapped in the upstage scenery, are all of one piece, not at all inconsistent with Stanislavsky's demands for an "unbroken line" of concentration intended to maintain an illusion of plausible reality on stage. Consequently, the devotee audience experiences and interacts with *râs lila* dramatic action as categorically *real*. And so we see the audience members who laugh, cry, shout, swoon, and tremble while actors re-pin their costumes, clean their fingernails, trip, and crack-up. In fact, *bhakti*, through highly disciplined practices, such as identified by Haberman, and through simple, day-to-day life, seeks to reorient the perspective of devotees in just this way, so that all action is stage action—the *râs lila* actor is truly Krishna, and the passing beetle is too.

The fact that the *râs lila* actors do not have to *do* much more than show up, while the performance goes on as an expression of absolute reality, indicates that the audience here has openly assumed in place of the actors much of the Stanislavskian responsibility to generate the realistic plausibility of the performance—a responsibility that the Western audience believes is almost entirely borne by the actor. The devotional life of Vrindavan orients the audience's relative point of view by revealing the comprehensive and pervasive quality of Krishna's play. This conceptual calibration contextualizes audience and actors, life and play, alike as functions of the same dramatic action. Furthermore, the Stanislavskian schooling inherent in Vrindavan devotion, which audience members receive in common with actors, makes audience members into actors of equal participation in the *râs lila* performance. Because of their own lives in the theatrical Vrindavan environment, patrons of the *râs lila*, as well as the actors, know how to live through a part and actively engage themselves accordingly in performances.

It may be that *râs lila* audiences and their religious experience tell us something about our own paradoxical engagement with dramatic fiction. Theatre patronage involves theatrical involvement. The paradox apparent in an audience's authentic emotional complicity with what is clearly fake derives more from that audience's own role-playing than from the artistic quality of the stage performance. Like the *râs lila* audience, the audience that *feels* as part of its encounter of *The Illusion* or *Trojan Women* itself creates much of its own experience, almost independently of the performance;

and, like the religious audience, the secular audience's own cultural conditioning, proclivities, and creative capacities combine in the theatrical moment to compensate for the gap between explicitly fake stage action and the world the audience regards as "real." The rationale for an audience's reaction to stage business as though it were real derives from the collaboration of the audience with the performers on a level that transcends the stage business, and, so, does occur in *reality*.

7. Conclusion

The Enlightenment killed God, and though religion does not depend on God's survival, it came through the Enlightenment hobbled. Religion's inscrutability set it against the eighteenth-century drive to comprehend, and did not find redemption among the genuine mysteries of Romanticism that further alienated the individual from the world and from his fellow man. In the twentieth century, religion in the West endures as a relic, the object of modern civilization's attachment to the roots of its culture, and postmodern civilization's disposition to approve anything without commitment. Religion now clings to Western culture as a curiosity, a peculiar quality that defies the conditions of contemporary life but will not disappear. In fact, the experience that sustains religion may not be so strange, so at odds, with modern life. At least, religious experience may not be any more strange, any more at odds, with modern life than other apparently groundless experiences that Western culture not only accommodates, but appreciates. *Râs lila* patrons little distinguish between the religious and the aesthetic: Krishna is an artist. The theatrical performance is of a piece with everything else as the product of Krishna's artistry, and the experience of the artistry of the performance is indistinguishably an encounter with Krishna. An individual's aesthetic experience of a performance of *Streetcar Named Desire* may not be an encounter with the Judeo-Christian God, but the mystery of the experience runs as deep. It is not merely the paradox of the satisfaction we take in something so distinctly unsettling as Blanche's undoing, or of the pleasure we feel in Stanley's brutality. Aesthetic experience per se eludes a coherent rationale, an empirical grounding. The *feeling* I have (if that is what it is) during a performance of *Streetcar*, what occurs between me and a Kandinsky painting, or between me and The Beatles' "When I'm Sixty-Four," is unpredictable because it arises from we-don't-know-where and is almost entirely incommunicable between me and another except through the media of the art in question. The devotee's experience of the icon, the chant, the ritual, circulates in a similar fashion. Religious and aesthetic experience similarly affect us, similarly defy reason, and similarly ground us without grounding. The close and enduring relationship between religion and art runs much deeper than their apparent dependency on each other for subject matter and means of expression. The mysterious experience that sustains each of these phenomena may be fundamentally the same, materializing variously as painting or prayer according to contingent circumstances. "The inner structures of the imagination," writes Harold Bloom, "prevail in religion as they do in poetry."[1]

Postmodernism has been eager to spin out the implications of what seems increasingly to be theatrical life. Van Gennep, Turner, Goffman, and others offer us ways of understanding our experience in theatrical terms. The problem we frequently encounter with thinking about the relationship between religious experience and aesthetic experience—especially aesthetic experience connected with theatre—has been its typically postmodern inclination to regard superficial correspondence as sufficient correlation. Norman A. Bert unpacks the declaration "theatre is actually religion" in this way:

> The myths executed in the theatre take the form of plays, and they are performed through spoken word and action—dialogue and business—, which parallel religious liturgy and ritual. In place of clergy, the theatre uses actors who wear the vestments we call costumes and utilize props in place of the tools of religious ritual. The whole performance takes place in the presence of, and on behalf of a community, the audience, and typically occurs in a theatre specifically constructed for the purpose—the temple of this religious endeavor.[2]

Although legitimate similarities between the performance of religion and theatre, the features Bert identifies are trivial, and may just as well identify the similarity between religion and professional sports. At its heart, Bert's analogy is only analogy, because it is primarily concerned with the elements of performance—costumes and implements—rather than with the activity of the individual. Anthony Kubiak pushes against Bert's premise with the same skepticism: "More than the perception that religion and theatre are connected through the mere act of performance that is common to each, there is something about the ontologies of both... the relationship in religious thought between the perception of the world as an illusion and the perception of the illusion as the real."[3] If, in the postmodern day, theatre is religion, it is on account of the way they operate similarly in the construction of reality, rather than through a cursory correspondence between features of their presentation.

KANT'S LEGACY

Even as it codified the skepticism that weakened the standing of religious experience in Western culture, Enlightenment rationality constructed the footings of an aesthetic appreciation of religious experience. Kant's aesthetic theory, as formulated in the *Critique of Judgment*, makes a very important move toward thinking of religion aesthetically (and vice-versa). Without directly addressing religion itself as a topic, Kant nevertheless opens a realm of possibility by locating aesthetics in the experiencing subject rather than in the experienced object. For Kant, "beauty" does not reside as a quality of an object to be grasped and appreciated by a subject who encounters it. Rather, "beauty" arises as a judgment the subject makes regarding an object, a judgment derived from the subject's "taste," or capacity to evaluate appeal within the context of a community of potential subjects. According to Kant, then, a subject's judgment tells us nothing about the essential character or composition of an object, so much as it tells us something about the subject, distinct from, and not impinging on, the object. The declaration "this object is beautiful," according to Salim Kemal's analysis of Kant's aesthetic theory:

> ...only seems to be about the object. In fact, the important feature of this saying is not about the object, neither the character it has as a result of its particular position in the nexus of determinate causes and natural laws, nor the purposes it can serve. Rather, the judgment 'The object is beautiful' is really an appraisal of the way the *subject's* faculty of taste is satisfied.[4]

Like the proverbial tree falling in the forest, the aesthetic object here is only understood as such by the subject who judges it so; which is to say, the aesthetic quality of an object is arbitrary, rather than essential. "Beauty" is not a feature of an object the way "sharpness" is a feature of a knife, but is an interpretation of a subject's experience of an object, after the fact of the experience. The object itself, as Kemal suggests, "is peripheral to the validity of aesthetic judgements..."[5]

Furthermore, reasons Kant, even though true aesthetic judgments are autonomous, a subject's "taste" is significantly conditioned by his or her place in a community of subjects. What Kant calls the *sensus communis* understands the place that aesthetic judgments have in a subject's moral imperative to regard fellow subjects as subjects, capable of making their own, autonomous judgments. Aesthetic judgments are valid when they can be confirmed by like subjects, so that the making and confirming of aesthetic judgments create, sustain, and promote community and the acknowledgement between subjects of their individual, independent subjectivity. Aesthetic agreement constructs a "community of taste" that does not mandate agreement among autonomous subjects, but, nevertheless, invites agreement and validates independent but like judgments.

One conclusion from the line of reasoning Kant develops about aesthetics is that individuals in communities determine how the experience of objects ought to be read, and independently of any particular qualities the objects may possess. *Râs lila* patrons demonstrate explicitly this Kantian principle in the way they attribute beauty to the often clumsy and haphazard performances of young actors. Beauty may not be an inherent quality of the actors or their performances, but is, rather, a reading of the experience of the performance in accordance with the principles of *bhakti* developed over long years of agreement among individuals in the community of devotees. A second conclusion developing from Kant's assertion that the object does not determine the aesthetic experience is that aesthetic experiences do not depend on any particular objects, but, given a community's confirmation, may attach themselves to anything. There is no objective "class" of beautiful objects, but, rather, a communal, aesthetic disposition of perception. We might consider again the pilgrim walking the *ban yatra*, who, in the midst of a torrential downpour, smiled broadly at David Haberman and declared, "What bliss this is!"[6] Even a potentially miserable object may be experienced as aesthetically pleasurable by an individual, who, in the confidence of the confirmation of a community, levies that judgment. For Kant, the *judgment* is aesthetic: our experience of aesthetically understood pleasure derives from the judgments we make, inspired by, but not contingent on, objects we encounter.

Kant opens Western aesthetics to the possibility that anything may be experienced aesthetically. The object does not determine a subject's aesthetic experience of it, but the encounter with an object (which includes a thoughtful consideration of the nature of the encounter) inspires a judgment, one quality of which is aesthetic pleasure that we experience as such. But if the object does not determine a subject's aesthetic experience, it likewise does not determine that a subject's experience of it be understood aesthetically. The *ban yatra* pilgrim's "bliss" is unquestionably a kind of aesthetic pleasure.[7] That bliss is also, however, a religious pleasure. In Braj, aesthetic and religious experience are not sharply distinguished: Krishna is an artist, and experiences of art are equally of the divine. *Râs lila* performances are both "beautiful" (aesthetic) and "spiritual" (religious) in the same moment, and in such a way that patrons hardly differentiate them. The temple activity (ostensibly religious activity as opposed to ostensibly artistic) similarly blurs the lines between art-experience and religion-experience. By separating experience and object, Kant points modern Western aesthetics in the same direction.[8] Our pleasurable experience of Michelangelo's *Pietà* may derive from a religious as well as an aesthetic judgment. We may similarly understand our experience of Spielberg's *Schindler's List*, or of The Beatles' "When I'm Sixty-Four," religiously, since the nature of these objects are neither determined by our judgments nor determine our judgments.

Furthermore, Kant's distinction between experienced object and experiencing subject provides for his empirical rationale concerning our construction of reality. As nature is a realm of "appearances" given form and meaning only by the categories of an individual's understanding, the character of an individual's experience of an object depends largely on the categories already inherent in the structure of the individual's mind. Thus, to borrow the words of Edgar A. Towne, "the human mind...will conceive of the reality it constructs as...reality itself."[9] In the context of this discussion, the human mind regards an object, and its experience of that object, as aesthetic or as religious in essence, depending on the a priori categories through which its perception of things flows. Theoretically, the categories of the "Braj mind," shaped by a cultural legacy it inherits, by the environment in which it develops, and by the activity it practices, provide for the apprehension of actor and God in one and the same object as reality itself, in a way that is impossible for the "London mind" (or the "Milwaukee mind").

Nevertheless, since Kant, there has been a distinct, though overlooked, tendency in Western thinking to conflate art and religion, to understand religious experience in aesthetic terms. The tendency has been stronger among American philosophers and theologians, perhaps, because, as Harold Bloom asserts, American religion has been more deeply invested in the value of personal experience as a measure of spirituality and religious authenticity.[10] Recent scholarship seems to be especially keen to understand religious experience aesthetically, to characterize spirituality as akin to the way we encounter, experience, and appreciate art.

THE (POST)MODERN REVISION

Facilitated by Kant, the primarily American disposition to speak of art and religion together derives largely from the early nineteenth-century writings of Jonathan Edwards, the primary voice in early America's attention to personal, spiritual experience as central to religion. Edwards sets in motion in the United States the modern, perhaps "modernist," revision of Kant's aesthetics that takes advantage of the line Kant draws between object and subject to validate subjective, personal experience of what must otherwise remain thoroughly transcendent. Like Kant, Edwards insists that beauty is the consequence of sense perception, subjective in the first instance, but conditioned by a "frame of mind" we might correlate with Kant's understanding of the mind's categories.[11] But Edwards can characterize the experience of the beauty as religious, since beautiful objects themselves do not insist on being read aesthetically. The experience of beauty passes through the a priori categories or frames of the mind on its way to comprehension and interpretation, and the structure of Edwards' mind, his "frame of mind," accommodates his experience religiously.

Edwards identifies beauty with God, even understanding God, in a tradition stretching back to Augustine, as "most beautiful."[12] In this respect, his concept keeps God in the world of human sense, almost in spite of the transcendence of God upon which Edwards insists, at least so far as to acknowledge the objects of direct experience from which we apprehend beauty at all. Ultimately, recognizing beauty is a prerequisite of knowing God. In J. Alfred Martin, Jr.'s assessment, "...Edwards and others see the beautiful as the category most naturally linked with the divine, and the esthetic as the most useful notion to employ in further characterization of the religious as such."[13] Edwards acknowledges aesthetic experience, the experience of beauty as such, as an empirical feature of human life, and understands that experience, insofar as the experience is "good," as an indication of supreme goodness.

At the doorstep of Modernism, Edwards retains the Kantian reliance on sense perception as the foundation of experience—both aesthetic and religious—but he looks ahead to an idealistic objectivity that exceeds the contingencies of Kant's *sensus communis*. In the midst of Modernism, John Dewey's idealistic aesthetics similarly try to accommodate our objective experience of nature to a more ineffable condition of perception. Although he wrote explicitly about religion, *A Common Faith* is generally regarded as less well-developed and less significant among Dewey's works. More important are his ideas about art, expressed in such works as *Art As Experience*, especially to the present discussion, since, as William M. Shea has shown, "Dewey's *Art As Experience* is no afterthought to his earlier pragmatism; it is its other side and its consummation."[14]

The essential notion in Dewey—well-articulated by William Shea, whose insightful argument I follow closely below—the notion that brings us a step closer to the (post)modern revision of Kant that hopes to unify religious and aesthetic experience for good, is, perhaps, the very thing that inhibits his writing about religion. Shea asserts that Dewey is "incapable of a constructive interpretation of actual religious languages and institutions."[15] Shea attributes this to Dewey's pragmatism. Esoteric religious beliefs, devotion to the supernatural, and the self-obsession of institutions inhibit genuinely ethical living. Martin concurs, suggesting that Dewey's tolerance of religion was tested by "ineffectual visions of Utopias" and "the religious and human evils of supernaturalism."[16] And yet, Dewey's sense of the aesthetic experience depended on a certain transcendent property, not, certainly, *supernatural*, per se, but not purely empirical either. Following Peirce, Dewey writes of aesthetic experience as having *quality*, a kind of character—even a *mood*—inherent to the experience, which the human subject perceives and appreciates, and through which the human subject understands. *Quality* is not an aspect of an aesthetic object, though it imbues the object and the whole circumstance it shares with a subject. In fact, *qualities* qualify all experience, but are "best experienced, directly and focally, in aesthetic experience."[17] That is, for Dewey, aesthetic experience does not arise strictly from the judgment levied by a subject, but "exists" in a nonmaterial way in the situation that includes an object and a subject.

Dewey's phenomenological aesthetic seems to depart from Kant by imputing something intangible to an object and its environment that is apart from the judgment of the subject. In fact, in spite of himself, Dewey recognizes just how "religious"—how other-worldly—his aesthetic theory is by identifying aesthetic experience with religious mysticism. "I have had occasion to speak more than once," Dewey writes in *Art As Experience*, "of a quality of an intense esthetic experience that is so immediate as to be ineffable and mystical."[18] It is not that Dewey accepted the concepts of God and transcendence of traditional mysticism, but that he accepted the legitimacy of experience *as it is experienced*, after all, "things are what they are experienced to be…"[19] The religious quality through which a mystic experiences God's presence corresponds in subjective terms with the aesthetic experience of the "whole," of existence as unified and complete (although existence could never be so condensed). Both mysteries defy reason but present themselves undeniably in direct, if noncognitive, experience.

In addition to articulating a clear, rather modernist correspondence between aesthetic and religious experience, Dewey formulates the beginning of a markedly postmodern understanding of the relationship between art and religion. Most importantly to Dewey, the aesthetic experience is *consummatory*. This means, first, that, like mysticism, the aesthetic experience provides a sense of the totality of nature, the unity and wholeness of existence. But, besides this more or less passive quality, the aesthetic experience, like mysticism, has an active aspect. Both experiences adjust individual perception and individuals themselves. Writing specifically of religion in *A Common Faith*, Dewey asserts that religious experience modifies a person: "There is a composing and harmonizing of the various elements of our being such that, in spite of changes in the special conditions that surround us, these conditions are also arranged, settled, in relation to us."[20] An obvious extension of his pragmatism, his interest in religion that changes the world of nature in positive ways, Dewey unmistakably characterizes the religious individual itself here as an artistic work. Religious experience has the capacity to fashion the individual and her sense of nature around her, not at all unlike aesthetic experience, which "adjusts" people to their natural environment, to the sense of the totality of their environment, and especially to "further adjustment through struggle."[21] On this account, Shea asserts that, although Dewey himself did not say as much explicitly, "Religion," for Dewey, "is an art."[22]

We can follow Shea's explication of Dewey just a little further to see the way Dewey anticipates the postmodern condition. Dewey's primary concern, of course, is making the world a better place. The "consummation" in religious and aesthetic experience—while "had"—is never conclusive since neither nature nor experience "ends"; rather, the consummatory experience drives our interaction with the world. "The vision must become an instrument of further vision...consummation is followed by action for the sake of further consummation."[23] That is, under the influence of religious and aesthetic experience, and seeking an ultimate consummation that eludes us, we act to transform our world so as to sustain the consummatory experience, to live in it.

Dewey's modernist interest in changing the world and his understanding of the instrumentality of experience to this end has a distinctly postmodern tone. The most recent artistic and intellectual period has been obsessed with nature, the world, with reality not as an objective thing but as a construction, with art and aesthetics as the principal agents—or culprits—behind reality's instability. Religion is often regarded as inimical to the postmodern ethic for insisting too strongly on ontological stability, definitive truth, and transcendent authority (the very things, incidentally, that alienated Dewey from institutional religion). But the tendency to recognize the affinity between types of experience—as opposed to, say, institutional dogma—features prominently in all sorts of thinking in this recent age that so eagerly seeks out and so readily accepts the interplay between ostensibly dissimilar phenomena. Accordingly, postmodern thinking has persistently acknowledged religious experience and, in a Deweyan sort of way, has conflated it with aesthetic experience as a mechanism of individual expression and of world construction.

IMAGINATION

Rather than in analogous components—costumes, stages, dialogue, and so on—theatre is religion (and vice-versa) in the similar means they both provide for shaping reality. The *râs lila* provides its devotee patrons with *playing space* in which they can live their ideal identities, through which, in turn, they make their world ideal. The similarities of costume and dialogue and so forth between an *abhishek* ritual in Radharama Temple and an *astayama lila* performance in Jaisingh Ghera's theatre are only objectifications or projections of their devotee patrons' intentional and active moves toward ideal life. That this ideal is culturally specific only confirms where the intersection of theatre and religion lies. The same playing spaces function differently—or not at all—for non-devotees, even though the similarities of costume and action remain. *Râs lila* performances and *bhakti* demonstrate explicitly something that postmodern thinking is still to understand: given the complicity of patrons, theatrically aesthetic experience and religious experience both involve a subject's perception, through which they both facilitate the subject's construction of the reality in which he lives, either momentarily or enduringly. The subject's experience is the thing, which Hamlet knew in spite of how he said it.

Developing Hjalmar Sundén's role theory as presented in the previous chapter, Jan van der Lans asserts an understanding of religious experience against the dominant, twentieth-century conceptions that involve objective cognition, feelings, and formalistic behavior, manifest in the work of William James and Rudolph Otto. "[The] concept 'religious experience'..." van der Lans suggests in opposition, "refers neither to an emotional state nor to religious behavior as such. It refers to a perceptual process.... the altered perception of the object-world."[24] This sort of religious experience is clear enough in Braj where the temple image is divine. We find the same kind of experience in the West, where certain devotees, we can confidently say, in a ritual such as the Catholic mass, perceive what seems—according to empirical data—to be there (wine) as something altogether different (the blood of Jesus), and *phenomenologically* so.

This discrete experience of the Eucharist is distinct from the ethics, feelings, commitments, and formalistic behavior of religious living, and is what informs Friedrich Schleiermacher's opinion that religion is based on our faculty of aesthetic appreciation.[25] The same experience is cunningly similar to a certain theatre-goer's perception of blood, where there is no blood, as *phenomenologically* on an actor's finger. The aesthetic experience here consists primarily of a perceptual alteration reminiscent of Martin Luther's assertion that faith "sees where nothing is to be seen, feels when there is nothing to be felt," as theatrical an understanding of religious faith as ever was formulated.[26] But the aesthetic experience is not limited to the transformation of objects any more than the devotee's experience of the mass is limited to the way the Eucharist appears. In aesthetic experience, as in religious, our apprehension of the whole changes and changes the whole. The mass can become pervaded by such a quality that the host is only of a piece with a situation that a devotee understands as sacred—a world objectively, empirically fraught with the spirit of God.

Nor is this kind of religious experience limited to the intentional, sculpted environments of temple and ritual. Consider the religious experience in routine circumstances that Alister Hardy relates in *The Spiritual Nature of Man*:

> One day I was sweeping the stairs down in the house in which I was working, when suddenly I was overcome, overwhelmed, saturated, no word is adequate, with a sense of most sublime and living LOVE. It not only affected me, but seemed to bring everything around me to LIFE. The brush in my hand, my dustpan, the stairs, seemed to come alive with love.... So utterly and overwhelmingly wonderful that one knew at once what the saints had grasped.[27]

Hardy, seemingly without prompt, suddenly perceives his situation in a wholly different way, unimposed by the situation itself, but evident in every minute, mundane object. He sees his situation not as the arrangement and function of objects, but as a manifestation of divine principle. Our situations, similarly, can become *beautiful*. Compare Hardy's basement experience with art critic Arthur Danto's description of the transformation of an American street corner:

> I have the most vivid recollection of standing at an intersection in some American city waiting to be picked up. There were used-car lots on two corners, with swags of plastic pennants fluttering in the breeze and brash signs proclaiming unbeatable deals, crazy prices, insane bargains. There was a huge self-service gas station on a third corner, and a supermarket on the fourth, with signs in the window announcing sales of Del Monte, Cheerios, Land o Lakes butter. Long Island ducklings, Velveeta, Sealtest, Chicken of the Sea.... Heavy trucks roared past, with logos on their sides. Lights were flashing. The sound of raucous music flashed out of the windows of automobiles. I was educated to hate all this. I would have found it intolerably crass and tacky when I was growing up an aesthete.... But I thought, Good heavens. This is remarkable![28]

Danto's perception of his environment—very mundane and even, at other times, repulsive—changes so that the "crass" signs for tuna fish and processed cheese, in conjunction with all the other elements of the situation, sparkle with new, unexpected force sufficiently stunning as to be best expressed by the subject with a meaningless exclamation.

Hardy and Danto characterize their experiences differently, as religious and as aesthetic, respectively, though their experiences coincide in many ways, especially with respect to their perception of ordinary objects as charged with new, surprising, and even strange significance. Their diverse readings attest not only to the understanding of such experiences as subject-centered, in the first place, but to the common root and common mechanism of development in religious and aesthetic experience. Returning to Kant, the "first moment" of aesthetic experience consists of a subject's self-assessment, rather than of an insight into the nature of an object. The sense of the beauty of an object, writes Salim Kemal in his explication of Kant, "is really an appraisal of the way the *subject's* faculty of taste is satisfied.... Every aesthetic judgement, then, of the form 'This is beautiful,' is really a disguised expression of the subject's feeling of pleasure or displeasure or 'of life.'"[29] Like the object of experience—the dustpan or the tuna advertisement—which does not "possess" a quality of beauty, the experience itself is without an essential quality. Though the experience may be "had," in the Deweyan sense of the sensing the whole that includes the subject and object, the *meaning* of the experience, which includes its aesthetic and/or religious character, only follows in a subsequent moment. Caroline Franks Davis asserts that religious experience—which, for her, may include aesthetic experience—only follows interpretation as such. "Experiences such as ecstasy, being in love, deliverance from danger or despair, aesthetic experiences, and inspiration must all be given a religious incorporated or reflexive interpretation if they are to count as 'religious experiences.'"[30] What Davis says of religious experience seems equally applicable to aesthetic experience. Beauty, or all those things implied by Danto's exclamation "This is remarkable!," must be given a reflexive interpretation in order to be regarded as aesthetic. No doubt, were their circumstances exchanged, Danto would have found Hardy's dustpan beautiful, and Hardy would have found love in the tuna advertisement.

This is not to deny the substantiality of the experience itself, any more than noting that two people separately finding the moon frightening and beautiful denies the existence of the moon. In John Searle's philosophical terms, experiences like Hardy's and Danto's, like the moon, have intrinsic factuality insofar as something *happens*. The experience also has something like Searle's "observer-relative" quality insofar as it inherits an ontological subjectivity from a subject.[31] In fact, the kinds of distinct experiences we *can* identify as aesthetic or religious (or both) submit to this characterization because of the teleological role they can play in affirming, reaffirming, and even constructing the world we live in.

Which brings Kant a last time to our discussion. Kant's doctrine of "disinterestedness" avers that aesthetic judgments depend on a subject's disregard for the utility, or teleological possibilities, of objects. The aesthetic distance involved in this doctrine, which gives a subject to appreciating an object apart from any uses it may have, adapts an object to be seen as other than it is or is intended. Kemal's indication of the implications of Kant's thought on this matter bring Danto's and Hardy's experiences to mind: "[We] might even see objects as churches, horses, or buildings...and then find them beautiful so long as we do not suppose that the object is beautiful or ugly *because* it is a church, horse, or building."[32] Nor so long as we think the tuna ad or dustpan is remarkable or full of love *because* it is a tuna ad or dustpan. We can read Danto's and Hardy's extraordinary experiences in a Kantian way, as arising from their momentary vision of the items in their situation as items *in themselves* apart from their mundane uses.

For Kant, the principal human faculty that permits this kind of dissociation is *imagination*, and its employment facilitates the understanding of experience *post facto* as religious and aesthetic by providing the means whereby a subject constructs reality. "The imagination..." writes Kant, "is very mighty when it creates, as it were, another nature out of the material that actual nature gives it.... We may even restructure experience...into something that surpasses nature."[33] Which is to say that while experiences such as Hardy's and Danto's arise from a momentary consideration of objects stripped of *use*, the experiences themselves do have use, as it is the remarkable experience that lends itself to our imagination's determination to remake our environments. The Braj devotee dispenses with the strictly material nature of the temple image, or of the rain on the Braj plain, or of the *rās līlā* actor, so as to experience these objects and phenomena, cognitively, as surpassing nature, so that a world that surpasses nature exists, cognitively, for the devotee. Hardy and Danto disregard the natural character of dustpans and tuna ads so as to experience these objects as hyper-real, reasonably (if not rationally) of a piece with a hyper-real world, cognitively, if only momentarily, perceived. The GC&SU undergraduate in attendance at *The Illusion* passes the literal appearance of classmates in costume so that a hyper-real situation impinges in a physical, visceral way.

That the Braj *bhaktin*'s, Hardy's, Danto's, *et aliorum*, hyper-real worlds do not coincide with respect to interpretive details, nor even, more importantly, with respect to their ultimate quality as religious or aesthetic, attests to the operation of the interpretive frames already at work in the lives of these subjects. The devotee who grows up in Vrindavan, as a *product* of Vrindavan, ingests and assimilates the interpretive mechanisms that read objects, phenomena, and experience together in the context of a hyperreality dominated by the transcendent Krishna. For the devotee, the experience, when it comes, is already always contextualized. Danto, the author of several books of art criticism and aesthetics, including such titles as *Embodied Meanings: Critical Essays and Aesthetic Meditations* and *The Transfiguration of the Commonplace*, clearly lives a life deeply informed, even dominated, by art, to the extent that his experience is ever already contextualized in an aesthetic hyper-world. We can say much the same of Hardy, the author of *The Spiritual Nature of Man: A Study of Contemporary Religious Experience*, whose experience is almost inevitably religious.

Perhaps religion and theatre do resemble each other with respect to their performative elements. But more significantly, religion and art, especially *theatrical* art, *coincide* in the way they both make reality. Luther and the eye that "sees where nothing is to be seen" gives way to Whitehead, who asserted, "the actual world is the outcome of the aesthetic order."[34] Extrapolating the theological tendency, postmodern thinking increasingly reiterates the premise that the reality that individuals inhabit does not derive exclusively from empirical, material stuff, but is no less real for developing from individuals' imaginative construction of their experience.

Take, for instance, the patently postmodern view of reality as expressed by Eugene G. d'Aquili and Andrew B. Newberg in a paper published just as the twentieth century was becoming the twenty-first, based on the interpretation of neurological data. "Suffice it to say," they write, "reality seems to consist fundamentally only of a vivid sense of reality, or, as some would say, reality is constituted by compelling presences."[35] Reiterating a fundamental principal of postmodernism, these two scientists—professionally practicing in psychiatry and radiology—conclude in lines reminiscent both of Dewey's "postulate of immediate empiricism" and of the postmodern President's interrogation of the meaning of *is*:

> ...spiritual and mystical states of reality [which occupy a place on an "aesthetic-religious continuum"] recalled in a baseline state as more certainly representing an objective condition than what is represented in the sensorium of the baseline state must be considered real. There can be no other conclusion

no matter how one comes at it. This may present many problems that must be worked out, but the essential or underlying reality of hyperlucid experiences must be said to be real or the word *reality* has no meaning whatsoever.[36]

Note that d'Aquili and Newberg do not suggest that subjects who recall hyperreal states from "baseline"—that state they define partly as the state "most of us are in at this moment"[37]—*can* recall those states from baseline; which is to say, subjects traverse the boundary without sacrificing their sense of what is real in either state. From baseline to hyperreal and back again, subjects move through realities rather fluidly, so that it should be no particular perplexity nowadays that people can conduct business with each other in the marketplace, pursue experiments in labs, and engage diplomats to argue over territory, while believing in God's grace, Krishna's bliss, and the infinite compassion of Avalokiteshvara.

Perhaps we come to this capacity for movement gradually, and to greater degrees depending on the cultural circumstances that equip us as we develop, but we do move comfortably between the perceptual modes necessary to sustain the various real worlds we inhabit. Perhaps our capacity to move between realities is a particularly postmodern talent. Van der Lans, at least, regards this ability as a particular hallmark of religion today:

> [One] of the characteristics of mature, authentic religiosity is that the individual is able to switch voluntarily from a profane to a religious frame of reference.... At moments when he does not need it the mature religious person is able to inhibit the usual pragmatic construction of reality and to experience reality religiously.[38]

The college student, who shows no sign of delusion or psychosis, who suddenly experiences revulsion at the frankly staged cannibalistic desecration of a corpse is no more a marvel in this postmodern age than the shifts individuals make between religious and mundane modes of perception. Our religion is theatrical and our theatre is religious, where we the subjects find ourselves sliding from state to state, as from reality to reality.

To the extent that they can be thought of as distinct *institutions*, religion and theatre offer the most powerful means of changing states. We fashion the many and varied practices of religion as well as the diverse practices of theatre to sustain departures from what d'Aquili and Newberg call *baseline*. Rituals and worship services, pilgrimages, icon veneration, meditation as well as theatre-going, workshops, script analysis, Stanislavskian acting, Method acting, Brechtian acting, and so on, mediate between the states we seek out. From the point of view of baseline, the theatrical significance of the priest's collar is not that it resembles in function the wig a drag queen dons for a show, but that the collar provides for the priest's role in different states and lends itself to others toward a similar purpose. The drag queen's wig is surely religious for doing the same thing. The ritual that is the *Rocky Horror Picture Show* may be described as religious in the way it resembles the sculpted, scripted participation of ritual. But there is nothing inherently religious about ritual itself, and so the comparison between the *Show* and ritual means little. The ritual is religious when its participants' perception of things alters so as to instigate a shift between cognitive states. The *Show* is genuinely (and undeniably) religious, not to mention *aesthetic*, when it provides an avenue by which participants perceive their situation as something hyperreal.

Such activities and practices are multiplying in the postmodern day in ways that increasingly defy clear distinctions between religion and theatre in the conduct of the activities themselves. Consider the relatively new phenomenon of Massively Multiplayer Online Role-Playing Games. MMORPGs, which depend on the very contemporary development of the Internet, only update humanity's very old inclination to find some alternative in which to live. The supposedly "virtual" worlds of these games intersect with the baseline of participants (dare we say, "devotees") in very complicated ways. In a notorious incident in early 2006, for instance, a group of gamers scattered around the surface of the baseline planet gathered as their virtual characters in the online *World of Warcraft* to hold a virtual funeral for a colleague who had really died (in the baseline world). While thus engaged in cyber-mourning, another group of gamers in their virtual and heavily armed roles descended on the cyber-funeral, slaughtering all the grieving, unarmed participants. Nothing actually *happened* in the baseline state of any of these individuals, but real outrage, anger, despair, and recriminations over this incident blazed in both the baseline and the cyber world. Another MMORPG, *Second Life*, offers gamers opportunities to purchase plots of virtual land so as to cyber-build and conduct cyber-business in a virtual, online economy. However, in recent months, plots of very virtual *Second Life* real estate have been bought and sold for five figure sums of very bankable U.S. currency. Century 21 and Coldwell Banker operate *Second Life* real estate offices—not for the purpose of buying *real* real estate, but real *virtual* estate in the *Second Life* world.

Such distinctly postmodern phenomena are both religious and theatrical, or something else, deeper, of which religion and theatre both are only particular manifestations. Seeking to satisfy an urge to experience, substantively, alternatives to the mundane, phenomenological world, both theatre and religion offer us role-playing opportunities through which we can alter our modes of perception so as to experience real alternatives. Their similar use of our propensity for role-play links religion and theatre indissolubly and connects them together with other secular and spiritual pastimes that also facilitate the development of realities through role-play. Our thinking in coming years about the activities and practices that constitute religion and theatre will have to account for the spirituality of *The Sims* and *Sim City* as much as for the theatricality of monasticism and the mysticism of a darkened theatre. The role-play that is available in emerging technology, as in the artistic and spiritual fixtures of culture, carries subjects to experience in ways that preexist civilization.

Notes

1. INTRODUCTION: *RÂS LILA* THEATRE AND ITS IMPLICATIONS

1. Maharaj-ji traces his lineage back to Narayan Bhatt, a sixteenth-century disciple of Caitanya, a mystic saint revered especially by the adherents of Gaudiya Vaishnavism—Krishna worship arising in Caitanya's Bengal-area homeland.
2. See T. R. Martland, *Religion As Art* (New York: SUNY Press, 1981).
3. Eugene G. D'Aquili and Andrew B. Newberg, "The Neuropsychology of Aesthetic, Spiritual, and Mystical States," *Zygon* 35, 1 (2000): 39–51.
4. The circumstances in which women occupy any public role in Vrindavan are equally rare. None of the several hundred shops that compose Vrindavan's several bazaars are operated by a woman, for example. My friend Raju, who operates a small shop in Loi Bazaar, told me there would be "chaos" in Vrindavan if women started operating shops and restaurants.
5. John Stratton Hawley, *At Play with Krishna: Pilgrimage Dramas from Brindavan* (Delhi: Motilal Banarsidass, 1992), 169–170.
6. Sylvain Levi, for example, found a correspondence between *râs lila* performances celebrating Krishna's birth and Christian nativity scenes. (*The Theatre of India*. vol I. trans. Narayana Mukherji [Calcutta: Writers Workshop, 1978], 28.)
7. Prabhudayal Mital, *Braj ki Râslîlâ* (Vrindavan: Vrindavan Shodh Samsthan, 1983), 114.
8. Donna Wulff, *Drama as Religious Realization: The* Vidagdhamâdhava *of Rûpa Gosvâmî* (Chico: Scholars Press, 1984), 20.
9. Ram Narayan Agrawal, conversation with the author, Mathura, India, February 7, 2002.
10. Srivatsa Goswami, conversation with the author, Vrindavan, India, February 12, 2002.
11. An American scholar related to me that while he was living in Vrindavan, the flat he rented from an ashram was burglarized. Upon hearing of the crime, the ashram director only replied with a smile, "Well, you know, Krishna is a thief."

12. Sudama Kutir, though a terrifically small venue, gives every musician a microphone. The "soundtrack" of the *râs lila* performance is blasted through preposterously large loudspeakers into the street outside, and can be heard a couple of blocks away, even over the abiding din of Vrindavan.
13. Scholars such as William Sax have written extensively on the religious content of the *ram lila*, and writers such as Richard Schechner have attempted to site the *ram lila* in the body of Western performance theory. See William S. Sax, "The Ramnagar Ramlila: Text, Performance, Pilgrimage," *History of Religions* 30 (1990): 129–153, and Richard Schechner, *Performative Circumstances from the Avant Garde to Ramlila* (Calcutta: Seagull Books, 1983).
14. One significant stylistic difference between Vrindavan-area *ram lila*s and the Varanasi *ram lila* is linguistic. Vrindavan *ram lila*s may be dominated by Brajbhasha, an archaic Hindi that dominated northern India a few centuries ago, but which now survives as a spoken language only within the boundaries of Braj itself.
15. Radhakamal Mukerjee, *The Cosmic Art of India* (New York: Allied Publishers, 1965), 1.
16. Theorists such as Keir Elam have contended that this kind of dual-nonduality is endemic in the very concept of theatre. Commenting on a passage from Shakespeare, Elam asserts that "sign vehicles on stage are perfectly interchangeable." *The Semiotics of Theatre and Drama* (New York: Taylor & Francis, 2002), 13.
17. Herbert Blau, *Take Up the Bodies: Theater at the Vanishing Point* (Urbana: University of Illinois Press, 1982), 249.
18. Schechner, *Performative Circumstances from the Avant Garde to Ramlila* (Calcutta: Seagull Books, 1983), 318.

2. THEATRE IS GOD

1. Charlotte Vaudeville, "Braj, Lost and Found," *Indo-Iranian Journal* 18 (1976): 199.
2. For a summary of several of the other relevant *râs lila* forms, see Donna Wulff, *Drama as a Mode of Religious Realization: The* Vidagdhamâdhava *of Rûpa Gosvâmî* (Chico: Scholars Press, 1984), 16–19.
3. Marjorie Boulton, *The Anatomy of Drama* (London: Routledge & Paul, 1960), 3.
4. Sometimes, many patrons pursue this course of worship. At some performances I have been concerned for Krishna's health as he ingests lump after lump of butter and sugar for the sake of his devotees.
5. John S. Hawley, "A Feast for Mount Govardhan," in *Devotion Divine: Bhakti Traditions from the Regions of India*, ed. Diana Eck and Françoise Mallison (Groningen: Egbert & Forsten, 1991), 172.
6. The disinterest and distraction that identifies the degree to which the young actors are, indeed, themselves on stage is notorious. In a *râs lila* I saw in

Udaipur in 2000, the boys playing Krishna and the *gopis* nudged and prodded each other while on stage, giggling at each others' dancing and fidgeting between the delivery of their lines such that the performance seemed more like a grade school talent show than a religious event. This onstage demeanor makes it clear that to whatever degree devotees regard them as divine, the *râs lila* actors even during the course of a performance are simply young boys in costumes. Still, even their lack of professional discipline helps to identify the actors as manifestations of Krishna, who, after all, given his own mischievous nature, would behave in precisely the same way were he playing himself on a stage. In *At Play with Krishna*, Hawley has noted the nature of the child actors on stage. "People do not believe in the *svarups* [the incarnation of God in the actors] in the way that children believe in Santa Claus," he writes, "they know perfectly well that these are normal children." These normal children are, nevertheless, the deities they represent—and partly because of their childhood. According to Hawley, for devotees "the best Krishna is the one who acts the most like himself, a child unbridled" (18).

7. Although he confirms that the word *salvation* is a fair approximation of such Vaishnava terms as *uddhara*, and is not "an arbitrary imposition of a term from Christian usage," Joseph T. O'Connell has noted the difficulty in using the term *salvation* in the context of a discussion of South Asian religion. "Salvation," he writes, "seems to me to have gained theological specification in the Christian tradition that deliverance has not gained, thus leaving 'deliverance' more open to academic definitions based on cross-cultural testimony . . ." ("Gaudiya Vaisnava Symbolism of Deliverance (*uddhara, nistara*, . . .) from Evil," *Journal of Asian and African Studies* 15, 1–2 (1983): 134).

   I have chosen to use the term *salvation* in addition to less colored terms such as *deliverance* and *liberation* in reference to Vaishnava concepts of divine assistance toward an ideal, spiritual end. I mean to retain the sense of divine mediation that is associated in English with the word *salvation*, and which is equally a part of *bhakti* theology.

8. The relationship between Krishna and the *gopis*, rooted as it is in infidelity, is more complicated than this, and mystification at the apparent impropriety inherent in Krishna's play with the *gopis* has been explicit in *bhakti* theology at least since the *Bhagavata Purana* in which King Parikshit marvels at how God himself can so violate moral law by cavorting with married women. But the various approaches to the apparent problem agree on the central place of the *gopis* in Krishna *bhakti*.

9. The Sanskrit vocabulary of *Bhagavata Purana* 10.33.17 strongly indicates a multilayered performance taking place here. Krishna has mystically multiplied himself so as to play with each *gopi* individually, though simultaneously, and the manner in which he dances, plays, and flirts with them is *svapratibimbavibhramah*—as though flirting with his own reflection. Krishna here imitates the *gopis*, who are imitating him.

10. For an eminently better translation of the *panchadhyaya*, see Graham M. Schweig, *Dance of Divine Love* (Princeton: Princeton University Press, 2005).

11. John Stratton Hawley and Srivatsa Goswami, *At Play With Krishna* (Delhi: Motilal Banarsidass, 1992), 14.
12. In fact, in the introduction to her partial translation and analysis of a drama written by Rupa Goswami, a figure important to the revival of Krishna devotion in the sixteenth century, Wulff speculates that Vishnu's *avatar*s or "embodied forms" may account for the broad variety of dramatic practices in Vaishnavism, which are entirely absent in Shaivism, even though Shiva has been always regarded as *nataraj*, or "lord of the dance." See Donna Wulff, *Drama as a Mode of Religious Realization: The* Vidagdhamâdhava *of Rûpa Gosvâmî* (Chico: Scholars Press), 8.
13. Barbara Stoler Miller, trans., *Bhagavad-gita* (New York: Columbia University Press, 1986), 98–99, 107.
14. Ganesh Vasudeo Tagare, trans., *Bhagavata Purana*, vol. IV (Delhi: Motilal Banarsidass, 1978), 1303–1304.
15. S. K. De, *Bengal's Contribution to Sanskrit Literature & Studies in Bengal Vaisnavism* (Calcutta: K. L. Mukhopadyaya, 1960), 115.
16. Wulff, 11.
17. The Bengali *sampradaya*s are those variations on *bhakti* doctrine that developed in the geographic region of India's Bengal State, and that are genetically descended from the medieval saint Caitanya and his disciples. Such sects, known as *Gaudiya* Vaishnavism and even Caitanyaism, are fiercely devotional, relying heavily on the *Bhagavata Purana* as a scriptural text, and regarding the child Krishna as the fully realized form of deity.
18. De, 143.
19. A. W. Entwistle, *Braj: Centre of Krishna Pilgrimage* (Groningen: Egbert Forsten, 1987), 71.
20. Avrum Stroll and Richard H. Popkin, *Philosophy and the Human Spirit* (New York: Holt, Rinehart and Winston, Inc., 1973), 239.
21. Tyrone Guthrie said as much, commenting on the relationship between plays as they exists on the page and on the stage, during a speech in New York sometime before 1962. "Dramatic criticism of the classics," he said, "is nearly always conducted on the assumption that there exists, probably in the mind of the critic, an ideal performance which completely realizes the intention of Shakespeare or Molière or Eugene O'Neill or whoever else. What they see on the stage is judged in comparison with that imagined ideal performance." From J. Robert Wills, *The Director in a Changing Theatre* (Palo Alto: Mayfield, 1976), 88.
22. Marvin Carlson, *The Haunted Stage: The Theatre as Memory Machine* (Ann Arbor: University of Michigan Press, 2003), 66.
23. I myself could do a fair imitation of Olivier's delivery as a child before knowing even who Olivier was, by way of Hawkeye Pierce/Alan Alda's delivery of these lines on the television show *MASH*.
24. Quoted in Carlson, 68.
25. What the devotee might derive from devotion is not the goal of devotion. The intention of devotion is God's pleasure, whatever the expense on the part of

the devotee. From the devotee's point of view, whatever personal benefits may be derived from devotional service to God are incidental. However, whether or not the devotee seeks after it, the inevitable product of devotion is the bliss that accompanies an understanding of God's nature and the devotee's relationship to it.

26. De, 113.
27. Ibid.
28. Margaret H. Case, *Seeing Krishna: The Religious World of a Brahman Family in Vrindaban* (New York: Oxford University Press, 2000), 366.
29. Joachim Wach, *Types of Religious Experience Christian and Non-Christian* (Chicago: University of Chicago Press, 1951), 32. In the second chapter of another work, *Comparative Study of Religion* (New York: Columbia University Press), Wach more fully connects this idea with philosophers and scholars preceding him, including Kierkegaard and Buber.
30. Thomas J. Hopkins summarizes the doctrine, thus: "The self is left in a state which the *Maitrî Upanishad* variously describes as 'release' (*mokṣa*) or 'isolation' (*kevalatva*). In this totally unqualified state, the true blissful nature of the self becomes clear; there is no distinction between the self and Brahman . . ." See *The Hindu Religious Tradition* (Belmont: Wadsworth, 1971), 66.
31. Clifford Hospital, "Bhakti and Liberation in the Bhagavata Purana," *Sciences Religieuses/Studies in Religion* 12.4 (1983): 402.
32. Quoted in Hospital, 404.
33. Richard Barz, *The Bhakti Sect of Vallabhacarya* (Faridabad: Thomson Press, 1976), 75.
34. According to Entwistle, the eschatology that *bhakti* theologians developed "meant that salvation was not seen as a state of total liberation or merging into a monistic absolute." Entwistle supports this assertion briefly with references to *Bhagavata Purana* 3.25.34, 9.4.67, 10.83.41–42, 11.14.14, and 11.20.34 (70).
35. Lance E. Nelson, "The Ontology of *Bhakti*: Devotion as *Paramapuruṣârtha* in Gauḍiya Vaiṣṇavism and Madhusûdhana Sarasvatî," *Journal of Indian Philosophy* 32 (2004): 349.
36. O'Connell, 131–132.
37. Srivatsa Goswami, conversation with the author, Vrindavan, India, March 31, 2002.
38. David R. Kinsley, *The Sword and the Flute: Kali and Krsna, Dark Visions of the Terrible and the Sublime in Hindu Mythology* (Berkeley: University of California Press, 1975), 68–69.
39. De, 114.
40. In *The Miracle Plays of Mathura*, Norvin Hein especially asserts the *Gita*'s emphasis on the religious value of performance, emphasizing what the *Gita* says about the worth of familiarity with Krishna's life. On pages 258–259, Hein writes:
    i. In Bhagavadgita 4:5 ff., Krishna says that he has been born many times and that the person who truly knows his wondrous births and actions

is not reborn but comes to him. Knowing Krishna's acts is of ultimate importance then as a means of salvation itself.

Hein then refers to *Bhagavad Gita* 10:8–9, where, he says, "we learn that enlightened men of the true spirit find contentment and joy 'enlightening one another and telling about Me constantly.'" Hein concludes, "The recitative dance drama, which was already in use, may have been among the customs here suggested whereby the devout told Krishna's story."

In Miller's translation, 4:5 reads: "He who really knows my divine/birth and my action, escapes rebirth/when he abandons the body—/and he come to me, Arjuna"; and 10:9 reads: "Thinking and living deep in me,/[wise men] enlighten one another/by constantly telling of me/for their own joy and delight."

The Sanskrit verbal root *budh*, which also gives us the word Buddha, supplies the word that Miller translates as *enlighten*.

Like Miller, who gives us the phrase *telling of me*, few translators emphasize the performative connotations of the verbal root *kath*. This root does, however, suggest such meanings as *narrate*, *report*, and *describe*. The cognate Sanskrit noun *katha* is the simple word for *story*. Kees W. Bolle gives us a fair translation of 10:9, which seems more appreciative of the stress Hein suggests the *Gita* places on telling *stories about Krishna*, as opposed to merely talking about Krishna: "They are happy and joyful, thinking of me,/their whole life going out toward me,/Instructing one another,/constantly narrating my acts" (*The Bhagavadgita: A New Translation* [Berkeley: University of California Press, 1979], 115).

41. Quoted in Hospital, 400.
42. That a spiritual reality may supersede a physical one may be more than mere theological contention. Eugene d'Aquili and Andrew Newberg assert that, neurologically speaking, "reality seems to consist fundamentally only of the vivid sense of reality . . . constituted by compelling presences." That is, subjects often affirm that what d'Aquili and Newberg call their "hyperlucid experiences" are "*more* real than baseline reality" on the basis of the vividness of their encounter with it. Nor, they conclude, is there any way to prove or disprove their claims. Hyperlucid experiences, they say, "must be said to be real or the word *reality* has no meaning whatsoever." ("The Neuropsychology of Aesthetic, Spiritual, and Mystical States," *Zygon* 35, 1 (2000): 50.)
43. David L. Haberman, *Acting as a Way of Salvation: A Study of Râgânugâ Bhakti Sâdhana* (New York: Oxford University Press, 1988), 6.
44. Haberman, 47.

3. KRISHNA, *LILA*, AND FREEDOM

1. John Stratton Hawley, *Krishna the Butter Thief* (Princeton: Princeton University Press, 1983), 212.

2. See Charlotte Vaudeville, "The Cowherd God in Ancient India," in *Pastoralists and Nomads in South Asia*, ed. Lawrence Saadia Leshnik and Günther-Dietz Sontheimer (Weisbaden: Otto Harrassowitz, 1975), 92–116.
3. See Alf Hiltebeitel, "Krsna at Mathurâ," in *Mathurâ: the Cultural Heritage*, ed. Doris Meth Srinivasan (New Delhi: Manohar, 1989), 93–102.
4. Consider the conglomerations of stories that make up the cycles of Christian saints in Europe. Saint Nicholas, for instance, at one time the historical Bishop of Myra, has become the hero of several distinct mythologies, including that of Santa Claus.
5. Alf Hiltebeitel, "Krsna at Mathura," in *Mathura: The Cultural Heritage*, ed. Doris Meth Srinivasan (New Delhi: Manohar, 1989), 95.
6. Lauri Honko, "The Problem of Defining Myth," in *Sacred Narrative*, ed. Alan Dundes (Berkeley: University of California Press, 1984), 47.
7. Hein, "A Revolution in Krsnaism: The Cult of Gopala," 307.
8. W. J. Johnson, trans. *The Bhagavad Gita* (New York: Oxford University Press, 1994), x.
9. *Srîmadbhagavadgîtâ*, 18: 41–44.
10. Vijay Nath, "From 'Brahmanism' to 'Hinduism': Negotiating the Myth of the Great Tradition," *Social Scientist* 29, 3–4 (2001): 21.
11. Hein, "Revolution," 298.
12. Ibid., 312.
13. Ibid.
14. Hawley, *Krishna the Butter Thief*, 214.
15. Ibid., 215.
16. Ibid., 192.
17. David L. Haberman, *Journey Through the Twelve Forests* (New York: Oxford University Press, 1994), 124.
18. Ibid., 197.
19. Ibid., 171.
20. Bettina Baümer, "The Play of the Three Worlds: The Trika Concept of *Lila*," in *The Gods at Play: Lila in South Asia*, ed. William Sax, 35.
21. Norvin Hein, "Lila," in *The Gods at Play: Lila in South Asia*, ed. Sax, 13.
22. Sax, "Who's Who in the *Pandav Lila*?," in *The Gods at Play: Lila in South Asia*, ed. Sax, 146.
23. Norvin Hein, "Lila," in *The Gods at Play: Lila in South Asia*, ed. Sax, 14.
24. Clifford Hospital, "*Lila* in Early Vaisnava Thought," in *The Gods at Play: Lila in South Asia*, ed. Sax, 29.
25. Baümer, 35.
26. Ibid., 46.
27. John B. Carman, "Some Concluding Reflections," in *The Gods at Play: Lila in South Asia*, ed. Sax, 226.
28. William Sax, "Who's Who in the *Pandav Lila*?," 147.
29. Donna M. Wulff, "The Play of Emotion: *Lilakirtan* in Bengal," in *The Gods at Play: Lila in South Asia*, ed. Sax, 110.

30. John Stratton Hawley and Shrivatsa Goswami, *At Play with Krishna: Pilgrimage Dramas from Brindavan* (Delhi: Motilal Banarsidass, 1992), 70.
31. John Stratton Hawley, *Krishna the Butter Thief* (Princeton: Princeton University Press, 1983), 192.
32. If we adopt religious terminology here, we might say the performances are the preeminent form of liberation.

4. ORIGINS OF CHILD PERFORMERS IN THE *RÂS LILA*

1. H. S. Jarret, trans. *'Ain-i-Akbari of Abulfazl-i-'Allami, 3* (Calcutta: Royal Asiatic Society of Bengal, 1948), 272.
2. Significantly, Abul Fazl's eyewitness description does not address the history of the performances he saw. While Hein rightly notes that Fazl's is the first concrete evidence we have of the presence of boys on the *râs lila* stage, Fazl's brief comments do not support the contention that he happened upon a newly developed manner of representing Krishna on stage. The only sure thing Fazl's account tells us is that boys were playing in the *râs lila* at the time of his writing.
3. Norvin Hein, *The Miracle Plays of Mathura* (New York: Yale University Press, 1972), 231–232.
4. Ram Narayan Agrawal, *Braj ka Râs Rangmanc* (New Delhi: National Publishing House, 1981), 92–93.
5. S. Kumar, conversation with the author, Vrindavan, India, March 27, 2002.
6. Kishori Saran Lal offers moderate vindication and accusation of Muslim rulers of this time period in his history of the Delhi Sultanate: "... by and large the fifteenth century Sultans of Delhi had not indulged in any senseless persecution. During this period the Sultanate was not so powerful as to be able to oppress the Hindus. It could not also antagonize the Hindu population in the interest of its own survival." *Twilight of the Sultanate* (New Delhi: Asia Publishing House, 1963), 190.
7. Hein, *Miracle Plays*, 116.
8. Ibid., 230.
9. Ibid., 229.
10. Ibid., 225.
11. Ibid., 230.
12. Ibid., 230.
13. The entry for the root *mâmgi* in *A Gurû Nânak Glossary* identifies the derivative *mâmgatu* as nothing more than "beggar." (C. Shackle, ed. *A Gurû Nânak Glossary* [London: University of British Colombia Press, 1981], 238.)
14. We would also note, though it is less relevant at this point since I am of the opinion that Dhruvdas's Ghamandi was not necessarily doing anything connected with the *râs lila*, that Hein's argument that the lack of a causative verb

in this verse indicates that the verse could not have regarded Ghamandi only as a director is weak. The nature of Brajbhasha, the nature of this verse, and the nature of directing/performing in this context all undermine the assertion that a causative verb would be necessary here to indicate that Ghamandi was not himself appearing on the stage of a performance for which he was organizationally and directorially responsible.
15. Prabhudayal Mital, *Braj ki Râslila* (Vrindavan: Vrindavan Shodh Samsthan, 1983), 56.
16. As indicated in the note on transliteration, *ras* and *râs* are different words. *Ras* descends from the Sanskrit term *rasa*, literally translated as juice or essence, a term the *Natyashastra* uses for a mystical sort of aesthetic experience. *Râs* may be derived from the Sanskrit verbal root *râ*, the use of which in the *Bhagavata Purana* has to do with giving and surrendering; *râs* may also be related to the verbal root *râs*, which appears in the *Mahabharata* to indicate howling or crying.
17. Agrawal, *Braj*, 101. Agrawal also corroborates my rendering of *vrindavan nij dham* as "from the region of the true Vrindavan" by subsequently describing this Ghamandi as *nijdham mankar* (contemplating the spiritual world) (103).
18. Hein, *Miracle Plays*, 225.
19. Ibid., 265. However, the summary of Jackson's paper in the *Transactions of the American Philological Society* indicates that the impersonation of deities by children is not a central concern, nor even any method of Sanskrit dramatic performance, but the many instances of child characters in Sanskrit dramatic literature (especially as those literary instances coincide with Shakespeare). The first conclusion to draw from Jackson's argument is that children did play children on the Sanskrit stage. Because there are precious few instances of Sanskrit drama concerning a child deity (which is almost exclusively a characteristic of Krishna, who, with one or two exceptions, does not appear in Sanskrit drama), it should be no wonder that instances of children representing deities in Sanskrit theatre do not present themselves; but to the degree that it is apparent that children played children on Sanskrit stages, it is spurious to suggest that the lack of instances in classical Sanskrit theatre in which children represent deities is an indication of a general disinclination in South Asian performance to employ children in divine roles suited to them by age. See A. V. W. Jackson, "Children on the Stage in the Sanskrit Drama," *Transactions of the American Philological Society* 27 (1896): v–vi.
20. Hein, *Miracle Plays*, 265–66.
21. Ibid., 263.
22. The *Bhagavata Purana* (800–1000, CE), a principal Vaishnava religious text—the most important collection of scripture for Krishna devotion—suggests that the dramatic representation of Krishna's life is a significant undertaking of religious practice. Hein's translation of *Bhagavata Purana* XI.11.23 reads:
    i. A believer, hearing the auspicious world-purifying tales of Me,
    ii. Chanting and surely remembering them, *constantly enacting My birth and deeds,*

iii. Undertaking duty, wealth, and enjoyment for My sake, with Me as refuge,
  iv. Obtains unshakable devotion for Me, the Eternal, O Uddhava! (262)
  With the injunction of scripture so firmly in place from such an early time, the likelihood that some such plays were occurring from the earliest days of the *bhakti* movement is greater than that they were not.
23. Hein, *Miracle Plays*, 230.
24. Agrawal finds himself similarly resigned. "Therefore, on the subject of the *râs*, it is a difficult task to say anything verifiable on a logical basis [*tarksamgat âdhâr par pramanikta se*]. So, we will here make an attempt to advance an opinion on this topic on the basis of the available material" (91).
25. Agrawal, *Braj*, 93.
26. Mital, 49–50.
27. Ram Narayan Agrawal, ed., *Râs-Lila: Ek Paricay* (New Delhi: Bharatiya Visva Prakashan, 1959), 7–8.
28. Vasant Yamadagni, *Râsalila tatha Râsanukaran Vikas* (New Delhi: Sangit Natak Academy, 1980), 159–60.
29. Hein, *Miracle Plays*, 224. Norvin Hein recounts, "The head of the sect [Vallabha] . . . impressed them by causing ten crowns of the type used by actors to descend miraculously from the sky." It appears that Hein misread a verse concerning the yogic exercise in which Vallabha engaged when entreated by Haridas for help in developing the *râs lila*. The verse as included in Yamadagni's *Râslila tatha Râsanukaran Vikas* reads:
  i. *pranayam cadhay roki das hum indri tab* |
  ii. *kuch chan piche kahyau sunau mere tum jan ab* ||
  iii. *nabh te utarat mukut sabai vishvas drdhavan* |
  iv. *sapt talvistarit jagamgat ati ng bar gan* || (154)
  Mital assumes that in this verse the adjective *das* (ten) modifies *indri* (senses), and thus elaborates on the way in which Vallabha caused by his spiritual power a single crown (*mukut*) to descend (50). The versions of the story offered by Agrawal (in both *Râs-Lila: Ek Paricay* and *Braj ka Râs Rangmanc*) and by Yamadagni also limit the number of miraculously falling crowns to one. See Agrawal, *Râs-Lila*, 7–8, *Braj*, 93, and Yamadagni, 154.
30. Agrawal, *Braj*, 93.
31. Ibid., 94.
32. Ibid., 102
33. Ibid., 94–95.
34. See Agrawal, *Râs-Lila*, 7–8.
35. The issue is further complicated by Gaudiya Vaishnavas, the followers of the Bengal Saint Caitanya, who prefer that Caitanya and his disciples, such as Narayan Bhatt, figure prominently in the history of the *râs lila*'s early development. The contribution of Narayan Bhatt, who settled in Braj at some time around 1550, will be taken up subsequently, but we would note here that the sixteenth- and seventeenth-century literature does not associate him directly

with Vallabha, Haridas, or Ghamanddev; furthermore, as Hein contends, "Nowhere in Nabhaji, Priyadas, Janakiprasad, the *Bhaktakalpadruma*, or the *Bhaktamalaharibhaktiprakasika* is there any statement that Narayan Bhatt was the actual inventor of the form of dramatic art which he promoted" (*Miracle Plays*, 229).

36. Yamadagni, 161.
37. This element of Ghamanddev's life, when combined with an estimate of the dates of Ghamanddev's theatrical activity proves more relevant to the current objective than an attempt to resolve the dispute over top billing, which continues among the Vrindavan sects that seek a degree of legitimacy in an exclusive association with *râs lila* as an institution.
38. Hein, *Miracle Plays*, 225.
39. See, for instance, Agrawal, *Braj*, 101. This is the beginning of the section of this book titled, "*Ghamanddev Kaun The?*" ("Who Was Ghamanddev?").
40. The agreement is generally held by scholars other than the few officially connected with and promoting the Nimbark sect.
41. See Vasant Yamadagni's assessment of the tradition, 161–162.
42. Agrawal, *Braj*, 104.
43. Mital, 56.
44. Agrawal, *Braj*, 103.
45. Mital, 56. Indeed, Agrawal and Mital sound rather similar on this point. Mital writes, "If the Nimbark sectarian Ghamanddevji had founded the *râslilanukaran*, he would have set it up in one of their [the Nimbarkites'] own towns, or would have set it up in 'Kundal' (Hariyana), his own center of power."
46. Agrawal, 103.
47. Ibid., 104.
48. Ibid., 103.
49. Hein's reading of the Nabhaji passage in question, which he finds in Growse, characterizes this Ghamandi as a "rigid ascetic" (*Miracle Plays*, 225). Again, this does not seem to be the same person whom the *Râs-Sarvasva* sends out to establish the *râs* all over Braj.
50. Mital, 56.
51. Hein seems to be guilty of precisely this kind of indiscriminate association. He persistently uses *Ghamandi*, the name appearing in the Braj chronicles we have mentioned, to refer to the Ghamanddev of the *Râs-Sarvasva*, though the verses from the *Râs-Sarvasva* included in Mital's book show that it prefers the name *Ghamand* (49) and *Ghamanddev* (51). The invariable use of *Ghamandi*, of course, serves Hein's theory, which is content to accept the Vrindavan Ghamandi as the Ghamanddev of *râs lila* fame in order to date the appearance of boy actors in Braj to the late sixteen hundreds.
52. Hein, *Miracle Plays*, 223.
53. Mital, 49.
54. The *Râs-Sarvasva*'s passage, which recounts this key development, not only marks it as a distinct event but lends the event a patently ritual air as it takes

pains to give equal due to Vallabha and Haridas. As included by Mital, the passage declares that Haridas costumed a boy as Radha and at the same time Vallabha dressed a boy as Krishna (50).
55. Agrawal, *Braj*, 94.
56. Mital, 51.
57. Agrawal, *Braj*, 104.
58. Mital notes this fact in his effort to disassociate Uddhav Ghamanddevacarya from Ghamandi. The Nimbark sect affirms that Uddhav Ghamanddevacarya was certainly the founder of the modern *râs lila*, but the few references to Ghamandi in the literature of the time do not make the same assertion. See Mital, 56.
59. Hein, *Miracle Plays*, 229.
60. Curiously, we might deconstruct the name *Ghamand* in the same way as we might deconstruct the name Homer. The meaning of the Greek word *homêros*—"joined together"—has contributed to theories that regard the Homeric poems as the product of a number of artists collected under Homer's name. The Hindi *ghamand* means pride, arrogance, conceit, and so on, and in this case, as is common, the termination *dev* is added to indicate that the name is borne by the individual only to refer to God as appropriately conceited. But the word *ghumad*, which aurally and on paper is little different from *ghamand* indicates an act of gathering or amassing.

The word *ghumad* is the root of the word *ghumadi* appearing in Dhruvdas's verse about Ghamandi, which indicates his state of dizziness or disorientation, presumably from constantly spinning his concentration around the fixed and central point of the transcendental Vrindavan, to which everything is attracted.
61. See Agrawal, *Râs-Lila*, 9, and *Braj*, 101.
62. Agrawal, 104.
63. Alan Entwistle, *Braj: Centre of Krishna Pilgrimage* (Groningen: Egbert Forsten, 1987), 254.
64. Entwistle, 255.
65. Hein, *Miracle Plays*, 227–228.
66. Entwistle, 255.
67. Hein, *Miracle Plays*, 225. Hein acknowledges the suggestion of the evidence that Ghamanddev was a contemporary of Narayan Bhatt, which would settle his dates closer to those proposed by Mital and Yamadagni. However, Hein reasons that the texts that suggest a connection with the two nevertheless posit Ghamanddev as preceding Narayan Bhatt chronologically, and persists in his estimate that Ghamanddev was a citizen of mid-sixteenth century Braj.
68. Agrawal, *Braj*, 97, 106.
69. Mital disputes the period of the mid-fifteen hundreds that Agrawal suggests for the reestablishment of the *râs lila* by arguing that, because of the Delhi Sultan Sikander Lodi's "religious oppression," this period was not conducive to the establishment of a Vaishnava theatre tradition (58). However, even if

Sikander Lodi's reign was as religiously oppressive as Mital suggests (though this is not at all established), Mital's dates are highly suspect, as Sikander is removed from the mid-sixteen hundreds not only by a successor in the Delhi Sultanate, Ibrahim Lodi, who ruled from 1517 to 1526, but by the complete fall of the Delhi Sultanate before the first Mughal emperor Babur, who controlled the area from 1526 to 1556. The mid-sixteen hundreds, then, sees the beginning of the reign of Akbar, whose generally progressive nature has already been noted. Consequently, Mital's objections to the period Agrawal asserts as the crucial time for the development of the *râs lila* seem unfounded. Yamadagni, too, suggests a later period as the crucial one in the *râs lila*'s history, but arrives at this date partly by postponing Narayan Bhatt's birth until 1588, and his arrival in Vrindavan until 1602 (175). But Yamadagni seems to accept the notion that Ghamanddev, whose name, at least, represents important developments in the *râs lila*, had a living association in Vrindavan with Narayan Bhatt (162).

70. In any case, the *bhakti* theology of Braj eschews the monistic concept of *moksha*, otherwise common to South Asian religion, which posits as man's ultimate objective the dissolution of identity. For an elaboration of this distinction in *bhakti*, see the subsequent chapter "'Salvation' Through Performance."
71. Hein, "Revolution," 312.
72. As opposed to the *Bhagavad Gita*'s adult Krishna who appeared as much as five hundred years earlier than this, in 200 BCE, who espoused adherence to *varnâsrama dharma*. At this time, North Indian Hindu hegemony was threatened by the control of the area by the non-Hindu Mauryan kingdom. In academic circles, the dispute continues as to whether the adult Krishna of the *Bhagavad Gita* and the child Krishna of the *Bhagavata Purana* are the same person.
73. Hein, "Revolution," 317.
74. David Haberman, *Acting as a Way of Salvation* (Delhi: Motilal Banarsidass, 1988), 41.
75. Edward C. Dimock, Jr., *The Place of the Hidden Moon: Erotic Mysticism in the Vaisnava Sahajiya Cult of Bengal* (Chicago: University of Chicago Press, 1966), 26–27.
76. Hein even identifies this tendency in early days of the so-called Hare Krishna movement in New York City. He suggests that the Indian founder of the movement "drew in youths who wanted above all to express their cultural disaffection by embracing an exotic religion. But they sought expression, also, for a view that natural impulses are holy" ("Revolution," 316). Of course, this is not a characterization of Krishna *bhakti* so much as a characterization of elements of the 1960s counterculture for whom *any* "other" way of life (which is to say, distinguished from Judeo-Christian traditions) could be an outlet for disaffection, be it Krishna *bhakti*, Transcendental Meditation, Taoism, Islam, Native American practices of worship, and even Communism. The appeal of the child Krishna in this particular case is not remarkable.

77. Agrawal, *Râs-Lîlâ*, 7.
78. Walid Ali Shah's *rahas*, contends Agrawal, evolved into the contemporary dance-drama forms *Bhagat* and *Swang*. Agrawal partly supports his argument by noting that in some places *Bhagat* and *Swang* are still confused with *râs lila*. See Agrawal, *Râs-Lîlâ*, 7.
79. Hein, *Miracle Plays*, 266.
80. Caitainya's ecstasies during such performances, as described in the *Caitanya Caritâmrta*, are famous. In one such case, after hearing a particular sloka, he "danced with this verse, deeply absorbed, and the people all around him were wet with the tears of *prema* of Prabhu. . . . Now he fell in a faint, and he had no more breath; and suddenly he stood up again and shouted. He was like a *simûlî* tree, thick with goose-flesh: sometimes his body blossomed [with it], and sometimes it abated. Bloody sweat came out of every pore of his body. . . . The third watch came, and still the dancing was not ended. A sea of *ânanda* welled up in all the people, and everyone forgot their bodies, their selves, and their homes" (Edward C. Dimock, Jr., trans., *Caitanya Caritâmrta* [Cambridge, MA: Harvard University Press, 1999], 898–899).
81. We can follow Hein's reasoning in this respect without accepting his insistence that the proto-forms of *râs lila* extant in Braj as the Bengali influence became prominent in the middle of the sixteenth century exclusively used adult performers. Just as he characterized the actor Vallabh as an adult, Hein maintains that in the early 1500s, Braj's Krishna actors "were necessarily non-juvenile because of the long training that their elaborate art required" (*Miracle Plays*, 269). International gymnastics and skating (not to mention music) competitions prove conclusively not only that children are perfectly capable of almost impossibly complex and demanding physical performance, but also that they may be better suited to it than adults.
82. Dimock, *Place*, 37.
83. The following chapter of this study examines in detail Haberman's work on *râgânugâ bhakti sâdhana*.
84. Entwistle, 66.
85. Dimock, *Place*, 164.
86. John S. Hawley and Srivatsa Goswami, *At Play with Krishna: Pilgrimage Dramas from Vrindaban* (Delhi: Motilal Banarsidass, 1992), 18.
87. Swami Ramprasad, conversation with the author, Vrindavan, India, November 16, 2001.
88. Vasant Yamadagni, conversation with the author, Vrindavan, India, March 13, 2002.
89. Dimock, *Place*, 159.
90. Ibid., 45.
91. Ibid., 154.
92. See note 76 above.

5. ACTING IN THE *RÂS LILA* AND REAL REALISM

1. Portions of this chapter appeared in the *Journal of Dramatic Theory and Criticism* 18, 1 (2003): 107–129.
2. Balwant Gargi, *Folk Theater of India* (Calcutta: Rupa & Co., 1991), 131.
3. Daya Prakash Sinha, *Lokrang: Uttar Pradesh* (Lucknow: UP Hindi Sansthan, 1990), 80.
4. In many ways, today's *râs lila* acting appears to be of precisely this kind.
5. It may be important to note here that Stanislavsky was not necessarily committed to Realism (capital "R") on the stage. Just as the focus and practices of his System changed and evolved over time, Stanislavsky's work in the theatre over several decades took advantage of a number of different presentational and representational styles. He remained committed throughout his life, however, to the concept that the essentially universal nature of man provided the link between actors and audience members. Even in the 1920s, when Stanislavsky experimented with highly stylized forms of staging, he maintained that he was seeking to express the inner substance of man. See David Allen, *Stanislavsky for Beginners* (London: Writers and Readers, 1999), 98–99.
6. Quoted in Allen, 131.
7. Not to be confused with the more specific concept of *affective memory*, which Stanislavsky flirted with for a short time and dropped. This is a process, at the core of the "Method" acting developed in the United States by Lee Strasberg, by which an actor compels the feelings associated with a personal memory to manifest themselves.
8. David L. Haberman, *Acting as a Way of Salvation: A Study of Râgânugâ Bhakti Sâdhana* (Delhi: Motilal Banarsidass, 1988), 68.
9. Haberman, 68.
10. Haberman makes it clear that this is the objective of *râgânugâ bhakti sâdhana* Among the many stories and anecdotes from Vrindavan devotees that he includes in his book is the following:
    i. When I was young I went to the hut of an old *bâbâ* by the name of Gaurânga Dâsa Bâbâjî who was at that time living in Vrndâvana. I found this *bâbâ* deep in meditation and decided to wait patiently for him to return. After a little while, Bâbâ muttered for me to help him from his hut to a chair under a verandah. I gave him my arm and assisted him to the verandah. I then sat quietly at the *bâbâ*'s feet. Some time later, Bâbâ came out of his meditative world and returned to this one. He soon asked, "Who helped me here?" I replied that I had. "But," said the *bâbâ*, "I was helped by a beautiful *gopî*. I touched her arm. Her skin was so beautiful and she wore beautiful bangles." (120–121)

    Inasmuch as such stories tell us what the intended goal of *bhakti* meditation is, we can see that it can result in a very literal inner transformation of a practitioner. I do not mean to suggest anything different concerning Haberman's

assessment of *râgânugâ bhakti sâdhana*. I would suggest only that, contrary to Haberman's reading, Stanislavsky himself would roundly reject acting that leads to such a transformation.
11. Toby Cole, ed. *Acting: A Handbook of the Stanislavsky Method* (New York: Crown, 1960), 27.
12. Colin Counsell, *Signs of Performance: An Introduction to Twentieth-Century Theatre* (New York: Routledge, 1996), 29.
13. Haberman, 75.
14. Ibid., 10.
15. Constantin Stanislavsky, *An Actor Prepares*, trans. Elizabeth Reynolds Hapgood (New York: Theatre Arts Books, 1936), 14. Emphasis mine.
16. Haberman, 68.
17. Ibid., 69–70.
18. Ibid., 72. I would suggest that the Sanskrit term *anubhâva* indicates precisely what Stanislavsky worked to keep actors from trying to imitate (or "taking on," as Haberman says here, indicating the assumption of a superficial, physical likeness). In their introductory remarks on their partial translation of the *Natyaśhastra*—the text that provides such aesthetic vocabulary as *anubhâva*—Masson and Patwardhan explain the term as "physical indices" of feeling (love, sorrow, anger, and so forth), and provide the examples, "trembling, sweating, etc. [sic]" (*Aesthetic Rapture:the Rasâdhyâya of the Nâtyaśâstra* [Poona: Deccan College, 1970], 23). Stanislavsky was certainly opposed to the development of character by imitation of such indices. In *An Actor Prepares*, he wrote:
   i. No matter how skillful an actor may be in his choice of stage conventions, because of their inherent mechanical quality he cannot move the spectators by them. He must have some supplementary means of arousing them, so he takes refuge in what we call theatrical emotions. These are a sort of artificial imitation of the periphery of physical feelings. (25)
Stanislavsky developed a system in order to generate emotional states in an actor, which would naturally produce such physical indices, so that an actor need not "take them on."
19. Stanislavsky, *An Actor Prepares*, 25.
20. Counsell, 29, referring to Stanislavsky's *An Actor Prepares*.
21. Nor is this the same practice adopted by Strasberg's Method. Throughout the long process of developing his System, during which time the System was many different things, Stanislavsky consistently sought a stage expression (emotion) that arose naturally from the immediate environment and circumstances of the stage.
22. Counsell, 30.
23. Haberman, 68.
24. Stanislavsky, *Creating a Role*, Elizabeth Reynolds Hapgood, trans (New York: Theatre Arts Books, 1961), 215.
25. Allen, 164.

26. Stanislavsky, *Creating a Role*, 216.
27. Haberman, 70.
28. Counsell, 35.
29. Ibid., 28.
30. Haberman, 124.
31. Ibid., 9.
    In a footnote, Haberman includes a favorite anecdote intended to support his contention about Stanislavskian acting's transformative power, as reported by Leslie Bennetts in the *New York Times* about Dustin Hoffman, who played a male actor impersonating a female actress in the film *Tootsie*. "I'm telling you," says Hoffman in the story, "if you are a woman for a month, the world is a different experience in ways you never imagine. . . . My wife tells me that playing the part altered me . . ." Setting aside for the moment the fact that Hoffman did not play a woman in the film (which fact greatly complicates the implication by Haberman's reasoning that the role may have transformed him into a woman), Hoffman is one of American film's poster boys for the acting "Method" of Lee Strasberg, an acting plan that has a historical relationship to Stanislavsky's System, but of which Stanislavsky himself was highly suspicious. See Haberman, 171.
32. J. L. Masson and M. V. Patwardhan, *Aesthetic Rapture: The Rasâdhyâya of the Nâtyaśâstra* (Poona: Deccan College, 1970), 35.
33. Masson and Patwardhan, 24.
34. Ibid., 23.
35. Christopher M. Byrski, *Concept of Ancient Indian Theatre* (Delhi: Munshiram Manoharlal Publishers, 1974), 18.
36. In the not too distant past—at least as recently as the 1950s, according to accounts by Vrindavan residents—*râs lila* actors underwent some rigorous acrobatic training. There is a living memory of child actors practicing acrobatic maneuvers on the sandy banks of the Yamuna river. This feature of *râs lila* training and performance has disappeared. It may be that an increasing interest in North Indian *kathak* dance as the physical inspiration for performance movement has supplanted the use of acrobatics. In noting current *râs lila* practices, which living directors themselves decry as responsible for a decline in the quality of the *râs lila*, Ram Narayan Agrawal writes, "With respect to *râs* dance, directors have noted the significance of *kathak*, and have injected bits of *kathak* into both dance and dramatic action. Some important troupes have begun to emphasize *kathak* dance over traditional dance." (*Braj ka Râs Ranmanc* [New Delhi: National Publishing House, 1981], 379)
37. Furthermore, seeking to understand Krishna's "motivation"—another central concept in the Stanislavskian System—is an exercise in futility since Krishna's actions, as asserted countless times in Vaishnava theological texts, and repeatedly emphasized by Vaishnava scholars and saints, are essentially motiveless. Krishna is engaged eternally in *play*, which, by theological definition and

otherwise, has no motive. As a consequence, a *ras lila* actor playing Krishna does not have an avenue of psychological character study open to him, even if he happened to be of a mind to pursue it.
38. Counsell, 28.
39. Monier Monier-Williams, ed. *A Sanskrit-English Dictionary* (Oxford: The Clarendon Press, 1899).
40. Haberman, 125.
41. Srivatsa Goswami, conversation with the author, Vrindavan, India, December 7, 2001.
42. David Shulman, "The Prospects of Memory," *Journal of Indian Philosophy* 26 (1988): 309–334, 316.
43. Robert L. Miller, "A Letter From the Editor," *Time Magazine*, August 15, 1988.
44. A. Whitney Sanford, "The Emotive Body in the *Astayâmalîlâ* Festival," *Arc* 25 (1997): 101–121, 110.
45. Haberman, 127–128.
46. Sanford, 110.
47. Donna Wulff, Drama as a Mode of Religious Realization: The Vidagdhamâdhava of Rûpa Gosvâmî (Chico: Scholars Press, 1984), 41.
48. Margaret Case, *Seeing Krishna: The Religious World of a Brahman Family in Vrindaban* (New York: Oxford University Press, 2000).
49. Barbara Stoller Miller, "Kâlidâsa's World and His Plays," in *Theater of Memory: The Plays of Kâlidâsa*, ed. Barbara Stoller Miller (New York: Columbia University Press, 1984), 323–324.
50. John Stratton Hawley and Srivatsa Goswami, *At Play with Krishna* (Delhi: Motilal Banarsidass, 1992), 20.
51. Hein, "Revolution in Krsnaism," 314. I would object, however, based only on personal experience, that toilet training "comes late" to an Indian child. Relative to the United States, toilet training comes surprisingly early to the child in India, where until very recently disposable diapers were unheard of, and where, in any case, few people use diapers of any sort. As a result, parents make efforts very early to train infants to recognize the appropriate places for relief, and are remarkably successful (though, admittedly, the places for such relief in India are more accessible than in the United States).
52. One such patron, an expensively dressed businessman, discovered while playing with my daughter that bouncing a baby on one's knee while giving the baby sips of Pepsi is not a good idea.
53. David G. Mandelbaum, "The Family in India," in *The Family, Its Function and Destiny*, ed. Ruth Nanda Anshen, rev. ed. (New York: Harper & Brothers, 1945), 104–105.
54. Hawley, Krishna the Butter Thief, 11.
55. Swami Fateh Krishna Sharma, conversation with the author, Vrindavan, India, January 6, 2002.

56. Vrindavan-wallas never found my insistence that my son was not God (*bhagwan*) but a demon (*rakshasa*) as humorous as I did.
57. Jeffrey R. Timm, "The Celebration of Emotion: Vallabha's Ontology of Affective Experience," Philosophy East & West 41, 1 (1991): 66.
58. Peter van der Veer, "The Power of Detachment: Disciplines of Body and Mind in the Ramanandi Order," *American Ethnologist* 16 (1989): 464.

    Although she does not use the term *bhâv*, Donna Wulff shows how Rûpa Goswami himself promoted the same kind of role-play among Krishna devotees. "[Rûpa] points out that . . . the aged king of Kurupurî, who had no son, is said to have worshipped the Lord in the image of Nandasuta (the son of Nanda, i.e., Kṛṣṇa, probably represented as a child), regarding him as hiw [*sic*] own son, and that he thus attained perfection . . ." (Wulff, 42).
59. van der Veer, 464.
60. Bollywood is the common term for the Hindi film industry based in Mumbai (formerly "Bombay"), which produces far more films annually than its namesake in California.
61. Fateh Krishna Sharma, conversation with the author, Vrindavan, India, January 6, 2002.
62. The way in which Swami-ji uses the term bhâv echoes the way Rûpa Goswami—whose theological treatises do not stray from the classical vocabulary of the Natyashastra—uses the term rati, as in *śrīkṛṣṇaviṣayā ratiḥ*, "love that has Krsna as its object." See Wulff, 197.
63. Yamadagni, conversation with the author, Vrindavan, India, March 15, 2002.
64. Conversation with the author, Vrindavan, India, December 21, 2001.

6. THEATRE IS RELIGION: THE ACTING AUDIENCE

1. Portions of this chapter appeared in the *Journal of Dramatic Theory and Criticism* 22, 2 (2008): 7–22.
2. A production of Kushner's adaptation of Corneille's *The Illusion* by the Theatre Program at Georgia College and State University in the Spring, 2004, directed by Marlene Johnson.
3. Donna Wulff, *Drama as a Mode of Religious Realization: The Vidagdhamâdhava of Rûpa Gosvâmî* (Chico: Scholars Press, 1984), 20.
4. William James, *The Varieties of Religious Experience* (New York: Simon & Schuster, 1997), 63.
5. The experience James relates here, as James acknowledges, "does not connect itself with the religious sphere." However, James includes it as representative of a kind of transcendent experience, which "may upon occasion" be identified by subjects as religious. I include this manifestation of the experience

on account of its close correspondence to the Eww-Effect of the Kushner production. See James, 64.
6. James, 60.
7. Colin Radford, "How Can We Be Moved by the Fate of Anna Karenina?" *Proceedings of the Aristotelian Society, Supplementary Volume* 49 (1975): 71.
8. At least, not suspension-of-disbelief as the phrase is colloquially employed. Coleridge, who coined the phrase, did not argue we could completely disbelieve, but wrote we are "never absolutely deluded—or anything like it . . ." (see Bernard Dukore, *Dramatic Theory and Criticism: Greeks to Grotowski* [Boston: Heinle, 1974], 588.)
9. Radford, "How Can We Be Moved By the Fate of Anna Karenina?" 71.
10. Just as we don't jump to the stage to prevent Mercutio's death, the religious Christian, for example, knows, even while he worships, that he cannot (and, perhaps, should not) interfere with the crucifixion. That the Christian recognizes Jesus as a historical reality and Mercutio as a character of fiction is precisely the issue. The audience member is affected in a real way by what happens to Mercutio, and it may be that the psychological mechanism by which that happens is similar to the way in which Jesus's passion, which is not happening in an immediate, temporal way, affects Christians.
11. Colin Radford, "Fiction, Pity, Fear, and Jealousy," *The Journal of Aesthetics and Art Criticism* 53, 1 (1995): 75.
12. Noël Carroll, *Beyond Aesthetics* (New York: Cambridge University Press, 2001), 234.
13. In addition to Turvey's various objections to Carroll's theory, we need not accept the proposition that the shudder one experiences at imagining a knife in one's eye is the same phenomenon as shedding a tear over Mercutio's death. Emotion is not necessarily the same as physical revulsion.

    In any case, we might reconsider whether the neutrality required by Carroll's "unasserted proposition" is possible. It is impossible to be neutral about the "truth value" of the proposition "Manhattan Island is made of pizza," which Carroll offers as an illustration. In fact, while one can imagine that Manhattan is made of pizza, one categorically cannot be neutral about this proposition's truth value, any more than we can suspend our disbelief about it. Similarly, we cannot be neutral with regard to Mercutio's stage death, since, however vividly we entertain the thought, we recognize clearly the kind of death involved (or, if we did not, as Radford suggests, we would jump on stage and try to interfere).
14. Malcolm Turvey, "Seeing Theory: On Perception and Emotional Response in Current Film Theory," in *Film Theory and Philosophy*, ed. Richard Allen and Murray Smith (Oxford: Clarendon, 1997), 434.
15. Carroll, 235.
16. Ibid.
17. Michael Weston, "How Can We Be Moved By the Fate of Anna Karenina?" *Proceedings of the Aristotelian Society, Supplementary Volume* 49 (1975): 92.

18. See especially chapter three of *Engaging Characters: Fiction, Emotion, and the Cinema* (Oxford: Clarendon, 1995).
19. Murray Smith, "Imagining from the Inside," in *Film Theory and Philosophy*, ed. Richard Allen and Murray Smith (Oxford: Clarendon Press, 1997), 415.
20. "In either minor or major ways," writes Smith, "fictions always break absolute alignment between character and viewer." See Smith, 424.
21. Kendall Walton, "Spelunking, Simulation, and Slime," in *Emotion and the Arts*, ed. Mette Hjort and Sue Laver (New York: Oxford University Press, 1997), 38.
22. Walton, 39.
23. Ibid.
24. Ibid., 42.
25. Nils G. Holm, "Sundén's Role Theory and Glossolalia," *Journal for the Scientific Study of Religion* 26 (1987): 384.
26. Holm, "Sundén's Role Theory," 384.
27. Quoted in Hjalmar Sundén, "Saint Augustine and the Psalter in the Light of Role-Psychology," *Journal for the Scientific Study of Religion* 26, 3 (1987): 375.
28. Sundén, 376.
29. Nils G. Holm, "Role Theory and Religious Experience," in *Handbook of Religious Experience*, ed. Ralph W. Hood, Jr. (Birmingham: Religious Education Press, 1995), 407–408.
30. Holm, "Role Theory," 401.
31. Ibid., 409.
32. Owe Wikström, "Attribution, Roles and Religion: A Theoretical Analysis of Sundén's Role Theory of Religion and the Attributional Approach to Religious Experience," *Journal for the Scientific Study of Religion* 26 (1987): 393.
33. With this myth in mind, at the temple of Shiva Gopeswar ("Lord of Gopis"), perhaps the only temple in Vrindavan not dedicated to Krishna or Radha, priests daily dress the monolithic representation of Shiva (*linga*) in a sari.
34. Vasant Yamadagni, conversation with the author, Vrindavan, India, March 15, 2002.
35. Margaret Case describes another *âstâyama lila* in her book *Seeing Krishna*, 111–150 (Chapters 7 and 8).
36. Krishna performances involving human actors may be as old as Krishna worship itself, going back to the time of the *Bhagavad Gita*. Even so, this *astayama lila* does strangely echo the legend that holds that in the sixteenth century Karahla's Ghamanddev began his career in *râs lila* performances by dressing up lumps of mud and arranging them in scenes from Krishna mythology. For more on the history of the *râs lila*, see the preceding chapter "Origins of Child Performers in the *Râs Lila*."
37. David L. Haberman, *Acting as a Way of Salvation* (Delhi: Motilal Banarsidass, 1988). Discussed in a previous chapter.
38. Wulff, 183–184.
39. Euro-American theatre is not alone in this regard. Various performance forms in Japan, China, Africa, South America, and many other forms in India itself

equally depend upon the actor's asserted stage presence. But because the present argument has to this point been specifically concerned with Stanislavskian theory, it will not stray too far from Stanislavskian territory.
40. Holm, "Role Theory," 409.
41. Role theory thus accounts for a cognitive state of *belief*, if such a state is, indeed, necessary to resolve the paradox of fiction.
42. Marvin Carlson, *The Haunted Stage: The Theatre as Memory Machine* (Ann Arbor: University of Michigan Press, 2003), 73.

7. CONCLUSION

1. Harold Bloom, *The American Religion: The Emergence of the Post-Christian Nation* (New York: Touchstone, 1992), 36.
2. Norman A. Bert, "Theatre Is Religion," *The Journal of Religion and Theatre* 1, 1 (2002): 2, 4.
3. Anthony Kubiak, "Virtual Faith," *Theatre Survey* 47, 2 (2006): 272.
4. Salim Kemal, *Kant's Aesthetic Theory: An Introduction* (New York: St. Martin's Press, 1992), 33.
5. Kemal, 97.
6. David L. Haberman, *Journey Through the Twelve Forests* (New York: Oxford University Press, 1994), 197.
7. Kant recognizes that features of nature, as well as art, could be experienced aesthetically, though he prefers art for the intentionality in it that facilitates the moral exercise of those who experience it. See Kemal, 135–151.
8. Of course, the Braj-style conflation of religion and aesthetics may have prevailed in the West during medieval days. If we think of medieval art and its appreciation in this way, we might then think of Kant's aesthetics as (perhaps unwittingly) reformulating archaic thinking for an enlightened age.
9. Edgar A. Towne, "Imaginative Construction in Theology: An Aesthetic Approach," *American Journal of Theology & Philosophy* 19, 1 (1998): 78.
10. Refer to the third chapter of *The American Religion* for the "doctrine of experience," as Bloom describes it, in endemically American religion.
11. Edwards uses the term in the following context: "The manner of being affected with the immediate presence of the beautiful idea, depends not on any reasonings about the idea after we have it, before we can find out whether it be beautiful or not; but on the frame of our minds, whereby they are so made that such an idea, as soon as we have it, is grateful, or appears beautiful," *The Nature of True Virtue* (Ann Arbor: University of Michigan Press, 1960), 99.
12. Edwards, 14.
13. J. Alfred Martin, Jr., "The Empirical, The Esthetic, and the Religious," *Union Seminary Quarterly Review* 30, 2–4 (1975): 113.
14. William M. Shea, "Qualitative Wholes: Aesthetic and Religious Experience in the Work of John Dewey," *The Journal of Religion* 60, 1 (1980): 34.

15. Shea, 32–33.
16. Martin, 117.
17. Shea, 35.
18. John Dewey, *Art As Experience* (New York: Penguin Putnam, 1934), 293.
19. John Dewey, "The Postulate of Immediate Empiricism," *The Journal of Philosophy, Psychology, and Scientific Methods* 2, 15 (1905): 394.
20. John Dewey, *A Common Faith* (New Haven: Yale University Press, 1934), 16.
21. Shea, 44.
22. Ibid., 47.
23. Ibid., 49.
24. Jan van der Lans, "Religious Experience: An Argument for a Multidisciplinary Approach," *The Annual Review of the Social Sciences of Religion* 1 (1977): 135.
25. "Religion and art," writes Schleiermacher, "stand together like kindred beings, whose inner affinity, though mutually unrecognized and unsuspected, appears in various ways." *On Religion: Speeches to Its Cultured Despisers*, trans. John Oman (New York: Harper & Brothers, 1958), 140.
26. I am following Ludwig Feuerbach's reading of Luther, who may not have been pleased with this liberal employment of his theology. Feuerbach follows Luther's words quoted here by calling faith, "the eye of the imagination." *The Essence of Faith According to Luther*, trans. Melvin Cherno (New York: Harper & Row, 1967), 77–78.
27. Quoted in Caroline Franks Davis, *The Evidential Force of Religious Experience* (Oxford: Clarendon Press, 1989), 59.
28. Quoted in Philip W. Jackson, *John Dewey and the Lessons of Art* (New Haven: Yale University Press, 1998), 89.
29. Kemal, 33–34.
30. Davis, 30.
31. John R. Searle, *The Construction of Social Reality* (New York: The Free Press, 1995), 12ff.
32. Kemal, 148.
33. Ibid., 139–140.
34. Quoted in Floyd L. Sampson, "An Aesthetic Approach to Religion," *Journal of Bible and Religion* 12, 4 (1944): 213.
35. Eugene G. d'Aquili and Andrew B. Newberg, "The Neuropsychology of Aesthetic, Spiritual, and Mystical States," *Zygon* 35, 1 (2000): 50.
36. D'Aquili and Newberg, 50.
37. Ibid., 42.
38. Van der Lans, 141.

Bibliography

Agrawal, Ram Narayan. *Braj ka Râs Rangmanc*. New Delhi: National Publishing House, 1981.
———. Conversation with the author, Mathura, India, February 7, 2002.
———. *Râs-Lila: Ek Paricay*. New Delhi: Bharatiya Visva Prakashan, 1959.
Allen, David. *Stanislavsky for Beginners*. London: Writers and Readers, 1999.
Allen, Richard and Murray Smith, eds. *Film Theory and Philosophy*. Oxford: Clarendon, 1997.
Anshen, Ruth Nanda, ed. *The Family, Its Function and Destiny*. New York: Harper & Brothers, 1945.
Barnes, Clive. "CSC Repertory Stages Successful Revival." *New York Times*, October 4, 1971, 53.
Barz, Richard. *The Bhakti Sect of Vallabhacarya*. Faridabad: Thomson Press, 1976.
Basham, A. L. *The Wonder That Was India*. New York: Grove Press, 1959.
Baümer, Bettina. "The Play of the Three Worlds: The Trika Concept of Lila." In *The Gods at Play: Lila in South Asia*, edited by William Sax. New York: Oxford, 1995.
Bennett, Susan. *Theatre Audiences: A Theory of Production and Reception*. New York: Routledge, 1997.
Bert, Norman A. "Theatre Is Religion." *The Journal of Religion and Theatre* 1.1 (2002): 1–11.
Bhagavata Purana. J. L. Shastri, ed. Delhi: Motilal Banarsidass, 1983.
Blau, Herbert. *Take Up the Bodies: Theater at the Vanishing Point*. Urbana: University of Illinois Press, 1982.
Bloom, Harold. *The American Religion: The Emergence of the Post-Christian Nation*. New York: Touchstone, 1992.
Bolle, Kees W., trans. *The Bhagavadgita: A New Translation*. Berkeley: University of California Press, 1979.
Bone, David W. "The Sea Across the Footlights." *New York Times Book Review and Magazine*, January 15, 1922, 3, 30.
Boulton, Marjorie. *The Anatomy of Drama*. London: Routledge & Paul, 1960.
Brecht, Bertolt. *Brecht on Theatre*. John Willett, ed. and trans. New York: Hill and Wang, 1964.

Buitenen, J. A. B. van., trans. *The Mahabharata*. Chicago: University of Chicago Press, 1973.
Byrski, Christopher M. *Concept of Ancient Indian Theatre*. Delhi: Munshiram Manoharlal Publishers, 1974.
Carlson, Marvin. *The Haunted Stage: The Theatre as Memory Machine*. Ann Arbor: University of Michigan Press, 2003.
Carman, John B. "Some Concluding Reflections." In *The Gods at Play: Lila in South Asia*, edited by William Sax. New York: Oxford, 1995.
Carroll, Noël. *Beyond Aesthetics*. New York: Cambridge University Press, 2001.
Case, Margaret. *Seeing Krishna: The Religious World of a Brahman Family in Vrindaban*. New York: Oxford University Press, 2000.
Chari, V. K. *Sanskrit Criticism*. Honolulu: University of Hawaii Press, 1990.
Cole, Toby, ed. *Acting: A Handbook of the Stanislavsky Method*. New York: Crown, 1960.
Coomaraswamy, Ananda K. "Lila." *Journal of the American Oriental Society* 61.2 (1941): 98–101.
Counsell, Colin. *Signs of Performance: An Introduction to Twentieth-Century Theatre*. New York: Routledge, 1996.
d'Aquili, Eugene G. and Andrew B. Newberg. "The Neuropsychology of Aesthetic, Spiritual, and Mystical States." *Zygon* 35.1 (2000): 39–51.
Davis, Caroline Franks. *The Evidential Force of Religious Experience*. Oxford: Clarendon Press, 1989.
De, S. K. *Bengal's Contribution to Sanskrit Literature & Studies in Bengal Vaisnavism*. Calcutta: K. L. Mukhopadhya, 1960.
———. *Early History of the Vaisnava Faith and Movement in Bengal, from Sanskrit and Bengali Sources*. Calcutta: Firma K. L. Mukhopadhya, 1961.
Dewey, John. *Art as Experience*. New York: Penguin Putnam, 1934.
———. *A Common Faith*. New Haven: Yale University Press, 1934.
———. "The Postulate of Immediate Empiricism." *The Journal of Philosophy, Psychology, and Scientific Methods* 2.15 (1905): 393–399.
Dimock, Edward C., Jr., trans. *Caitanya Caritâmrta*. Cambridge, MA: Harvard University Press, 1999.
———. *The Place of the Hidden Moon: Erotic Mysticism in the Vaisnava Sahajiya Cult of Bengal*. Chicago: University of Chicago Press, 1966.
Dundes, Alan, ed., *Sacred Narrative*. Berkeley: University of California Press, 1984.
Eck, Diana. *Darshan*. Chambersburg: Anima, 1981.
Eck, Diana and Françoise Mallison, eds. *Devotion Divine: Bhakti Traditions from the Regions of India*. Groningen: Egbert & Forsten, 1991.
Edwards, Jonathan. *The Nature of True Virtue*. Ann Arbor: University of Michigan Press, 1960.
Elam, Keir. *The Semiotics of Theatre and Drama*. New York: Taylor & Francis, 2002.

Entwistle, A. W. *Braj: Centre of Krishna Pilgrimage*. Groningen: Egbert Forsten, 1987.
Feuerbach, Ludwig. *The Essence of Faith According to Luther*. Michael Cherna, trans. New York: Harper & Row, 1967.
Fish, Stanley. *Is There a Text in This Class?* Cambridge, MA: Harvard University Press, 1980.
Gargi, Balwant. *Folk Theater of India*. Calcutta: Rupa & Co., 1991.
George, David E. R. *India: Three Ritual Dance-Dramas*. Cambridge: Chadwyk Healey, 1986.
Goffman, Erving. *Frame Analysis: An Essay on the Organization of Experience*. New York: Harper Colophon Books, 1974.
Goswami, Srivatsa. Conversation with the author, Vrindavan, India, December 7, 2001, December 12, 2002, and March 31, 2002.
Haberman, David L. *Acting as a Way of Salvation: A Study of Râgânugâ Bhakti Sâdhana*. Delhi: Motilal Banarsidass, 1988.
———. *Journey Through the Twelve Forests*. New York: Oxford University Press, 1994.
Hawley, John Stratton. "Every Play a Play Within a Play." In *The Gods at Play: Lila in South Asia*, edited by William Sax. New York: Oxford, 1995.
———. "A Feast for Mount Govardhan." In *Devotion Divine: Bhakti Traditions from the Regions of India*, edited by Diana Eck and Françoise Mallison. Groningen: Egbert & Forsten, 1991.
———. *Krishna the Butter Thief*. Princeton: Princeton University Press, 1983.
Hawley, John Stratton and Donna Marie Wulff. *The Divine Consort: Radha and the Goddesses of India*. Berkeley: University of California Press, 1982.
Hawley, John Stratton and Shrivatsa Goswami. *At Play with Krishna: Pilgrimage Dramas from Vrindaban*. Delhi: Motilal Banarsidass, 1992.
Hein, Norvin. "Lila." In *The Gods at Play: Lila in South Asia*, edited by William Sax. New York: Oxford, 1995.
———. *The Miracle Plays of Mathura*. New York: Yale University Press, 1972.
———. "A Revolution in Krsnaism: The Cult of Gopala." *History of Religions* 25.1 (1985): 296–317.
Hiltebeitel, Alf. "Krsna at Mathura." In *Mathura: The Cultural Heritage*, edited by Doris Meth Srinivasan. New Delhi: Manohar, 1989.
Hjort, Mette and Sue Laver, eds. *Emotion and the Arts*. New York: Oxford University Press, 1997.
Holm, Nils G. "Role Theory and Religious Experience." In *Handbook of Religious Experience*, edited by Ralph W. Hood, Jr. Birmingham: Religious Education Press, 1995.
———. "Sundén's Role Theory and Glossolalia." *Journal for the Scientific Study of Religion* 26.3 (1987): 383–389.
Honko, Lauri. "The Problem of Defining Myth." In *Sacred Narrative*, edited by Alan Dundes. Berkeley: University of California Press, 1984.

Hood, Ralph W., Jr. *Handbook of Religious Experience*. Birmingham: Religious Education Press, 1995.
Hopkins, Thomas J. *The Hindu Religious Tradition*. Belmont: Wadsworth, 1971.
Hospital, Clifford. "Bhakti and Liberation in the Bhagavata Purana." *Sciences Religieuses/Studies in Religion* 12.4 (1983): 397–405.
———. "Lila in Early Vaisnava Thought." In *The Gods at Play: Lila in South Asia*, edited by William Sax. New York: Oxford, 1995.
Isacco, Enrico. *Krishna the Divine Lover*. London: Serindia Publications, 1982.
Jackson, A. V. W. "Children on the Stage in the Sanskrit Drama." *Transactions of the American Philological Society* 27 (1896): v–vi.
Jackson, Philip. *John Dewey and the Lessons of Art*. New Haven: Yale University Press, 1998.
James, William. *The Varieties of Religious Experience*. New York: Simon & Schuster, 1997.
Jarret, H. S., trans. *'Ain-i-Akbari of Abulfazl-i-'Allami, 3*. Calcutta: Royal Asiatic Society of Bengal, 1948.
Kemal, Salim. *Kant's Aesthetic Theory: An Introduction*. New York: St. Martin's Press, 1992.
Kinsley, David R. *The Divine Player*. Delhi: Motilal Banarsidass, 1979.
———. *The Sword and the Flute: Kali and Krsna, Dark Visions of the Terrible and the Sublime in Hindu Mythology*. Berkeley: University of California Press, 1975.
Kubiak, Anthony. "Virtual Faith." *Theatre Survey* 47.2 (2006): 271–276.
Kumar, S. Conversation with the author, Vrindavan, India, March 27, 2002.
Lal, Kishori Saran. *Twilight of the Sultanate*. New Delhi: Asia Publishing House, 1963.
Levi, Sylvain. *The Theatre of India*. Narayana Mukherji, trans. Calcutta: Writers Workshop, 1978.
Mandelbaum, David G. "The Family in India." In *The Family, Its Function and Destiny*, edited by Ruth Nanda Anshen, rev. ed. New York: Harper & Brothers, 1945.
Martin, J. Alfred, Jr. "The Empirical, The Esthetic, and the Religious." *Union Seminary Quarterly Review* 30.2–4 (1975): 110–120.
Masson, J. L. and M. V. Patwardhan. *Aesthetic Rapture: The Rasâdhyâya of the Nâtyasâstra*. Poona: Deccan College, 1970.
McGregor, R. S. *The Round Dance of Krishna and Uddhav's Message*. London: Luzac & Company, 1973.
Metz, Christian. *Film Language: A Semiotics of the Cinema*. Michael Taylor, trans. New York: Oxford University Press, 1974.
Miller, Barbara Stoler, trans. *Bhagavad-gita*. New York: Columbia University Press, 1986.
———. "Kâlidâsa's World and His Plays." In *Theater of Memory: The Plays of Kâlidâsa*, edited by Barbara Stoller Miller. New York: Columbia University Press, 1984.

———, ed. *Theater of Memory: The Plays of Kâlidâsa.* New York: Columbia University Press, 1984.
Miller, Robert L. "A Letter From the Publisher." *Time Magazine,* August 15, 1988.
Mital, Prabhudayal. *Braj ki Râslila.* Vrindavan: Vrindavan Shodh Samsthan, 1983.
Monier-Williams, Monier, ed. *A Sanskrit-English Dictionary.* Oxford: The Clarendon Press, 1899.
Mukerjee, Radhakamal. *The Cosmic Art of India.* New York: Allied Publishers, 1965.
Nelson, Lance E. "The Ontology of *Bhakti*: Devotion as *Paramapuruṣârtha* in Gauḍiya Vaiṣṇavism and Madhusûdhana Sarasvatî." *Journal of Indian Philosophy* 32 (2004): 345–392.
O'Connel, Joseph T. "Gaudiya Vaisnava Symbolism of Deliverance (uddhara, nistara,...) from Evil." *Journal of Asian and African Studies* 15.1–2 (1983): 124–135.
Preciado-Solis, Benjamin. *The Krsna Cycle in the Puranas.* Delhi: Motilal Banarsidass, 1984.
Radford, Colin. "Fiction, Pity, Fear, and Jealousy." *The Journal of Aesthetics and Art Criticism* 53.1 (1995): 71–75.
———. "How Can We Be Moved by the Fate of Anna Karenina?" *Proceedings of the Aristotelian Society, Supplementary Volume* 49 (1975): 67–80.
Ramprasad, Swami. Conversation with the author, Vrindavan, India, November 16, 2001.
Rig Veda. Barend A. Van Nooten and Gary B. Holland, eds. Cambridge, MA: Harvard University Press, 1994.
Sampson, Floyd L. "An Aesthetic Approach to Religion." *Journal of Bible and Religion* 12.4 (1944): 211–216.
Sanford, Whitney A. "The Emotive Body in the *Astayâmalîlâ* Festival." *Arc* 25 (1997): 101–121.
Sartre, Jean-Paul. *The Psychology of Imagination.* New York: Philosophical Library, 1948.
Sax, William, ed. *The Gods at Play: Lila in South Asia.* New York: Oxford, 1995.
———. "The Ramnagar Ramlila: Text, Performance, Pilgrimage." *History of Religions* 30 (1990): 129–153.
———. "Who's Who in the Pandav Lila?" In *The Gods at Play: Lila in South Asia,* edited by William Sax. New York: Oxford, 1995.
Schechner, Richard. *Performative Circumstances from the Avant Garde to Ramlila.* Calcutta: Seagull Books, 1983.
Schleiermacher, Friedrich. *On Religion: Speeches to Its Cultured Despisers.* John Oman, trans. New York: Harper & Brothers, 1958.
Schweig, Graham M. *Dance of Divine Love.* Princeton: Princeton University Press, 2005.

Searle, John R. *The Construction of Social Reality.* New York: The Free Press, 1995.
Shackle, C., ed. *A Gurû Nânak Glossary.* London: University of British Colombia Press, 1981.
Sharma, Swami Amicand. Conversation with the author, Vrindavan, India, December 21, 2001.
Sharma, Swami Fateh Krishna. Conversation with the author, Vrindavan, India, January 6, 2002.
Sharpe, R. A. Review of *Paradoxes of Emotion and Fiction*, by Robert J. Yanal. *British Journal of Aesthetics* 41 (2001): 234–236.
Shea, William M. "Qualitative Wholes: Aesthetic and Religious Experience in the Work of John Dewey." *The Journal of Religion* 60.1 (1980): 32–50.
Shulman, David. "The Prospects of Memory." *Journal of Indian Philosophy* 26 (1988): 309–334.
Singer, Milton, ed. *Krishna: Myths, Rites, and Attitudes.* Chicago: University of Chicago Press, 1968.
Sinha, Daya Prakash. *Lokrang: Uttar Pradesh.* Lucknow: UP Hindi Sansthan, 1990.
Smith, Murray. *Engaging Characters: Fiction, Emotion, and the Cinema.* Oxford: Clarendon Press, 1995.
———. "Imagining from the Inside." In *Film Theory and Philosophy*, edited by Richard Allen and Murray Smith. Oxford: Clarendon Press, 1997.
Srîmadbhagavadgîtâ. Rajdeo Mishra, ed. Varanasi: Sampurnanand Sanskrit University, 1990.
Srinivasan, Doris Meth, ed. *Mathura: The Cultural Heritage.* New Delhi: Manohar, 1989.
Stanislavsky, Constantin. *Creating a Role.* Elizabeth Reynolds Hapgood, trans. New York: Theatre Arts Books, 1961.
———. *An Actor Prepares.* Elizabeth Reynolds Hapgood, trans. New York: Theatre Arts Books, 1936.
Stroll, Avrum and Richard H. Popkin. *Philosophy and the Human Spirit.* New York: Holt, Rinehart and Winston, Inc., 1973.
Sundén, Hjalmar. "Saint Augustine and the Psalter in the Light of Role-Psychology." *Journal for the Scientific Study of Religion* 26.3 (1987): 375–382.
Swann, Darius. "The Braj Ras Lila." *Journal of South Asian Literature* 10(2–4) (1975): 21–44.
Tagare, Ganesh Vasudeo, trans. *Bhagavata Purana, vol. IV.* Delhi: Motilal Banarsidass, 1978.
Thielemann, Selina. *Rasalila: a Musical Study of Religious Drama in Vraja.* New Delhi: APH Publishing Corporation, 1998.
Tian, Min. "'Alienation Effect' for Whom? Brecht's (Mis)interpretation of the Classical Chinese Theatre." *Asian Theatre Journal* 12.2 (1997): 200–222.
Timm, Jeffrey R. "The Celebration of Emotion: Vallabha's Ontology of Affective Experience." *Philosophy East & West* 41.1 (1991): 59–75.

Towne, Edgar A. "Imaginative Construction in Theology: An Aesthetic Approach." *American Journal of Theology and Philosophy* 19.1 (1998): 77–103.
Tull, Herman. *The Vedic Origins of Karma.* Albany: SUNY Press, 1989.
Turvey, Malcolm. "Seeing Theory: On Perception and Emotional Response in Current Film Theory." In *Film Theory and Philosophy*, edited by Richard Allen and Murray Smith. Oxford: Clarendon, 1997.
Ubersfeld, Anne. "Mother Courage in France," Frank Collins, trans. *Modern Drama* 42.2 (1999): 198–206.
Van der Lans, Jan. "Religious Experience: An Argument for a Multidisciplinary Approach." *The Annual Review of the Social Sciences of Religion* 1 (1977): 133–143.
Van der Veer, Peter. "The Power of Detachment: Disciplines of Body and Mind in the Ramanandi Order." *American Ethnologist* 16.3 (1989): 458–470.
Varadpande, Manohar Laxman. *Krishna Theatre in India.* New Delhi: Abhinav Publications, 1982.
Vaudeville, Charlotte. "Braj, Lost and Found," *Indo-Iranian Journal* 18 (1976): 195–213.
Wach, Joachim. *Comparative Study of Religions.* New York: Columbia University Press, 1963.
———. *Types of Religious Experience Christian and Non-Christian.* Chicago: University of Chicago Press, 1951.
Walton, Kendall, "Spelunking, Simulation, and Slime." In *Emotion and the Arts*, edited by Mette Hjort and Sue Laver. New York: Oxford University Press, 1997.
Weston, Michael. "How Can We Be Moved by the Fate of Anna Karenina?" *Proceedings of the Aristotelian Society, Supplementary Volume* 49 (1975): 81–93.
Wikström, Owe. "Attribution, Roles and Religion: A Theoretical Analysis of Sundén's Role Theory of Religion and the Attributional Approach to Religious Experience." *Journal for the Scientific Study of Religion* 26.3 (1987): 390–400.
Wills, J. Robert. *The Director in a Changing Theatre.* Palo Alto: Mayfield, 1976.
Wulff, Donna M. *Drama as a Mode of Religious Realization: The* Vidagdhamâdhava *of Rûpa Goswâmî.* Chico: Scholars Press, 1984.
———. "The Play of Emotion: Lilakirtan in Bengal." In *The Gods at Play: Lila in South Asia*, edited by William Sax. New York: Oxford, 1995.
Yamadagni, Vasant. Conversation with the author, Vrindavan, India, March 13, 2002 and March 15, 2002.
Yamadagni, Vasant. *Râsalila tatha Râsanukaran Vikas.* New Delhi: Sangit Natak Academy, 1980.
Yanal, Robert J. *Paradoxes of Emotion and Fiction.* University Park: Pennsylvania State University Press, 1999.

Index

Abhinavagupta, 97, 98
  see also Natyashastra
acting
  by audience, 10, 115, 118, 124, 134–5, 140–1, 156–8
  by children, 12, 13, 16, 17, 58–64, 72–3, 78–81, 99, 137, 161, 175
  emergence of actor in, 111, 125–7, 135, 138–40
  representational (mimesis), 11, 17–18, 26, 29–30, 32, 39, 45, 52–4, 79–80, 84, 90–5, 99, 112–13, 115–16, 161, 173, 174, 175
  see also anubhâva; avatar; bhâv; lila; Stanislavsky, Constantin
Adi Granth
  see Guru Granth Sahib
Akbar (Mughal emperor), 58–9, 77, 166, 171
anubhâva, 91, 94, 108, 110, 174
  see also bhâv
arati, 4–6, 16, 26, 28, 39, 103, 128, 144, 145, 163, 168
Arjuna, 30–2, 39, 47–50, 164
  see also Bhagavad Gita; Pandavas
art and religion
  see religion and art
astayama lila, 133, 151, 179
Aurangzeb (Mughal emperor), 60, 73
avatar, 30, 32–3, 36, 39, 45, 162

Babur (Mughal emperor), 77, 171
Bade Thakur (râsdhâri), 12, 165
Barsana (Braj village), 12, 23, 67, 75
Bergeron, Brad (actor), 116
Bhagavad Gita, 30, 39, 40, 45, 46, 48, 49, 78, 162, 163, 165, 171, 179
Bhagavata Purana, 27–9, 31–2, 33, 36, 38, 40–1, 106, 161, 162, 163, 167, 171
bhakta
  see bhakti
Bhaktamal, 61, 71, 169
bhakti
  bliss in, 10–11, 36–8, 41–2, 43–4, 51, 55, 61, 146, 156, 163
  devotion, 9, 13, 15, 24, 37, 38, 118, 140, 151, 161
  see also bhâv
  Hindu practice, 13, 15, 25, 33, 36, 51, 55, 58, 66, 70, 76–82, 101, 105, 140, 146, 155, 162, 171
  see also Gaudiya Vaishnavism; Nimbark Vaishnavism; Pushtimarg Vaishnavism
  liberation through, 15, 37–40, 161, 163, 171
  see also bhâv; râgânugâ bhakti sâdhana
bhâv, 110–12, 126–7, 132, 134, 174
  see also anubhâva; bhakti
Bhramar Ghat (Vrindavan), 108

Braj, 5, 6, 7, 8, 16, 23, 25, 28, 33, 43, 44, 49, 50–2, 55–6, 57–9, 60–75, 78–81, 88, 101, 104, 105, 106, 118, 122, 135, 137, 146, 147, 151, 160, 169, 170, 171, 172
  transcendent aspect, 17, 33, 51, 91, 94, 137, 154, 155
  see also pilgrimage

Caitanya, 70, 75, 76, 79, 80, 159, 162, 172
  attitudes toward women, 80–1
  Caitanya Caritâmrta, 80, 172
  see also Gaudiya Vaishnavism
children, regard for, 108–10
  see also acting: by children

Danto, Arthur (author), 152–3, 154, 155
devotion
  see bhakti; bhâv
Dewey, John, 148–50, 153, 155
Dhruvdas, 61–3, 68–71, 166, 170
Doordarshan, 8, 46
Dwarka, 45

Edwards, Jonathan, 147–8, 180
emotion memory
  see Stanislavsky, Constantin
Eww-Effect, 115–16, 118–19, 124–5, 130, 178

Fazl, Abu (chronicler), 58, 60–1, 63, 166
freedom 38, 44, 49, 50–6
  see also bhakti; lila; moksha

Gaudiya Vaishnavism, 32, 33, 39, 76, 80–1, 88, 159, 162, 168
  see also bhakti; Nimbark Vaishnavism; Pushtimarg Vaishnavism
Ghamanddev (Vaishnava saint), 58, 66–74, 82, 169, 170, 171, 179

  see also Ghamandi; Uddhav Ghamanddevacarya
Ghamandi (Vrindavan performer), 61–4, 70, 71, 72, 74, 166–7, 169, 170
  see also Ghamanddev; Uddhav Ghamanddevacarya
Gitagovinda, 78
gopi, 2, 6, 9, 11–12, 13, 25, 27, 28–30, 32, 40, 41, 50, 58, 59, 60, 63, 64, 67, 72, 74, 85, 125, 127, 132–3, 161, 179
Govardhan, 23, 27, 29, 49, 51
Gray, Spalding, 35, 139
Growse, F. S., 8, 169
Gupta Empire, 49, 76
Guru Granth Sahib, 8, 60, 65
Guru Nanak, 60–1, 62, 65, 74

Hamlet, 34–5, 134
Hardy, Alister (author), 152–5
Haridas (Vaishnava saint), 66–8, 70, 73, 75, 168, 169, 170
Harivamsa, 49, 53
Harivyas Devacarya (Vaishnava saint), 69
Hein, Norvin, 9, 27
Hinduism
  See bhakti; Gaudiya Vaishnavism; Nimbark Vaishnavism; Pushtimarg Vaishnavism
Holi, 1, 10, 12, 16
Homer, 74, 170

Ibrahim Lodi (Delhi sultan), 77, 171
Islam, 58–9, 77, 166

Jaipur, 111
Jaipur Mandir, 132
Jaisingh, Raja (Rajput ruler), 73
Jaisingh Ghera (Vrindavan ashram), 1–2, 4–5, 8, 10, 12, 14, 133, 151
James, William, 37, 118–19, 127, 151, 177

janmashtami (festival), 8, 16
jhanki, 6–8

Kalidasa (Sanskrit playwright), 108
Kaliya (mythic demon), 27
Kamsa (mythic king of Mathura), 45, 52
Kant, Immanuel, 19, 119, 145–9, 153, 154, 180
Karahla (Braj village), 67–76, 79, 81–2, 179
katha (performance), 106
katha (Sanskrit word), 164
kathak (dance), 9, 59, 85, 175
kathakali (theatre), 27
Kaufman, Andy, 17–18
kirtan (devotional activity), 13, 54, 75
Krishna
  as actor, 18, 26, 32–3, 39, 80, 140, 146
   see also avatar
  butter thief, 11–12, 36, 39, 43–4, 49–50, 159
  daily schedule, 24, 103–5, 108, 133
  Gopal (child), 2, 13, 15, 16, 27, 31–2, 33, 36, 39–41, 43, 44, 45, 46, 47–8, 49–51, 76, 77–8, 79, 80, 109–10, 161, 162, 167, 171
  irrational, 48–50, 51–2, 55–6
  kshatriya in Mahabharata, 27, 30–2, 39–40, 45–7, 48–9, 50, 54, 163–4, 171
  theme, 15, 28, 44–8, 51–2, 55–6
  transcendent aspect, 18, 20, 31–2, 33, 36, 38, 39, 40–2, 44–6, 55, 71, 77–8, 100, 105, 133, 134, 137–8, 146, 155, 161, 164, 170

Levi, Sylvain, 8, 159
liberation
  see moksha

lila (play), 4, 6, 10–11, 13, 15, 28, 30–3, 39, 40, 41–2, 49, 52–4, 55–6, 80, 81, 103, 104, 105, 112–13, 115, 127, 132, 134, 137, 138–40, 161, 175
  see also freedom

Mahabharata, 45–7, 48, 50, 52, 54, 167
Maharaj-ji, 1–2, 4, 8, 37, 159
maharâs dance, 6, 9–10, 29
massively multi-player online role-playing games
  see virtual worlds
Mathura, 8, 9, 12, 23, 44, 47, 60, 66–7, 70, 72
Malik (family of Vrindavan), 103
memory
  see smarana
metatheatre, 4, 26–32, 41
method acting, 86, 156, 173, 175
Mirabai (poet), 12, 27
moksha, 15, 18, 26, 28, 37–9, 41–2, 76, 161, 163, 164, 166
  see also bhakti; freedom
mukut, 25, 66–9, 72, 168
myth
  see Krishna: theme

Nabhaji (poet), 61–2, 71, 169
Nanda (Krishna's adoptive father), 44, 50, 63, 89, 177
  see also Vasudeva; Yashoda
Narada (mythic sage), 11, 63
Narayan Bhatt (Vaishnava saint), 61, 75, 159, 168–9, 170, 171
Natyashastra, 18, 97, 110, 167, 174, 177
  see also Abhinavagupta
Neech (Braj village), 70
Nimbark Vaishnavism, 69–73, 169, 170
  see also bhakti; Gaudiya Vaishnavism; Pushtimarg Vaishnavism
nô (Japanese theatre), 27

Otto, Rudolph, 151

Panchadhyaya (portion of the Bhagavata Purana), 28–9, 161
pandav lila, 54
Pandavas (Mahabharata characters), 46–7
   see also Arjuna
paradox of fiction, 3, 19, 116–27, 128, 130, 132, 135, 140–1
Pavlov, Ivan Petrovich, 92, 94–5, 101
peacock dance, 10, 30
pilgrimage, 11, 16, 51, 57, 69, 70, 74–5, 81, 106, 146, 156
play
   see lila
prasad, 13, 24, 26, 43, 133
Purushottam Goswami
   see Maharaj-ji
Pushtimarg Vaishnavism, 38, 72, 110
   see also bhakti; Gaudiya Vaishnavism; Nimbark Vaishnavism; Vallabha (Vaishnava saint)
Putana (mythic character), 27, 29

Radha, 2, 5, 6–8, 9, 12–13, 27, 40, 62–3, 64, 66, 72, 79, 80, 85, 106, 108, 113, 133, 170, 179
   see also Krishna
Radharaman (Vrindavan temple), 24, 36, 107, 151
râgânugâ bhakti sâdhana, 79, 88–9, 90–1, 93, 96–8, 101, 104–5, 134, 173–4
rahas dance, 78, 172
   see also Walid Ali Shah
Rajasthan, 2, 27
   see also Jaipur
Ram, 17, 47, 111
Ramanuja (Vaishnava saint), 101, 105
ram lila, 16–17, 160
   at Ramnagar, 16–17
râs lila (Manipur), 25

Râs-Sarvasva, 66–9, 71–3, 169
rasa, 18, 97, 167
râsdhâri (director), 4, 11, 26
reality, experience of
   see paradox of fiction
religion and art, 3–4, 9, 18–19, 25, 117–20, 125, 128, 135–7, 140–1, 143–4, 150, 152–3, 155–8
   see also Danto, Arthur; Dewey, John; Edwards, Jonathan; Hardy, Alister; Kant, Immanuel
religious experience
   see religion and art
Ribot, Théodule (psychologist), 100–1
Rocky Horror Picture Show (motion picture), 157
Role Theory of Religious Experience, 127–32, 135–7, 151, 180
Rupa Goswami (Vaishnava saint), 19, 79–80, 91, 97, 104, 134, 162
   see also râgânugâ bhakti sâdhana
Russell, Bertrand, 33–5

salvation
   see moksha
Sanskrit Drama, 12, 64, 167
   see also Kalidasa; Natyashastra
shakta (Sahajiya) sect, 78–9
Sharma, Fateh Krishna (râsdhâri), 1, 4–6, 8, 10, 12, 111, 126–7, 133, 177
Shiva (Siva), 11, 54, 62, 79, 132, 162, 179
Shroud of Turin, 102
Sikander Lodi (Delhi sultan), 77, 170–1
smarana, 96, 100–10
   see also Stanislavsky, Constantin
Srivatsa Goswami
Stanislavsky, Constantin, 87, 100, 101, 173, 174
   acting System, 84, 86, 87–98, 104, 140, 174, 175

emotion memory, 84, 87–8, 89, 90–1, 92, 95, 100–1, 173
  see also smarana
method of physical actions, 93–4
psycho technique, 92–3
running score, 88, 95–6, 104
Sudama Kutir (Vrindavan ashram), 11, 85, 160
Sundén, Hjalmar
  see Role Theory of Religious Experience
svarup, 16–17, 59, 61, 66, 161
  see also acting; avatar; Krishna
Swami-ji
  see Sharma, Fateh Krishna

technology (influence on râs lila), 8, 9, 11, 160
Trojan Women (Greek tragedy), 83–4, 140
  Andromache (character), 2, 111, 127, 139

Uddhav Ghamanddevacarya (Vaishnava saint), 69–72, 170
  see also Ghamandi; Ghamanddev

Vallabh (Vrindavan dancer), 61–3

Vallabha (Vaishnava saint), 38–9, 66–8, 70, 72, 73, 75, 76, 168, 169, 170
  see also Pushtimarg Vaishnavism
Varanasi, 16–17, 160
Vasudeva (Krishna's father), 36, 44–5
vidushaka, 12
  see also Sanskrit drama
vipralambha (love in separation), 28
virtual worlds, 157–8
Vishnu, 30, 45, 162
  see also avatar
Vishram Ghat (Mathura), 66–9, 72
Vrindavan
  see Braj; Krishna

Walid Ali Shah (Lucknow ruler), 78, 172
Webb, Cort (actor), 116
Wilson, H. H. (Sanskrit scholar), 8
World of Warcraft
  see virtual worlds

Yamuna (river), 6, 29, 44, 67, 83, 132, 175
Yashoda (Krishna's adoptive mother), 11, 31–2, 39, 44, 49–50, 63, 89

GPSR Compliance

The European Union's (EU) General Product Safety Regulation (GPSR) is a set of rules that requires consumer products to be safe and our obligations to ensure this.

If you have any concerns about our products, you can contact us on

ProductSafety@springernature.com

In case Publisher is established outside the EU, the EU authorized representative is:

Springer Nature Customer Service Center GmbH
Europaplatz 3
69115 Heidelberg, Germany

www.ingramcontent.com/pod-product-compliance
Lightning Source LLC
LaVergne TN
LVHW011824060526
838200LV00053B/3892